GAINES & COLEMAN

FLORIDA REAL ESTATE EXAM MANUAL

FOR SALES ASSOCIATES AND BROKERS

30TH EDITION

LINDA L. CRAWFORD

Dearborn™
Real Estate Education

This publication is designed to provide accurate and authoritative information in regard to the subject matter covered. It is sold with the understanding that the publisher is not engaged in rendering legal, accounting, or other professional service. If legal advice or other expert assistance is required, the services of a competent professional person should be sought.

President: Roy Lipner
Vice-President of Publishing and Product Development: Evan Butterfield
Managing Editor, Product Development: Kate DeVivo
Senior Development Editor: Tony Peregrin
Director of Production: Daniel Frey
Senior Managing Editor, Production: Jack Kiburz
Production Artist: Maria Warren
Creative Director: Lucy Jenkins
Cover Design: Gail Chandler

Published by Dearborn™ Real Estate Education,
a division of Dearborn Financial Publishing, Inc.®
30 South Wacker Drive, Suite 2500
Chicago, IL 60606-7481
(312) 836-4400
www.dearbornRE.com

Printed in the United States of America.

07   08   10 9 8 7 6 5 4 3 2 1

ISBN-13: 978-1-4195-8877-8
ISBN-10:   1-4195-8877-X

Contents

How to Use This Manual

The *Florida Real Estate Exam Manual for Sales Associates and Brokers* provides a concise, focused approach to preparing for the Florida real estate license exams, and is designed to aid both sales associate students and broker students. You can review key concepts in a relatively short span of time and work through a variety of practice questions. The State of Florida does *not* use national real estate exams. The license exams are developed by the Bureau of Education and Testing within the Florida Department of Business and Professional Regulation. The material in this book is specifically designed to prepare you for Florida's license exams.

The Key Point Reviews contain the most important concepts explained in the textbook, *Florida Real Estate Principles, Practices & Law (PP&L)*, and will reinforce the information learned in the sales associate course. Sales associate *and* broker candidates are tested on material from the sales associate prelicense course so it is important to study this material to prepare for the license exam.

It may seem a little odd that the Key Point Reviews are not in numerical order. Instead, we have grouped the chapters by topics: real estate law; Florida real estate license law; general real estate law; and real estate principles and practices. The chapters listed in the Contents refer to the chapters of *PP&L*. Because a good portion of the state exam concerns Florida license law, we have grouped these chapters together to make exam preparation easier.

This edition has been revised to further assist broker candidates with preparing for the broker license exam. The sample exam questions (starting on page 103) indicate the chapter in the sales associate textbook, *PP&L*, that corresponds to the sample questions. We have also included the corresponding chapters in the broker textbook, *Florida Real Estate Broker's Guide*. If there is a set of questions that are particularly troubling for you, refer to the corresponding chapters in *PP&L* and the *Broker's Guide* for additional study. This edition also features math problems exclusively designed for broker candidates. Broker candidates should be proficient in solving *all* of these math problems, including the investment problems that follow the general math problems.

■ SUCCESSFUL EXAM-TAKING STRATEGIES

This section of the book lays out a strategy for answering multiple-choice questions. You need a proven strategy (or plan) for taking and passing the exam on the first try. Part of a successful strategy is learning how to become "test wise." It also involves understanding a test writer's objectives. If you understand how questions are constructed and are familiar with the subjects that are tested, you are well on your way to reaching your goal on exam day.

■ KEY POINT REVIEWS

The key point reviews are a no-nonsense approach to reviewing the most important concepts in *PP&L.* The key point reviews are organized into two parts. The first part covers Florida real estate license law and general real estate law (chapters 2, 3, 4, 5, 6, 21, 7, 8, 9, 11, and 20). Sales associate candidates *and* broker candidates need to study these chapters carefully to prepare for the state license exams! Part two covers real estate principles and practices (chapters 1, 10, 12, 13, 15, 16, 17, 18, 19, and 14). The principles and practices chapters cover primarily sales associate material. However, broker candidates are tested on sales associate material! Broker candidates should study all of the material in this manual to properly prepare for their state license exam.

Each chapter in this manual begins with a Key Term Review. Each key term features a straightforward definition. Terminology is a big part of testing! Study each of the terms carefully.

Key Concepts follows Key Terms. Key Concepts lists the most important concepts found in each chapter. The background material and explanations have been cut out and just the highlights are presented here. If a concept seems foreign to you, go back to *PP&L* for a complete explanation. The purpose here is to help you focus on the exam and bring the most important concepts in each chapter together in a simple, straightforward review.

At the end of some of the chapters in this book you will find Important Dates and Time Periods to Remember. Some of the license exam questions require you to recall a certain number of days (for example, a licensee has just ten days to notify the DBPR of a change in mailing address). The most important dates and time periods are featured at the end of each chapter (if applicable). These time periods should be memorized as part of the exam preparation process.

Important Formulas to Remember appears at the end of the real estate principles and practices chapters described earlier. This section features many of the types of math calculations that may appear on your exam. The formula and a sample problem have been worked for you. Be sure to master the various types of math calculations. If math is not your "bag" so to speak, consider purchasing a copy of the author's *Real Estate Math: What You Need to Know,* published by Dearborn™ Real Estate Education. It provides numerous practice problems with the solutions so that you can study step-by-step how to perform each type of math problem.

■ FLASH CARD CD-ROM BONUS!

An interactive Flash Card CD-ROM is located in the back of this book to help you master the definitions of important real estate terms. With the CD-ROM you can choose which topics, and how many terms associated with those topics, you would like to review, allowing you effectively to focus your study time.

■ PRACTICE QUESTIONS

This section of the manual is made up of five parts totaling nearly 650 practice questions. The first part consists of multiple-choice questions on license law followed by general real estate law. Sales associate candidates *and* broker candidates will benefit from studying the law questions. The practice questions use the same type of item format that is used on the license exam. Many of the practice questions are difficult. Do not let that deter you! You want to be prepared for whatever you find on the license exam. The purpose here is to help you stretch. Just can't figure out the answer to a tough practice question? No worries—an explanation to every practice question is in the back of this manual. Reading the explanation to each practice question after you have taken the practice quiz is part of test preparation.

The second part of the practice questions section contains real estate principles and practices multiple-choice questions. The principles and practices questions (as well as the law and math questions) are presented in the same chapter sequence as is used in the Key Point Reviews section of the manual.

The third part of this section is made up of math problems. Each math area is represented. A step-by-step math solution is provided for every math calculation! This edition also features math problems exclusively designed for broker candidates. Broker candidates should be proficient in solving all of these math problems, including the broker investment problems on page 157.

Practice Exam 1 and Practice Exam 2 are found in parts four and five of the sample question section. These are 100-question practice exams. The exams have been carefully constructed to match the proportion of principles and practices, license law, and math questions on the state license exam. Every effort has been made to ensure that the practice exams are approximately as difficult as the typical Florida state license exam.

■ ANSWER KEYS

Answer Keys to ALL of the practice questions appear at the end of this book. The answer keys to the two practice exams are cross-referenced to the appropriate chapter in *PP&L*. This will help you focus on those areas where you need additional review. The answer key explanations and solutions give you immediate feedback on what you answered right and wrong on all test items. In addition, a Math Cross-Reference Key lists the math testing areas by name and chapter number.

Every effort has been made to provide you with a great study tool. But success doesn't come easy. It takes hard work and determination. So pull up a chair and get a cup of coffee or your favorite beverage and get to work. I know you can accomplish your goal!

Best of luck,

Linda L. Crawford

November 2006

Successful Exam-Taking Strategies

■ PURPOSE

The main purpose of this section of the *Exam Manual* is to help you master a strategy for success. A *strategy* is a plan or method for achieving a specific goal. An effective strategy is what successful persons develop and use. This section of the book is designed to show you proven strategies to help you succeed on the Florida real estate license exam.

■ STATE LICENSE EXAM PROCESS

If you have not already done so, you will need to submit a license application to the Division of Real Estate (DRE). The application form and information concerning application fees are posted at the DRE's Web site at *www.state.fl.us/dbpr/re/forms/index.shtml.* Once your application has been approved by the DRE, a file of authorized candidates is electronically submitted to the test vendor, Promissor. The test vendor loads the candidate authorization file into its reservation system and then mails authorization letters to each eligible candidate. Upon receipt of the authorization letter, candidates are eligible to reserve an exam date and location through Promissor.

■ SCHEDULING YOUR TEST DATE

Exam reservations may be made by calling Promissor Customer Care at 888-204-6289 Monday through Friday from 8:00 AM to 11:00 PM, Saturday 8:00 AM to 5:00 PM, and Sunday from 10:00 AM to 4:00 PM (EST). Telephone reservations must be made at least three business days prior to the exam date. Candidates will receive a confirmation number at the time of the call. (Jot down the confirmation number because you will need it when you go to the test center.)

If candidates prefer, they can fax their reservation form (enclosed with the authorization letter) to (888) 204-6291. Internet reservations may be made at Promissor's Web site at *www.catglobal.com.* Fax and Internet reservations must be made at least four business days before the exam date.

When making your exam reservation, you will be asked to indicate a desired test center location. Test centers are located throughout the state. To find the location nearest to you, visit Promissor's Web site. Addresses, days and hours of operation, and directions to each test site are posted on the Web site.

Candidates are charged an examination fee payable directly to Promissor. You will be instructed to pay the fee with a major credit card or electronic check at the time you make your test reservation. Examination fees are posted on Promissor's Web site. Payments are not accepted at the test center. Choose your test date and location carefully. Candidates who wish to cancel or change an examination reservation may do so without penalty up to four business days before the examination. Candidates who are absent from or late for an examination, or who change or cancel their reservations without proper notice, will be charged the full examination fee.

WHAT TO BRING ON EXAM DAY

Allow sufficient time to arrive at the test center 30 minutes prior to your exam time. You will be required to show the test administrator two forms of signature identification, one of which must be a photo ID. You will also need to take your course completion slip (Certificate of Pre-licensing Education Completion). If you mailed the original completion slip with your license application, bring a photocopy of it to the test center. You will also be asked for the confirmation number that was given to you when you made your test reservation. Although it is not required, it is recommended that you bring with you the official authorization notice that Promissor mailed to you.

You are allowed to bring a simple nonprogrammable electronic calculator. The calculator cannot have an alphabet keyboard. It must be a silent calculator. Put fresh batteries in your calculator on exam day and run a few simple calculations on your calculator to verify that it is working properly. It is best is avoid using a solar powered calculator because the light may be insufficient for sustained use. Cell phones and pagers are *not* allowed in the testing center.

■ COMPUTER-BASED EXAM

You will take your exam on a computer. Each test question will be displayed on the computer screen. You will record your answer to each question by clicking the answer choice (A, B, C, or D) with your mouse. Your answer choice will be highlighted so that you immediately know the answer choice that is recorded electronically. Read every answer choice before choosing the answer!

You can go forward or backward through the test, mark test questions for review, and change answers. A summary screen, which can be accessed at any time during the exam, informs the candidate of the number of test questions answered, the number unanswered, and/or the number of questions skipped. The time remaining is displayed on the computer screen.

The PC (computer) you will be using is easy to operate. However, it is *strongly recommended* that you take the tutorial provided before the exam starts to familiarize yourself with the equipment. The tutorial takes about 15 minutes. It provides sample test questions so that you can familiarize yourself with how to indicate your answer choice and how to navigate through the exam. The tutorial explains all of the test features such as how to turn the exam clock on and off and how to access the summary screen.

A STRATEGY FOR A PAPERLESS EXAM

The computer will automatically keep track of any questions you skip. For this reason, it is recommended that you plan on going through the entire exam at least twice. On the first time through, answer the easy questions first. These are the test questions that you are familiar with and are confident that you know the correct answer. There are three types of test questions for which you should press "next screen" and pass up until the second time through. They are:

1. unfamiliar questions for which the correct answer is not obvious;
2. lengthy questions that fill up much of the computer screen; and
3. math questions (it is most efficient to do all of the math questions at one time when you have your calculator and scratch paper ready).

Your strategy is to use your time efficiently and to get every point possible. Therefore, answering the questions that are easiest for you first is a strategic way of maximizing your score. Once you have finished the first pass, it is time to take a second pass through the exam. Go to the summary page on your testing device. Press "Review Unanswered," and the test questions left unanswered will come up one after the other. Now it is time to finish the examination and add to your total score.

■ ORDER OF TEST QUESTIONS

Your exam is made up of three broad categories (law, principles and practices, and math). Math questions are sprinkled throughout the exam. The questions have no particular order and they are *not* arranged from "easy" to "difficult" (or vice versa). This is why the strategy of answering the easy questions first is so important. Broker candidates will complete a composite closing statement. The closing statement problem is read from the computer screen and the broker candidate completes a paper and pencil composite closing statement form.

■ PREPARING FOR SUCCESS

Knowing how to study increases your knowledge of the subject. Knowing how to take exams helps raise your score when you are tested on that subject. Now it's time to prove to yourself and to the Florida Real Estate Commission that you have mastered the subject areas of real estate principles and practices, law, and math. The strategies that are described below will help build your test taking skills. You *can* raise your score. Here is how to do it!

■ DEVELOP A POSITIVE ATTITUDE

Research shows that optimists do much better than pessimists in classes, on exams, and at work. Pessimism and optimism are *not* fixed at birth. Attitude is learned, so pessimism can be unlearned. The night before and the day of the exam, put yourself in a positive frame of mind. Reject any negative thoughts, such as "I'm not sure I'm ready" or "I don't think I'll pass," because they are self-defeating and can contribute to failure. Too much test anxiety can seriously interfere with your ability to succeed on the exam. On the other hand, a little anxiety can increase your mental processes. Adopt a positive attitude toward the exam. The exam is based on information you have already studied and been tested on in class. Use the many memory aids from your course to help you recall important facts, terms, and concepts. Maintain a confident outlook. Put yourself in the exam driver's seat. Acknowledge that there are easy *and* difficult questions to answer. Don't panic if you draw a blank on a question. Visualize yourself as relaxed and in control of the situation. See yourself as working all the way through the exam with good concentration and energy. Stay in control to maximize your exam results. The power of positive thinking applies in the test-taking arena just as it does throughout life's activities. Picture yourself leaving the test center with your PASSING notice!

■ CONTROL ANXIETY

Again, some pre-exam anxiety is natural and helpful. It "psychs" you up, it sharpens your senses, it gets the adrenaline flowing. But too much worrying gets in the way of your timing, as will anger, resentment, disgust, and a lot of other counterproductive emotions. Prepare an antipanic strategy!

If you become uptight or tense, use relaxation techniques to reduce the effect. Move your muscles (for example, briefly let your arms hang at your sides or shake or rotate your arms and hands). Relax with a sigh. Take a deep breath and hold it for a second or two. Close your eyes, clear your mind, relax your body (but don't fall off your chair). Practice this five-second "exam-jitters eliminator" *before* exam day so that you can personally experience the benefits should you need the technique on exam day.

■ BUDGET YOUR TIME

Allotted exam time (currently three and one-half hours) is at a premium for most examinees and must be used wisely. Although everyone feels the pressure of time, not every examinee makes good use of it. Too many start right off answering questions, acting like a motorist with the gas pedal to the floor and no trip itinerary! The goal is to pass the exam, so you cannot afford to rush blindly. Successful carpenters "measure twice, cut once." The following suggestions will help you improve your exam score by using time more efficiently.

One useful technique for planning your test-taking time is to set a mental *halfway point* on the exam as well as on your watch. Think in terms of three hours for taking and one-half hour for reviewing your exam. Because you are taking a 100-question exam with each question counting as one point, be sure that you have finished about 50 questions midway through the three-hour period. Continue to work at the remaining questions in the next hour and a half and use the remaining one-half hour for review. Keep track of the passing time, but don't panic if you get slightly off schedule. Work swiftly but intelligently. Don't linger too long over difficult questions—skip and return to them. Do not get uptight or rush if you see other examinees finishing early or before you. Studies prove that students who turn in their exams early include high *and* low scorers. To stay on your preplanned time schedule, be emotionally as well as academically prepared.

Toward the end you may feel you are running out of time, that if you only had more time you could answer all the questions. As mentioned earlier, everyone feels time-pressured. Try to keep that thought from hurting your exam-taking schedule. You have allowed time for going back to questions you couldn't answer or were unsure of on the first pass. Go over difficult questions you marked for review. Do *not* leave any questions unanswered (we can't say this enough) because then your chances of getting the correct answer are zero!

YOUR PERSONAL STRATEGY

Because different exam-taking strategies work for different people, some of the strategies in this section may not work for you. Follow those techniques that seem best for *you*. Do not consider the ideas set forth here to be a lock-step guide to follow—take the ones that make sense to you. Using *your common sense* throughout is the single best guide. Why? Because some of the situations described in exam questions are simply facts of everyday life and experience. *For example:*

An acre consists of
- A.   208 cubic feet.
- B.   360 degrees.
- C.   5,280 feet.
- D.   43,560 square feet.

Stop and answer the question. Using common sense as well as common knowledge, you know answer A is a measure of volume, answer B is a circular measure, and answer C is a linear measure. An acre is a *surface* measure of area, so answer D is correct. You didn't even have to know the numbers, although as familiar "traps," each side of an acre is approximately 208 feet, a circle has 360 degrees, and a mile is 5,280 feet in length. When answering a multiple-choice question, your common sense, sound reasoning, personal experience, and known information all come into play.

■ QUESTION TERMINOLOGY

If you do not know the parts and functions of an exam question, you begin with one strike against you. Because only multiple-choice formats are used on the exam, you need to understand that the first part of a question is called the *stem* or *lead-in*. It may come in the form of a question ("Which statement best defines a title search?"), an incomplete sentence ("A title search is defined as:"), or a direction ("Select the definition that best describes a title search."). The stem provides the information needed to determine the correct answer. The four possible answers are called *choices, alternatives, options,* or *responses*. One of the four choices will be the correct (or best) answer; the other three will be incorrect answers called *distractors* or *throwaways*. They are called distractors because their purpose is to distract (divert) your attention away from the correct option.

Occasionally, distracting or irrelevant information may also appear in the stem of a question to test your knowledge of the key point or formula being examined. Distractors in the lead-in may appear to you to be tricky or unfair, but if you know the course material and read carefully, you will not be misled by such distractors. *For example:*

> A property sold for $95,000. The new owner applied for and was granted a $25,000 homestead tax exemption. The property was assessed for $85,500, which is 90 percent of its selling price. If the tax rate is 28.8 mills, how much will the property taxes be?
> A. $2,216.16
> B. $2,016.00
> C. $1,742.40
> D. $1,568.16

Stop now and work the problem. To solve this property tax problem, subtract allowable tax exemptions from the assessed value and multiply the result by the tax rate: ([$85,500 – $25,000] × .0288). The price the property sold for is a distractor, as is the phrase, "which is 90 percent of its selling price." Both are irrelevant to solving this problem. Answers A, B, and D are also distractors—wrong answers in this case. Math questions are often designed so that each wrong answer can be arrived at if you fail to read the question carefully or do not know the correct way to solve the problem. Answer A ([$85,500 × .90] × .0288), answer B ([$95,000 – $25,000] × .0288), and answer D ($1,742.40 × .90) above demonstrate this. Like life, an exam is full of "red herrings." Now you see how important it is to know the component parts and structure of a question and, in the case of a math problem, to also know how to solve it.

■ MORE ABOUT MATH QUESTIONS

Another important strategy is to read the math exam question and then make a mental estimate of the answer. So often teachers are amazed at how students calculate a number that is not plausible. *Estimating* the answer first before *calculating* the answer will send up a red flag if the number you calculate isn't in the estimated ballpark. An important word of caution—the incorrect answer choices typically are the results of common mistakes, such as reversing dividend and divisor, failing to carry the math calculation to the final step, failing to convert inches to feet or feet to yards, misplacing the decimal point, and so forth. So if you mentally estimate how big a number should be *before* you calculate the answer, you are less likely to fall for one of those red herrings!

■ RESTATE THE STEM

If you have difficulty understanding the meaning of a question, mentally restate the stem from its present form into another form. If the stem is in the form of an incomplete statement, recast it into a question if that helps you. *For example*, if the stem reads, "A deed is defined as a/an:" then put the stem in question form: "How is a deed defined?" Or, "How do you define the term 'deed'?" If the stem is in the form of a question, rephrase it in the form of a complete or an incomplete statement. *For example*, if the lead-in is "Which condition may result from a change of zoning?" reword it mentally to, "A change in zoning may result in:". By rephrasing a sentence that has a confusing or complex word order, you can analyze the stem more easily and determine the correct answer more readily.

Caution: When changing the form of a stem, be certain *not* to change the meaning!

■ FOREIGN QUESTIONS

You may also come across one or two questions that might just as well have been written in a foreign language you've never seen or heard! It may be a genuinely difficult question. It may represent a blind spot in your learning. It may be a point never covered in class. In a 63-hour course (in fact, 60 "classroom hours" plus exam, translates into 50 hours of class time, given the "50-minute hour"), thousands of facts and hundreds of concepts are covered in a short time. Therefore, not everything can be taught or learned in that period, realistically speaking. Keep in mind that a "foreign" question represents only 1 out of 100 points. Choose the correct answer using a process of elimination (common sense plus sound reasoning and your own knowledge). Don't panic and bog down. Minimize the effect this one question has on your overall positive approach to the exam.

■ THE BEST ANSWER

On the state license exam, the three basic approaches to structuring the stem are: find the correct answer, find the incorrect answer, and find the best answer. When you are asked to select the "best" (or "most accurate") answer or description of the situation (as opposed to the "correct" answer), you are being alerted to the strong possibility that more than one answer is correct. Your strategy, as with all questions, is to read the lead-in carefully, think of the correct answer, and read the four choices given. Because only one of the choices is the "best" answer, you must systematically eliminate the other three. *For example*:

Checks, townships, and sections are
- A.   units of measurement.
- B.   measurements of areas.
- C.   measured by surveyors' tapes.
- D.   metric measurements.

Stop and answer this question. You look at A above and it seems to be correct. The same holds true for B. Answer C is too limiting. Answer D seems ridiculous. So you reexamine A and B and determine that, whereas A is a "correct" answer, it is not as specific a description of the lead-in as is B. Thus answer B is the best choice.

■ THE INCORRECT ANSWER

Whenever you come across an exam instruction that requires you to find the incorrect answer among the choices, apply the lead-in to each listed answer, one at a time, and determine if each choice is T or F. *For example:*

Select the incorrect answer. A broker retains a buyer's deposit in an escrow account until the
  A.   transaction is concluded.
  B.   deposit is forfeited by the buyer.
  C.   FREC issues an escrow disbursement order (EDO).
  D.   buyer changes his/her mind after the seller's acceptance of the offer.

Answer the question by choosing T or F for each choice. If necessary, keep track of this on the scrap paper provided at the test center. For answer A, you should have written a T because this is the typical time at which a deposit is released. For answer B, you know that when a buyer forfeits a deposit for whatever the reason, this too constitutes a "correct" time to release a deposit. So, you should have put down a T. For answer C, an "escape procedure" has been used due to conflicting demands on escrowed funds, and the broker is therefore required to release the deposit. You should have marked T for answer C. Finally, for answer D, the buyer is bound by acceptance of his/her offer, and since the seller accepted it, answer D is the choice you were looking for—the incorrect answer (the broker should not release a buyer's deposit under the conditions specified).

■ GUESSING

It is important to understand that there is *no* penalty for guessing on the state license exam. This means that wrong answers are *not* subtracted from right answers to arrive at your exam score. However, not answering a question is counted as a wrong answer! Therefore, make certain that all 100 questions have been answered. Now let's see what intelligent guessing—not wild haphazard guessing—can do to raise your score.

With careful reading, rereading, common sense, and logic, you will find you are able to eliminate one, perhaps two, of the wrong answers in almost every case. Educated guessing on the remaining possible answers increases your chances of correctly handling a difficult question and scoring an overall 75 or higher. You have 25 chances to be wrong and still pass the state license examination and receive your license. An illustration of guessing at the correct answer, but doing so using common sense and solid reasoning, might help you understand this strategy. *For example:*

Inflation by itself
  A.   makes it possible for more people to buy homes.
  B.   is good for the overall economy.
  C.   has no effect on buying power.
  D.   decreases buying power.

Stop and answer this question. In thinking about the concept of inflation and analyzing your four choices, answer A makes no sense; B is silly; C can't be right; and D makes sense, and it is correct.

Another guessing strategy arises with an answer that contains an *unfamiliar* word or words. This may be a distractor. In other words, do *not* assume that a word or term that is foreign to you is probably the correct answer. More often, the unfamiliar is a deliberate distractor—an incorrect answer.

■ IMPROVING YOUR ODDS

When you haven't a clue as to the correct answer, don't mentally flip a coin or throw a dart! Instead, remember that *the correct answer to every question is right in front of you* on the exam! You don't have to cope with fill-in-the-blank or essay-type questions. Sure, the right answer is carefully hidden among the group of wrong answers (distractors), but you have a one-in-four, or 25 percent, chance of choosing the correct answer. If you can eliminate just one choice for whatever the reason, you increase your odds of getting credit for a correct answer to one in three, or 33⅓ percent. If you can eliminate two choices, you raise your odds to 50 percent. Theoretically, if you know the answers to only 72 questions (failing) but make educated guesses at the remaining 28, you could end up with a score ranging from 79 to 86, which would be passing! Making the odds work in *your* favor is using your head.

■ IGNORING THE ANSWERS

Most test-takers read a question stem and immediately look at all four answers. For some, this approach causes no problems. For others, it causes unnecessary tension and confusion over every question. Common errors are often used as incorrect choices (distractors), so to prevent individual question anxiety, try not reading the four choices while reading the stem. After you have read the stem one or more times, think about (or calculate) the correct answer. Then read the four choices and see if your thought-out answer is there. The result of using this approach could be to reduce your nervousness, heighten your confidence, and raise your score.

■ HANDLING NEGATIVES

The shock of encountering questions that are worded in unexpected and awkward ways can scare and frustrate anyone. On the state license exam *negatives* in the stem or in a choice (for example, "not" or "un-" or "except") are typically in uppercase letters for emphasis. A negative in a stem is asking you to respond in the opposite manner from an affirmative statement. Whereas usually you eliminate incorrect answers to a question, in the case of a negative in a stem, you *discard the correct answers*. Therefore, be alert for a negative, particularly one found in the stem of a multiple-choice question. *For example:*

Escape procedures available to a licensee for resolving conflicting demands on escrowed funds do NOT include
  A. mediation.
  B. arbitration.
  C. subpoena.
  D. lawsuit.

Stop and answer this question. Because of the word "NOT" in the stem, you need to rule out the correct answers (A, B, and D), and thus C is the answer to this negatively worded question.

The form of a negative question may be shaped by the word "except," which is usually in uppercase letters. Use the same strategy by ruling out the correct answers, or put another way, choose the one answer that is different from the other three. *For example:*

> Which feature does NOT affect the size of the monthly payments for adjustable-rate mortgages?
> A. Index rate used by the lender
> B. Margin used by the lender
> C. Principal borrowed by the mortgagor
> D. Assumability of the loan

Stop and answer the question. From your knowledge of the components of adjustable-rate mortgages, you know that the index, margin, and principal affect the monthly payment amount. So you reject the correct answers and are left with D as your answer choice.

■ CLUES IN STEMS AND CHOICES

A clue may come from the use of "general qualifiers" or "absolute words" in the choices. *For example:*

> When reconciling value, an appraiser
> A. usually weighs the quantity and quality of the relevant data/information.
> B. must select the highest price in terms of cash equivalency.
> C. gives the most weight to the median indicator of value.
> D. always chooses the mean of the three indicators of value.

Stop and answer the question. Because qualifiers, such as "usually" (as well as "generally," "tends to," "most," and "some") *lessen* the strength of a statement or answer, they are often clues to a correct response. Because absolutes such as "always" (as well as "all," "entirely," and "never") *tighten* a statement or answer, they are often hints to an incorrect response (distractor). In the example, "usually" is a clue to the right answer (A), whereas clues to wrong answers are "must" (B) and "always" (D). Answer C is incorrect as a result of your knowledge of the subject area being tested.

Other strategies could be lumped under the heading "clues in stems and choices," but it is unnecessary to cover them in light of the higher quality of questions now appearing on real estate license examinations.

■ DESPERATION STRATEGIES

Originators of exam questions generally find it easier to create the wrong answers than the right (or best) answers. Consequently, test-writers sometimes have a tendency to qualify the correct answer with extra words to ensure its preciseness. Therefore, the correct choice is sometimes the longest answer among the four choices because it is more detailed. However, recognize this as a desperation strategy, one that should be used only if you "draw a blank."

By this same reasoning, you may be able to increase your odds by dismissing the shortest answer. But again, this is very nearly "blind guessing," as is the tactic of throwing out answers A and D on the grounds that test-writers tend to "hide correct answers in the pack." A similar, but equally blind, approach is to eliminate the highest and lowest answers to a math problem. These three strategies are in the same league as the longest-answer approach—rash moves indeed!

■ EXAM RESULTS

Exams are graded at the test site and candidates are given a grade notice at that time. The grade notice includes pass/fail information, and failure notices include a breakdown of the points scored in each major subject area. An initial inactive license is mailed directly to licensees following notification of a passing score. Sales associate applicants may legally begin to operate as licensees once they notify the DRE of their employer's name and address by filing the appropriate DRE form.

■ EXAM-TAKING REMINDERS

Start your review several weeks, or at least several days, before the exam. Get plenty of rest the night before the exam. Be careful of "cramming" to the point that you are drained and unable to think clearly on exam day. Study smart, not necessarily more. Wear comfortable clothing and shoes to the test center. Remember to bring whatever materials are required. Don't arrive hungry or too full—eat "appropriately" beforehand. Be at the test center a little ahead of the start time. Make a "pit stop" before you go into the exam room. Be mentally and physically prepared; listen to, understand, and follow all verbal and written instructions. Budget your exam time by preparing a preplanned approach. Read every word of every question (stem as well as choices). Think before you answer. Answer the question asked—not the one you expected or hoped would be on the exam. Check and recheck. Answer all 100 questions even though you don't know the answer to every question on the exam—no one knows it all. Review your work as time permits. Remember that the objective is a passing score, not necessarily a perfect score.

The preceding strategies constitute neither solutions nor substitutes for learning and knowing the required subject matter. They are offered as guides to improve your exam-taking ability and to assist you in passing the state license examination. Put these strategies to work for you by systematically progressing through the review outlines that follow, answering the math questions, and taking the two practice 100-question exams.

REAL ESTATE LAW, FLORIDA REAL ESTATE LICENSE LAW

License Law and Qualifications for Licensure
(Chapter 2)

■ KEY TERM REVIEW

Broker is a person who, for another and for compensation, performs real estate services.

Broker associate is an individual who meets the requirements of a broker but who chooses to work (operate) in real estate under the direction (employ) of another broker.

Caveat emptor is a policy of let the buyer beware (buyer is responsible for own knowledge in real estate transactions).

Compensation is anything of value or a valuable consideration, directly or indirectly paid, promised, or expected to be paid or received.

License is a written document issued by the DBPR that serves as *prima facie evidence* (valid on its face) that the person is licensed on the date shown.

Mutual recognition agreement is a transactional agreement between Florida and another state that provides for the two states to recognize each other's real estate license education.

Owner-developer is an unlicensed entity that sells, exchanges, or leases its own property.

Prima facie evidence is a legal term used to refer to evidence that is good and sufficient on its face to establish a given fact or prove a case.

Real estate services include any real estate activity involving compensation for performing the service for another.

Reciprocity is the practice of mutual exchanges of privileges. Some states have reciprocal arrangements for recognizing and granting licenses to licensed real estate professionals from other states.

Registration is the process of submitting information to the DRE that is entered into the Division's records.

Sales associate is a person who performs real estate services for compensation but who does so under the direction, control, and management of an active broker or owner-developer.

Withhold adjudication occurs when the court determines that a defendant is not likely to again engage in a criminal act and that the ends of justice and the welfare of society do not require the defendant suffer the penalty imposed by law. After such determination, the court may withhold adjudication of guilt, stay (stop) the imposition of the sentence, and place the defendant on probation.

■ KEY CONCEPTS IN CHAPTER 2

■ **Two types of real estate licenses**

— Sales associate is the introductory level; sales associates must work under the direction, control, and management of a broker or an owner-developer; sales associates must be registered under one broker or one owner-developer

— Broker licenses require additional education and experience

■ **Broker associates** are licensed as brokers but choose to work under the direction of a broker/employer

■ **Owner-developer** is an unlicensed entity that sells, exchanges, or leases its own property

— Sales staff must hold active real estate licenses to be paid commission

— Sales staff is exempt from licensure if paid strictly on salaried basis

■ **Application requirements**

— Background information required concerning whether the applicant has been convicted of a crime, pled guilty to a crime, or pled *nolo contendere* (no contest)

— Must disclose prior conviction even if court action (*adjudication*) was withheld

— Disclose any name or alias not signed on the application, including a maiden name

■ **Applicant must**

— be 18 years of age or older

— have earned a high school diploma (or equivalent)

— be of good character

— have not violated Chapter 475 within one year prior to application

■ **Time limits for application and pre license education**

— The license application expires two years after it is received by the DBPR

— If applicant does not pass the state license exam within two years after the course completion date, the course completion expires and the applicant must again complete the pre license education course

■ **Nonresident application requirements**

— U.S. citizenship is *not* required

— Applicants do *not* have to be residents of Florida

— Nonresident applicants must sign the *irrevocable consent to service* section on the application which allows legal action to be initiated in Florida

— Resident licensees who move out of the state (become nonresidents of Florida) must notify the Commission within ten days of the change of address *and* comply with all nonresident requirements within 60 days

■ **Change in mailing address** requires licensee to inform the DBPR in writing within ten days

■ **Mutual recognition agreements** recognize the education and experience that real estate licensees have acquired in another state or nation

— Applies exclusively to *nonresidents* licensed in other jurisdictions

— Requires applicants to pass a 40 question Florida-specific real estate law exam with a grade of 75 percent or higher

■ **Florida resident**

— A person who has resided in Florida continuously for a period of four calendar months within the preceding year

— The test used to determine whether an applicant for licensure qualifies as a nonresident under mutual recognition

■ **Post-licensing requirement**

— Florida sales associates *must* complete the 45-hour post-licensing course *before the expiration* of the initial sales associate license

— Failure to complete the post-licensing requirement prior to the expiration date will cause the license to become null and void

■ **Continuing education requirement** requires 14 hours of continuing education each subsequent licensure period following the initial license period

■ **Attorneys** who are active members of The Florida Bar are exempt from FREC Course I (for sales associates) and continuing education (but not post-licensing education)

■ **Individuals with a four-year degree in real estate** are exempt from FREC Course I, FREC Course II, and post-licensing education (but not continuing education)

■ **Prima facie evidence**

— A legal term used to refer to evidence that is good and sufficient on its face to establish a given fact or prove a case

— A real estate license indicates the licensee's name, issue date, and expiration date and serves as *prima facie evidence* that the licensee holds a current and valid license

■ **Real estate services (A BAR SALE)**

— **A** Advertise real estate services

— **B** Buy

— **A** Appraise

— **R** Rent or provide rental information or lists

— **S** Sell

— **A** Auction

— **L** Lease

— **E** Exchange

■ **A real estate license is required** if a person performs any real estate service for compensation *or the implied intent* to collect compensation, unless specifically exempt

■ **Real estate attorneys** may *not* receive compensation for performing real estate services, including referral of clients and prospects, *unless* they also have a real estate license

■ **Individuals exempt from licensure**

— Property owners who buy, sell, exchange, or lease their own real property (person who sells or leases real estate that he or she does *not* own is *presumed* to be acting as a real estate licensee)

— Part owners *provided* they do *not* receive a larger share of the profits than their proportional investment

— Business entities that sell, exchange, or lease their own real property

— Salaried employees of business entities who sell, exchange, or lease real property for their employer *provided* they are *not* paid a commission or compensated on a transactional basis

■ **A real estate license is not required** for the following

— Selling cemetery lots

— Renting a mobile home lot in a mobile home park

— Radio and television announcers

— Attorneys-at-law and certified public accounts when working as attorneys or CPAs

— Attorney-in-fact (person with a *power of attorney*) for execution of instruments only

— Selling personal property only such as mortgage brokers selling mortgages (personal property) even though the mortgages are secured by real property

— Personal representatives (such as receivers or trustees) when designated by a will or by court order

— Salaried managers of condominiums and cooperative apartment complexes (co-ops) *provided* the rentals are for periods of one year or less

— Leasing agents of an apartment complex who work in an on-site rental office in a leasing capacity *provided* they are paid a salary

— Owners of time-shares who sell the time-share *provided* the person *owns* the time-share for his or her own use and occupancy

— See textbook, *Florida Real Estate Principles, Practices & Law,* for other exemptions

■ IMPORTANT DATES AND TIME PERIODS TO REMEMBER

■ **Ten days.** Number of days to notify the DBPR regarding a change of mailing address, change of employer, or change of business address

■ **60 days.** Number of days to notify the DBPR if a licensee becomes a nonresident and to file *irrevocable consent to service*

■ **Up to one year.** Salaried managers of condominium or cooperative units who prepare rental agreements with a duration of up to one year are exempt from real estate license

■ **More than one year.** Mangers of condominiums or cooperatives who prepare lease agreements with a duration longer than one year must be licensed

■ **Two years.** Time period after which the license application expires

■ **Two years.** Time period after which the pre license course expires

License Law and Administration
(Chapter 3)

■ KEY TERM REVIEW

Canceled means to become void without disciplinary action.

Current mailing address is the current residential address a licensee uses to receive mail through the U.S. Postal Service.

Executive powers of the Florida Real Estate Commission (FREC) include the power to regulate and enforce license law.

Group license is issued to a sales associate or broker associate employed by an owner-developer who owns properties in the name of various entities.

Ineffective refers to a license that exists, but the licensee cannot use it because it is either inactive or has been suspended.

Involuntary inactive status results when a license is not renewed at the end of the license period.

Multiple licenses refers to when a broker holds more than one broker's license.

Promulgate means to enact rules and regulations.

Quasi-judicial powers of the FREC include the power to grant or deny license applications, to determine license law violations, and to administer penalties.

Quasi-legislative powers of the FREC include the power to enact administrative rules and regulations and to interpret questions regarding the practice of real estate.

Void means to no longer exist.

Voluntary inactive is the license status that results when a licensee has applied to the DBPR to be placed on inactive status.

■ KEY CONCEPTS IN CHAPTER 3

- ■ **The Florida Real Estate Commission (FREC)** is made up of
  - — Four licensed real estate brokers who have held active licenses for the past five years
  - — Two consumer members

- One licensed broker or sales associate who has held an active license for the past two years

- At least one member 60 years or older

■ **Seven Florida Real Estate Commissioners**

- Appointed by the governor, subject to confirmation by the Florida Senate

- Appointed to four-year terms

- May *not* serve more than two consecutive terms

- Paid $50 per day per diem

■ **Commission powers** include three general areas

- Executive power to regulate and enforce license law

- Quasi-legislative power to enact and revise administrative rules

- Quasi-judicial power to grant or deny applications and administer penalties

■ **Specific duties of the FREC**

- Adopt a seal

- Foster the education of applicants and licensees

- Make determinations of violations

- Regulate professional practices

- Create and pass rules and regulations

- Establish fees

- Grant and deny applications for licensure

- Suspend and revoke licenses, and impose administrative fines

■ **FREC *may not* impose imprisonment as a punishment**

■ **The Director of the Division of Real Estate (DRE)** is appointed by the Secretary of the DBPR, *subject to* FREC approval

■ **Licensees must notify the DBPR of a change in current mailing address within ten days**

■ **Active status** required to operate as a licensee; the licensee must have an active license at the time the service of real estate was *performed*—however, the licensee may be inactive at the time payment is *received*

■ **Licensees** must complete applicable post-licensing education or continuing education *before* renewing a license

- When a licensee signs and returns the renewal application the licensee is attesting to have completed the education requirement

■ **Two types of inactive status**

- Voluntary inactive—A licensee has timely renewed but chooses not to engage in the real estate business; licensee requests to be placed in this status and he or she may renew as voluntary inactive indefinitely

— Involuntary inactive—A licensee fails to renew; the license becomes null and void after two years

■ **Members of U.S. Armed Forces who have licenses in good standing** are exempt from license renewal while on active duty and for six months thereafter—If the military duty is out of state, the exemption also applies to a licensed spouse (*Note:* The exemption does *not* apply if the licensee engages in real estate services for profit during that period.)

■ **Void license** means the license no longer exists

— When a license is involuntary inactive for more than two years, the license becomes null and void

— A license becomes void when it has been revoked

— A person who no longer wants to engage in the real estate business can voluntarily cancel being licensed; when a license is canceled it becomes null and void

■ **Ineffective license** exists, but the licensee cannot use it

— Real estate licensees with an inactive license may not perform real estate services

— A real estate license is ineffective during the period of license suspension

■ **Ten days to notify the Commission**

— Broker or a registered school changes business address

— Sales associate, broker associate, or real estate instructor changes employer

— The licenses *cease to be in force* (business cannot be conducted) until the FREC receives proper notification

■ IMPORTANT DATES AND TIME PERIODS TO REMEMBER

■ **Ten days.** Number of days to notify the FREC regarding a change of business address

■ **Ten days.** Number of days a sales associate, broker associate, or an instructor has to notify the FREC of a change of employer

■ **Six months.** Grace period after discharge from military duty to renew license

■ **Two years.** Time period after which involuntary inactive license becomes null and void

Brokerage Relationships and Ethics
(Chapter 4)

■ KEY TERM REVIEW

Agent is a person entrusted with another's business; the person authorized by the principal to act on the principal's behalf.

Customer is a member of the public who is or may be a buyer or a seller of real property and may or may not be represented by a real estate licensee in an authorized brokerage relationship.

Designated sales associates are two real estate licensees from the same brokerage company designated to represent the buyer and the seller as single agents in *nonresidential* transactions.

Dual agent refers to a broker who represents as a fiduciary both the buyer and the seller in a real estate transaction; dual agency is illegal in Florida.

Fiduciary occurs when a broker is in a relationship of trust and confidence with the broker as agent and the seller or the buyer as principal.

Fraud is the intent to misrepresent a material fact or to deceive to gain an unfair advantage or to harm another person.

General agent is authorized by the principal to handle the affairs related to a business or trade, or to handle all the business at a certain location; for example, a property manager.

Misrepresentation is the misstatement of fact or the omission or concealment of a factual matter.

Principal is the seller (or the buyer, but not both) in a single agent relationship; the principal authorizes the agent to act on the principal's behalf; while the principal is responsible for the actions of the agent.

Residential sales are defined in Florida license law to mean the sale of improved residential property of four or fewer units, the sale of unimproved residential property intended for use as four or fewer units, or the sale of agricultural property of ten or fewer acres.

Single agent is a broker who represents either the buyer or the seller (but not both) and has a fiduciary relationship with the party represented.

Special agent is authorized by the buyer or the seller to handle only a specific business transaction or to perform a specific act; a broker who has a single agent relationship is a special agent with limited power or authority.

Transaction broker is a broker who provides limited representation to a buyer, a seller, or both in a real estate transaction, but who does *not* represent either party in a fiduciary capacity or as a single agent.

Universal agent is authorized by the principal to perform all acts that the principal may personally perform and that may be lawfully delegated.

■ KEY CONCEPTS IN CHAPTER 4

- ■ **Three types of agency relationships in general business dealings**

  — Universal agent is authorized to perform all acts

  — General agent is authorized to perform only acts related to a business

  — Special agent is authorized to perform a specific act

- ■ **Three brokerage relationship options in Florida**

  — The broker may work as a transaction broker for the buyer and/or the seller (presumed relationship)

  — The broker may work as a single agent for either the buyer of the seller (but *not* for both in the same transaction)

  — The broker may act in a no brokerage relationship (the broker doesn't represent either the buyer or the seller)

- ■ **Although dual agency was allowed at one time in Florida, dual agency is now illegal**

- ■ **Duties and obligations of the brokerage relationship law** apply to *all* real estate transactions

- ■ **Written disclosures are required in residential real estate transactions** *only*

- ■ **Disclosure requirements do *not* apply to**

  — Nonresidential transactions

  — Rental or leasing of real property, unless there is an option to purchase property improved with four or fewer residential units

  — Auctions

  — Appraisals

  — Business enterprises or business opportunities unless improved with four or fewer residential units

- ■ **Transaction broker provides limited representation**

  — The buyer or seller is *not* responsible for the acts of the licensee

  — Parties give up their right to undivided loyalty

  — Allows licensee to facilitate the transaction by assisting both buyer and seller

- ■ **Duties of a transaction broker**

  — Dealing honestly and fairly

  — Accounting for all funds

  — Using skill, care, and diligence in the transaction

  — Disclosing all known facts that materially affect the value of residential real property and are not readily observable to the buyer

  — Presenting all offers and counteroffers in a timely manner

— Exercising limited confidentiality, unless waived in writing by a party

— Providing any additional duties that are mutually agreed to with a party

■ **Single agent relationship**

— Fiduciary relationship

— Broker *agent* and seller (or the buyer) *principal*

— Full disclosure and loyalty to the principal

■ **Single agent relationship duties**

— Dealing honestly and fairly

— Loyalty (Act solely in the best interest of the principal)

— Confidentiality

— Obedience (Must obey all *lawful* instructions of the principal)

— Full disclosure

— Accounting for all funds

— Using skill, care, and diligence in the transaction

— Presenting all offers and counteroffers in a timely manner

— Disclose all known facts that materially affect the value of residential real property and are not readily observable

■ **Subagents** are persons authorized to assist and represent the agent

— Sales associate is an agent of the broker

— In a single agent relationship, the broker is an agent of the principal

— Because a sales associate is an agent of the broker, the sales associate is a *subagent* of the principal

— Sales associates and broker associates owe the same fiduciary obligations to the principal as does their broker

■ **No brokerage relationship duties**

— Dealing honestly and fairly

— Disclosing all known facts that materially affect the value of residential real property that are not readily observable to the buyer

— Accounting for all funds entrusted to a licensee

■ **Transition to another relationship** is accomplished with the *Consent to Transition to Transaction Broker,* which requires the buyer's or seller's signature (or initials) before the licensee may change from one brokerage relationship to another

■ **Written disclosure requirements for residential transactions**

— The proper disclosure notice must be given to the party before, or at the time of, entering into a listing agreement or an agreement for representation, or before the showing of property, whichever occurs first

— The disclosure document may be separate or incorporated into another document

— Signature is *not* mandatory (*except* Content to Transition to Transaction Broker Notice)

— Broker must retain disclosure documents for five years on all residential transactions that result in a written contract to purchase

■ **Designated sales associates**

— This applies to nonresidential sales *only*

— Buyer and seller must each have assets of at least $1 million

— Broker designates one sales associate to work with buyer as a single agent and another to work with seller as a single agent

— Broker facilitates and advises designated sales associates

— Buyer and seller must request the arrangement

— Buyer and seller must sign disclosure notice

■ **Ways to terminate a brokerage relationship**

— Fulfillment of brokerage relationship's purpose (performance)

— Mutual agreement

— Expiration of terms of the agreement

— Broker renouncing relationship by giving notice (resignation)

— Principal or customer revokes

— Death of either party

— Destruction or condemnation of the property

— Bankruptcy of the principal or customer

■ **Elements for a cause of action for fraud**

— The licensee made a misstatement or failed to disclose a material fact

— The licensee either knew or should have known that the statement was not accurate or that the undisclosed information should have been disclosed

— The buyer relied on the misstatement

— The buyer was damaged as a result

■ IMPORTANT DATES AND TIME PERIODS TO REMEMBER

■ **Five years.** Period required to retain brokerage relationship disclosures for all transactions that result in a written contract

Real Estate Brokerage Operations
(Chapter 5)

■ KEY TERM REVIEW

Arbitration is a process whereby, with the consent of all parties to the dispute, the matter is submitted to a disinterested third party who makes a binding judgment.

Blind advertisement is advertising that fails to disclose the licensed name of the brokerage firm and that provides only a post office box number, telephone number, and/or street address.

Commingle is the illegal practice of mixing a buyer's, seller's, tenant's, or landlord's funds with the broker's own money or mixing escrow money with the broker's personal funds or brokerage funds.

Conflicting demands occur when the buyer and seller make demands regarding the disbursing of escrowed property that are inconsistent and cannot be resolved.

Conversion is the unauthorized control or use of another person's personal property.

Corporation is an artificial person or legal entity created by law and consisting of one or more persons that is formed by filing articles of incorporation.

Deposit is a sum of money, or its equivalent, delivered to a real estate licensee as earnest money, payment, or partial payment in connection with a real estate transaction.

Earnest money deposit also referred to as a *good-faith deposit* or *binder deposit* is money given as good faith to accompany an offer to purchase or lease real property.

Escrow account is an account for the deposit of money held by a third party in trust for another for safekeeping.

Escrow disbursement order (EDO) is a determination by the FREC of who is entitled to disputed funds.

General partnership is an association of two or more persons for the purpose of jointly conducting a business together and each to share the profits and losses of the business.

Good faith is a party's honest intent to transact business, free from any intent to defraud the other party, and generally speaking, each party's faithfulness to his or her duties or obligations as set forth by contract.

Interpleader is a legal proceeding whereby the broker, having no financial interest in the disputed funds, deposits with the court the disputed escrow deposit so that the court can determine the rightful claimant.

Kickback occurs when a broker receives money from someone other than the buyer or the seller such as for referring a buyer or seller to a particular vendor for services.

Limited liability company is a form of business organization that offers the best features of a corporation and a partnership; members of a LLC are protected from personal liability as in a corporate form of ownership and the tax advantages of a partnership.

Limited liability partnership features protection from personal liability in much the same way as limited partners in a limited partnership.

Limited partnership consists of one or more general partners and one or more limited partners.

Mediation is an informal, nonadversarial process intended to reach a negotiated settlement that is *not* binding.

Ostensible partnership (or quasi partnership) exists where the parties do not form a real partnership but act or do business in such a manner that the public, having no knowledge of the private relations of the parties, would reasonably be deceived into believing that a partnership exists. (Note: Brokers *may* share office space *provided* they make true status known on signs, telephone listings, advertising, and so forth.)

Point of contact information refers to any means by which to contact the brokerage firm or individual licensee including mailing address(es), physical street address(es), e-mail address(es), telephone number(s), or facsimile (FAX) telephone number(s); the brokerage firm's name must be above, below, or adjacent to the point of contact information.

Policy manual is a collection of office rules and regulations created to inform sales associates and employees of the standards and procedures in that particular office. (Note: A policy manual is an important document in brokerage offices regardless of size.)

Puffing is the term used to describe a licensee's boasting of a property's benefits.

Sole proprietorship is a business owned by one person with no legal separation between the owner and the business.

Telephone solicitation is the initiation of a telephone call for the purpose of encouraging the purchase of, or investment in, property, goods, or services.

■ KEY CONCEPTS IN CHAPTER 5

■ **Brokerage offices**

— Active brokers required to have an office and to register the office with the DBPR

— Must be at least one enclosed room in a building of stationary construction

— Office may be in broker's residence *provided* the entrance sign is displayed and local zoning permits business in residence

— Sales associates must be registered and work out of the broker's office or branch office and may *not* open their own offices

■ **Branch office**

— Each branch office must be registered (two-year period)

— A *temporary shelter* in a subdivision being sold by a broker is not a branch office if the shelter is intended only for the protection of customers and sales associates (if business records are maintained at location and sales associates are assigned to location then it must be registered as a branch office)

— Branch office registrations are *not* transferable to another location

■ **Active real estate brokers must display an entrance office sign** with the

— Name of the broker

— Trade name (if any)

— Words "Licensed (or Lic.) Real Estate Broker"

— Name of the business and the name of at least one active broker (if business entity)

— Names of sales associates (if included) separate from the broker's names and identified as sales associates or broker associates

■ **Advertising**

— Advertising must be worded so that a reasonable person will know that he or she is dealing with a licensee

— Blind advertisement prohibited

— Internet advertising must include point of contact information

— Advertising on the Internet must include the brokerage firm's name adjacent to, above, or below the point of contact information

— If licensees include their personal name in an advertisement, they must use their last name as registered with the FREC

— Yard signs, classified ads, and promotional advertising must include name of real estate brokerage firm

— False advertising is a second-degree misdemeanor

■ **Licensee selling property "by owner"**

— A licensee who owns property and is selling the property "by owner" may place a classified ad

— Licensees are *not* required to indicate in the ad that they are licensees

— Licensees should disclose to prospective buyers that they are licensed at the first point of meaningful negotiation

■ **Escrow or trust accounts**

— Sales associates must deliver earnest money deposits to their broker no later than the end of the next business day

— Brokers must place deposits into their escrow account no later than the end of the third business day
    Example—sales associate receives a deposit on Wednesday (no legal holidays involved); sales associate must turn over to broker by end of business on Thursday and broker must deposit by end of business on Monday

— Broker must be a signatory on broker's escrow account

— Broker must reconcile the broker's escrow account each month

— Escrow account may be an interest-bearing or a noninterest-bearing account; if interest-bearing must secure the written permission of all interest parties and broker must get written authorization as to who is entitled to interest earned

— Broker's escrow accounts are maintained at Florida commercial banks, savings associations, and credit unions

— Alternatively attorneys and title companies with trust powers may hold the funds instead of the broker (but *not* in stock or bond brokerage house)

— If an attorney or title-closing agent will hold the deposit, the broker is still required to deliver the funds to the escrow agent within the same time frame required for depositing funds into a broker's escrow account

■ **Broker must reconcile escrow account each month**

— Brokers may not commingle (mix) escrow deposits with business funds or personal funds

— Broker must be a signatory on broker's escrow account

— Broker must review, sign, and date monthly reconciliation

— Broker is allowed to place up to $1,000 of personal funds in sales escrow accounts

— Broker is allowed to place up to $5,000 of personal funds in property management escrow account

— Broker is accountable for reviewing the brokerage's escrow accounting procedures to ensure compliance with Florida law

■ **Conflicting demands and good-faith doubt**

— Broker must notify the FREC, in writing, within 15 business days

— Broker must institute one of four settlement procedures within 30 business days from the time the broker received the conflicting demands

■ **Three exceptions to notice requirements**

— Sale of HUD-owned property utilizing a HUD contract

— If buyer of a residential condominium unit gives written notice of buyer's intent to cancel the contract as authorized by the Condominium Act

— If buyer in good faith fails to satisfy the terms specified in the financing clause of a contract

■ **Four settlement procedures (MALE)**

— **M**   Mediation

— **A**   Arbitration

— **L**   Litigation

— **E**   Escrow disbursement order (EDO)

- ■ **Requirements concerning rental lists**
  - — Rental list must include a notice to prospective tenant concerning repayment
  - — If rental information is in error 100 percent refund
  - — If unable to find a suitable rental 75 percent refund
  - — Demand for refund must be made within 30 days following the day of purchase
  - — Violation is a first degree misdemeanor

- ■ **Broker must be authorized in contract** in order to place a lien on real property for nonpayment of commission

- ■ **Broker may not pay a commission or referral fee to an unlicensed person**
  - — Finder's fee exception—A property management firm or an owner of an apartment complex may pay a finder's fee (referral fee) of up to $50 to an unlicensed person who is a tenant of the apartment complex
  - — Broker may pay a licensed foreign broker a fee so long as the licensed foreign broker does not violate Florida law
  - — All deposits and other funds must be collected in the name of the broker/employer with the express consent of the broker/employer

- ■ **Facts regarding kickbacks**
  - — A *kickback* is an unearned fee paid to a licensee associated with a real estate transaction for non-real estate services
  - — Prior to the payment and receipt of the kickback, the buyer and seller must be fully informed of facts regarding the kickback
  - — Kickbacks must not violate RESPA
  - — Kickbacks are *not* allowed for title and casualty insurance transactions
  - — Person receiving the kickback must be properly licensed if a license is required to perform the service (In Florida, real estate licensees must also be licensed as mortgage brokers to be legally paid a fee for referring prospects to a mortgage lender)
  - — Licensees are prohibited from sharing commission with an unlicensed person (Exception if sharing commission with a buyer or seller in a real estate transaction)

- ■ **Business entities that may register as a brokerage entity**
  - — *Sole proprietorship* (features unlimited liability and no formal requirement to create)
  - — *General partnership* (each partner is responsible for all business debts)
  - — *Limited partnership* (created by filing agreement with the state and features unlimited liability for general partners and limited liability for limited partners; words "Limited" or abbreviation must be used in name and limited partners make cash or property investment but *not* managerial services)
  - — *Limited liability partnership* (protection from personal liability for acts of another partner or employee)

- — *Corporation* (features separate legal entity from the owners and is formed by filing Articles of Incorporation and must include "company" or "incorporated" or abbreviation in name (*Note:* Sales associates and broker associate may *not* be officers or directors of a brokerage corporation; broker associate must change status to broker before becoming an officer or director.)

- — *Limited liability company* (protection from business debts)

■ **Real estate brokerage general partnership**

- — The partnership must register with the FREC under the partnership name

- — At least one partner must be licensed as an active broker

- — Partners who deal with the public and perform real estate services must be licensed as active brokers

- — Sales associates and broker associates may *not* be general partners in a real estate brokerage partnership

■ **Real estate brokerage limited partnerships**

- — The limited partnership must register with the FREC under the limited partnership name

- — General partners who deal with the public and perform real estate services must be licensed as active brokers

- — All other general partners must register with the FREC for identification purposes

- — Sales associates and broker associates may *not* be general partners in a real estate brokerage limited partnership

- — Sales associates and broker associates may be limited partners in a real estate brokerage limited partnership (regarded in same light as stockholders in a corporation)

- — Limited partners are not required to register with the FREC

■ **Real estate brokerage corporations**

- — The corporation must register with the FREC under the corporation name

- — At least one officer or director must be licensed as an active broker

- — Active Florida brokers, inactive Florida brokers, and unlicensed people may serve as officers and directors of a real estate brokerage

- — Officers and directors who deal with the public and perform real estate services must be licensed as active brokers

- — All officers and directors who are not licensed must be registered with the FREC for identification purposes

- — Sales associates and broker associates may *not* be an officer or director in a real estate brokerage corporation

- — Sales associates and broker associates may be shareholders of a real estate brokerage corporation

■ **Business entities that may *not* register**

— Corporation sole (churches)

— Joint venture (an agreement to participate in one or a limited number of transactions)

— Business trust (for example Real Estate Investment Trust—REIT)

— Cooperative association

— Unincorporated association

■ IMPORTANT DATES AND TIME PERIODS TO REMEMBER

■ **End of next business day.** Time period for sales associates to turn funds over to broker

■ **End of third business day.** Time period for broker to deposit funds into escrow account

■ **Ten business days.** Number of days to notify the FREC if the broker requested an EDO and the escrow dispute is either settled or goes to court before the EDO is issued

■ **15 business days.** Number of days to notify the FREC of conflicting demands or good faith doubt

■ **30 business days.** Number of days to institute settlement procedure after receiving conflicting demands

■ **Five years.** Time period to preserve broker's business records (two years after litigation if longer than five years)

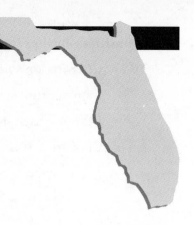

Complaints, Violations, and Penalties
(Chapter 6)

■ KEY TERM REVIEW

Administrative complaint is an outline of allegations of facts and charges against the licensee.

Breach is the breaking of a promise or obligation.

Citations (specified fines) involve fines that range from $100 to $1,000 per offense for violations that have been specified in the citation rule for which there is no substantial threat to the public health, safety, and welfare.

Commingle is to mix the money of a buyer or seller with a broker's own money.

Complaint is an alleged violation of a law or rule.

Concealment is the withholding of information.

Conversion is the unauthorized control or use of another's personal property.

Culpable negligence is failing to use the care a reasonable person would exercise.

Failure to account for and deliver is the act of failing to pay money to a person entitled to receive it.

Formal complaint (or *administrative complaint*) is an outline of charges against a licensee.

Fraud is intentional deceit for the purpose of inducing another to rely on information to get the person to part with some valuable thing or to surrender a legal right.

Legally sufficient means that a complaint contains facts indicating that a violation of federal or Florida statute, or DBPR or FREC rule.

Material fact is a piece of information that is relevant to a person making a decision and that affects the value of the real property.

Misrepresentation is an untrue statement of fact or the concealment of a material fact.

Moral turpitude is conduct contrary to honesty, good morals, justice, and accepted custom.

Notice of noncompliance may be issued for a first-time minor violation (licensee has 15 days to correct minor infraction).

Probable cause is reasonable grounds (sufficient facts and evidence) to warrant prosecution.

Recommended order contains the administrative law judge's findings, conclusions, and recommended penalty.

Stipulation is an agreement as to the penalty reached between the attorneys for the DRE and the licensee or licensee's attorney.

Subpoena is a command to appear at a certain time and place to give testimony.

Summary suspension is an emergency suspension that must be issued by the DBPR Secretary or his or her designee.

■ KEY CONCEPTS IN CHAPTER 6

- ■ **Seven steps to complaint process** (quasi-judicial procedure)
  - — Filing the complaint
  - — Investigation
  - — Probable cause
  - — Formal complaint
  - — Informal hearing or formal hearing
  - — Final order
  - — Judicial review (appeal)
- ■ **Complaint is filed with the DBPR**
  - — Complaint must be legally sufficient
  - — DBPR may issue a notice of noncompliance for a first-time offense of a minor violation
- ■ **Investigation** of the complaint
  - — Complaint must be in writing and legally sufficient
  - — Anonymous (unsigned) complaint is accepted if complaint is substantial
- ■ **Probable Cause Panel**
  - — Composed of two members of the FREC
  - — Closed to the public
  - — Purpose to determine whether probable cause exists
  - — If probable cause not found, may dismiss case or dismiss with letter of guidance
- ■ **Formal complaint is issued if probable cause is found**
  - — Also called an *administrative complaint*
  - — Specifies the alleged violation
- ■ **Informal hearing**
  - — Licensee signs *election of rights* and does *not* dispute allegations of material fact and requests an informal hearing before the FREC for final action of the complaint
  - — Held during regular Commission meeting
  - — Probable cause members do not participate in informal hearing
  - — Licensee *must* agree that there is no dispute of the material fact to choose informal hearing

■ **Formal hearing**

— Respondent/licensee signs *election of rights disputing* allegations of material fact and requests a formal hearing to determine the facts

— Formal hearing is mandatory if licensee/respondent disputes the allegations

— Administrative law judge hears testimony and submits a recommended order to the FREC containing findings of fact, conclusions of law, and recommended penalty, if applicable

■ **Final order**

— Probable cause members do not participate

— Commission may accept, reject, or modify the conclusions of law in the administrative law judge's recommended order

— Effective 30 days after final order is issued

— Licensee may operate during complaint process and during 30-day period

— Summary (emergency) suspension issued by DBPR Secretary in serious cases to suspend licensee immediately

■ **Right to appeal (judicial review)** must be filed within 30 days with District Court of Appeals

— Licensee may request appeals court to stop (*stay*) enforcement of penalty

— *Writ of Supersedes* stops (stays) enforcement of penalty

■ **Licensee may continue to operate pending appeal provided**

— Licensee has filed an appeal

— An *order of stay* is requested

— Request for stay is granted (*Writ of Supersedes* is issued)

■ **Grounds for denial, suspension, and revocation** (Refer to Table 6.1 in your textbook, *Florida Real Estate Principles, Practices & Law*)

■ **Administrative penalties that are imposed by the FREC**

— Deny an application

— Letter of reprimand

— Notice of noncompliance as a first response to a minor violation

— Citations involve fines of $100 to $1,000 per offense

— Probation

— Administrative fine of up to $5,000 per count or separate offense for violating Chapter 475 and Chapter 455

— Suspension for up to ten years

— Revocation with prejudice (*Revocation without prejudice* applies to license issued in error)

■ **First-degree misdemeanor** is a criminal penalty punishable in a court of law by a fine of not more than $1,000 and/or by imprisonment for not more than one year

— Failing to provide accurate and current rental information for a fee

- **Second-degree misdemeanor** describes all other violations of Chapter 475
  - $500 fine and/or 60 days imprisonment
- **The FREC must report criminal violations to the state attorney**
  - The FREC must inform the Division of Florida Land Sales, Condominiums, and Mobile Homes of disciplinary action taken against a real estate licensee
- **Unlicensed practice of real estate for compensation is a felony of the third degree**
- **Recovery Fund**
  - Separate account used to reimburse people who have suffered monetary damages as a result of license law violations by a licensee
  - Claim limited to $50,000 per transaction
  - Claims against one licensee may not exceed in total $150,000
  - Fee collected from licensees when fund drops below $500,000; collection is discontinued when the fund exceeds $1 million
  - License is automatically suspended upon payment from the fund until the fund is reimbursed (including interest)
- **Persons NOT eligible to seek reimbursement from Recovery Fund**
  - Spouse of the person the judgment is against (judgment debtor) or the spouse's personal representative
  - Licensee who acted as a single agent or a transaction broker in the transaction may not make a claim for unpaid commission
  - Anyone who bases the claim on a real estate transaction in which a licensee owned or controlled the property and was dealing for his or her own account (not acting as a licensee)
  - Anyone who makes a claim against a licensee with an inactive real estate license at the time of transaction
  - Judgment was issued against a business entity and not an individual

■ IMPORTANT DATES AND TIME PERIODS TO REMEMBER

- **15 days.** Number of days to correct minor infraction listed in notice of noncompliance
- **30 days.** Number of days after which a final order becomes effective
- **30 days.** Time period to file an appeal
- **60 days and/or $500 fine.** Penalty for second-degree misdemeanor
- **One year and/or $1,000 fine.** Penalty for first-degree misdemeanor
- **Two years.** Time period allowed to file claim against recovery fund
- **Ten years.** Maximum period of suspension

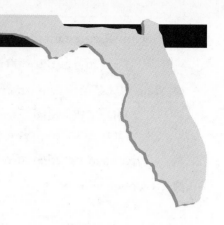

Case Studies in Real Estate
(Chapter 21)

■ KEY CONCEPTS IN CHAPTER 21

This review of chapter 21 is designed to provide a means for discussing, via the case study approach, selected topics in licensing, agency, and brokerage using actual situations commonly encountered in the real estate business. The cases appear in *Florida Real Estate Principles, Practices & Law.* Additional materials such as the real estate rules and statutes may be needed to complete the review of this topic. Each case study number is followed by a synopsis of facts. Compare the violations with the penalties listed in Table 6.1, chapter 6 of *Florida Real Estate Principles, Practices & Law.*

#1. Respondent advertised and showed a home listed for rent with her brokerage firm. The owners refused to rent the home to the prospective tenants because they were black. Respondent violated a duty imposed upon her by law; Section 475.25(1)(b). An agent is required to lawfully obey the principal, answer any questions that are asked, or follow any instructions given. They are not required to break the law. The fiduciary duty stops at the point when asked a question regarding race or any other discriminatory category. The licensee can lawfully refuse to answer questions regarding a prospective tenant's or buyer's race because it is an unlawful question.

#2. Respondent conspired to conceal true purchase and sale price for purpose of aiding buyer to obtain a mortgage. (Fraudulent actions; conspiracy to commit fraud; misrepresentation; concealment; and dishonest dealing by trick, scheme, or device)

#3. Respondent contracted to buy house listed by his employer-broker. Prior to closing, respondent contracted to sell to buyers not informed of identity of the actual owners. Both sales closed within minutes of each other without the broker's principal or the buyers learning of the circumstances. (Breach of fiduciary duty, concealment of material facts, fraudulent misrepresentation, violation of a duty imposed by listing contract, and failure to place deposit immediately with employer)

#4. Respondent obtained listing and was advised by seller-principal that a ten-year partially amortized mortgage lien with a balloon payment existed. Respondent failed to mention this in MLS listing or discussions with selling sales associate, buyers, or closing agent. (Fraudulent and dishonest dealing by trick, scheme, or device; concealment; and culpable negligence)

#5. Respondent negotiated lease for absentee owners and substituted personal check for lessee's payment, which she collected. Respondent's check was not honored by bank. Additional amount collected by respondent was not forwarded to owners until more than nine months later when full restitution was made. (Conversion, violation of duty imposed by law, and breach of fiduciary duty)

GENERAL REAL ESTATE LAW
Federal and State Housing Laws
(Chapter 7)

■ KEY TERM REVIEW

Annual percentage rate (APR) includes the interest rate and other loan costs and represents the true yearly cost of credit.

Blockbusting is to use entry, or rumor of entry, of a protected class into a neighborhood to persuade owners to sell.

Civil Rights Act of 1866 prohibits any type of discrimination based on *race* in *all* real estate transactions (sale or rental) without exception.

Fair Housing Act created protected classes of people and prohibits discrimination when selling or renting certain residential property.

Good faith estimate of closing (settlement) costs lists the charges the buyer is likely to pay at closing.

Redlining is to deny loans or insurance coverage by a lender or insurer or presenting different terms or conditions for homes in certain neighborhoods.

Servicing disclosure statement discloses to the borrower whether the lender intends to service the loan or transfer it to another lender or servicing company.

Special information booklet contains consumer information regarding closing services the borrower may be charged for at closing.

Steering is channeling protected-class homeseekers away from areas that are not mixed with that class into areas that are.

Triggering terms include certain credit terms or specific financing information.

■ KEY CONCEPTS IN CHAPTER 7

- ■ **Civil Rights Act of 1866**
  - — Prohibits racial discrimination
  - — Applies to all real estate transactions
- ■ **Fair Housing Act (Title VIII of the Civil Rights Act of 1968)** established protected classes
  - — Race
  - — Color

— Religion

— Sex

— National origin

— Familial status (families with children younger than 18 and pregnant women)

— Handicap status (physical or mental impairment that interferes with day-to-day activity)

— No protection is given to individuals based on age, occupation, marital status, or sexual orientation

■ **Housing under Fair Housing Act** includes sale or rental of housing, financing of housing, and brokerage services, specifically

— Government-owned residential property

— All privately owned residential property if a real estate licensee is employed

— Residential property owned by a person who owns four or more residential units

— Residential property when the owner, during the past two years, sells two or more houses in which the owner did not reside

— Multifamily dwellings of five or more units

— Multifamily dwellings of four or fewer units if the owner does not reside in one of the units

■ **Prohibited activities**

— Refusing to rent to, sell to, negotiate with, or deal with a member of a protected class

— Quoting different terms or conditions for buying or renting

— Advertising that housing is available only to people of a certain race, color, religion, sex, national origin, handicap status, or familial status

— Steering protected-class homeseekers away from areas that are not mixed with that class into areas that are (channeling)

— Blockbusting (inducing a person to sell or lease because the area is "in transition"; use of entry or rumor of entry of a protected class to persuade homeowners to sell)

— Redlining (denying loans or insurance coverage or offering loans or insurance coverage with different terms or conditions for homes in certain neighborhoods)

— Denying membership in or use of any real estate service, brokers' organization, or MLS

— Making false statements concerning the availability of housing for inspection, rent, or sale

■ **Certain housing for older persons** is exempt from familial status protection under the Fair Housing Act provided one of two situations exists

— All units must be occupied by persons 62 years of age or older

— At least 80 percent of the units are occupied by one or more persons 55 years of age or older

■ **HUD prosecutes Fair Housing complaints**

— If seller or landlord asks licensee to violate Fair Housing Laws, licensee must refuse to list the property, or terminate the existing listing

— The FREC may institute an administrative proceeding against a licensee found guilty of a discriminatory act

■ **Americans with Disabilities Act of 1990**

— Purpose is to ensure that persons with disabilities have access to public transportation, commercial facilities, and public accommodations

— ADA requirements implemented for new construction

■ **Florida Uniform Land Sales Practices Act** applies to developments of 50 lots or greater

— Requires public offering statement and other disclosures

■ **Consumer Credit Protection Act (Truth-in-Lending Act)**

— Implemented by Federal Reserve Regulation Z

— Requires lenders to disclose the annual percentage rate

■ **Advertisements containing triggering terms must disclose**

— Amount or percentage of down payment

— Terms of repayment

— Annual percentage rate

■ **Equal Credit Opportunity Act (ECOA)** prohibits discrimination on the basis of race, color, religion, national origin, sex, marital status, *age*, or *receipt of public assistance*

■ **Real Estate Settlement Procedures Act (RESPA)** was enacted to ensure buyers are informed regarding the amount and type of charges they will pay at closing

— Uniform settlement statement (HUD-1) at or before closing

— Information booklet concerning settlement costs at time of loan application or within three business days

— Estimate of settlement costs at time of loan application or within three business days

■ **Florida Residential Landlord and Tenant Act to protect against unconscionable landlord**

■ **Landlord must maintain security deposits and advance rent**

— Separate noninterest-bearing escrow account

— Separate interest-bearing account and pay tenant 5 percent interest or 75 percent of interest earned

— Separate account is *not* required if the landlord posts a surety bond for the lesser of the amount of the funds or $50,000 (pay tenant 5 percent interest)

■ **If a real estate broker holds the funds on behalf of a landlord, the broker must abide by real estate license law concerning escrowed funds**

■ **Residential landlord to comply with building, housing, and health codes**

■ IMPORTANT DATES AND TIME PERIODS TO REMEMBER

- **Three business days.** Number of days to give information booklet concerning settlement costs to loan applicant (or at time of loan application)

- **Three business days.** Number of days to give loan applicant an estimate of settlement costs (or at time of loan application)

- **Seven business days.** Time period allowed to cancel agreement under the Florida Uniform Land Sales Practices Act

- **30 days.** Number of days to inform tenant regarding how funds are being held

Property Rights: Estates, Tenancies, and Multiple Ownership Interests
(Chapter 8)

■ KEY TERM REVIEW

Bylaws are a recorded document that consists of the rules and regulations of a condominium.

Concurrent ownership means ownership by two or more persons at the same time.

Condominium ownership is a single unit consisting of the vertical and horizontal space in a multiunit structure plus a proportionate share of the common elements.

Cooperative is a multiunit dwelling owned by a corporation, owners purchase shares in the corporation and receive a proprietary lease.

Declaration is a recorded document that creates the condominium.

Elective share consists of 30 percent of the decedent's net estate, in addition to homestead property.

Estate for years is basically a written lease with a definite termination date.

Estate in severalty occurs when title to property is held by one person.

Fee simple estate is the most common type of ownership; it is the most comprehensive collection of property rights and may be inherited.

Fixtures are objects that were personal property but have been permanently attached to or made part of real property by attachment.

Freehold estate is an ownership interest for an indefinite period of time.

Homestead law provides certain types of protection and benefits to homeowners regarding their permanent residence.

Joint tenancy is an ownership interest between two or more persons with right of survivorship.

Land refers to the surface of the earth and to everything attached to it by nature.

Leasehold estate is a less-than-freehold estate; it is an interest in real property in which ownership is for a definite period (measured in calendar time).

Life estate is a freehold estate that ends with the death of a named person; ownership for the life of a person.

Littoral rights are associated with land abutting tidal bodies of water such as an ocean, sea, or lake.

Marital assets are assets acquired during marriage.

Personal property or chattel is any tangible item that is *not* real property and that is movable.

Proprietary lease is the document that entitles a shareholder in a cooperative to possession of a unit.

Real estate refers to the land and all improvements permanently attached to land.

Real property includes all real estate plus the legal bundle of rights inherent in the ownership of real estate.

Remainderman is the third party to whom a property is transferred at the end of a life estate (*vested* if named; *contingent* if not named).

Right of survivorship means that when one co-owner dies, his or her share goes to the surviving co-owner(s) and not to the deceased tenant's heirs.

Riparian rights are associated with land abutting the banks of a river, stream, or other watercourse.

Separate property is nonmarital assets.

Tenancy at sufferance exists when the tenant, after rightfully being in possession of the rented property, continues possession after his or her right has ended; a *holdover* tenant.

Tenancy at will is a leasehold in which the tenant holds possession of the premises with the owner's permission but without a fixed term.

Tenancy by the entireties is an estate created by a husband and wife who take title together at the same time.

Tenancy in common is an interest in real property in which two or more persons hold title to the property with equal or unequal interests in the estate.

Tenants in common is the most frequently used form of co-ownership except for husband-and-wife ownership.

Time-share ownership involves an undivided interest in a living unit according to the number of weeks purchased.

Trade fixture is an item of personal property attached to real property that is owned by a tenant and used in a business that is legally removable by the tenant.

Undivided interest is an interest in the entire property, rather than ownership of a particular part of the property.

■ KEY CONCEPTS IN CHAPTER 8

- ■ **Nature of property**
  - — *Land* refers to the surface of the earth and items attached by nature
  - — *Real estate* includes land and all human-made improvements
  - — *Real property* includes real estate plus the legal bundle of rights
- ■ **Physical components (rights) of real property**
  - — Surface
  - — Subsurface
  - — Air
- ■ **Surface rights** include water rights
  - — Riparian—associated with land abutting the banks of a river, stream, or other watercourse

— Littoral—associated with land abutting tidal bodies of water such as an ocean, sea, or lake

■ **Definitions** associated with water rights

— *Accretion* is the process of land build-up from water-borne rock, sand, and soil

— *Alluvion* is the resulting new deposits of land caused by accretion

— *Erosion* is the gradual loss of land due to natural forces

— *Reliction* is the gradual receding of water, uncovering additional land

■ **Personal property** is also known as chattel

— Anything that is *not* real property

— Real property becomes personal property by *act of severance*

■ **Fixtures** were personal property but have been permanently attached to and made part of real property

■ **Tests to decide if an item is a fixture (IRMA)**

— **I** Intent of the parties

— **R** Relationship between the parties

— **M** Method of annexation

— **A** Adaptation of the article

■ **Bundle of rights (DUPE)** (real property ownership rights) include the right of

— **D** Disposition (right to sell or give away)

— **U** Use (right to control)

— **P** Possession (right to occupy)

— **E** Exclusion (right to quiet enjoyment)

■ **Freehold estates** are estates of ownership

— *Fee simple* (absolute) estate is the most comprehensive estate and it is inheritable

— *Life estate* is measured for a person's lifetime

— *Estate in reversion* occurs when property returns to the grantor

— *Remainder estate* occurs when property goes to a third party known as a remainderman

■ **Nonfreehold estate (leasehold)** are estates of possession measured in calendar time

— *Estate for years* is a written lease agreement with a specific starting and ending date

— *Tenancy at will* is either an oral agreement or one that has no specific beginning and ending date

— *Tenancy at sufferance* occurs when the lease period has ended and the tenant is a holdover

■ **Sole ownership** occurs when title to property is held by one person; an *estate in severalty*

■ **Co-ownership** means title to real property is shared by two or more persons (concurrent ownership)

— Tenancy in common

— Joint tenancy

— Tenancy by the entireties

■ **Features of tenancy in common**

— Two or more people

— Undivided possession

— Interest equal or unequal percentage

— Take title at same time or at different times

— Heirs inherit (*no* right of survivorship)

■ **Features of a joint tenancy (PITTS)**

— **P**   Each joint tenant has undivided **P**ossession

— **I**   Each joint tenant has equal **I**nterest

— **T**   Joint tenants take title at the same **T**ime

— **T**   Joint tenants are all named on the same **T**itle

— **S**   Must expressly state right of **S**urvivorship

■ **Features of tenancy by the entireties**

— Husband and wife take title together

— Undivided possession

— Right of survivorship

— Same title, same time

— Only available to husband and wife

■ **Homestead** benefits and protections

— Protection from forced sale for certain debts

— $25,000 tax exemption

— Size restriction of one-half acre inside a city or 160 acres outside a municipality

— Protection of the family (if a married person dies and the family homestead was titled in the deceased person's name only, by operation of law, the surviving spouse receives a life estate and the children [lineal descendants] receive a remainder estate)

■ **Condominium documents**

— Declaration of condominium contains legal descriptions of the units and once recorded creates the condominium

— Articles of incorporation of the association create the corporate entity responsible for operating the condominium

— Bylaws of the association describe operational requirements and provide for the administration of the association

— Frequently Asked Questions and Answers (FAQs) inform prospective purchasers about restrictions on the leasing of a unit, information concerning assessments, and whether the unit owners or the association are obligated to pay rent or land-use fees for recreational facilities

— Estimated operating budget details estimates of various common expenses that are to be shared by the unit owners

- **Time-share ownership**

  — *Interval ownership* is fee simple ownership

  — *Right-to-use* is a leasehold interest

■ IMPORTANT DATES AND TIME PERIODS TO REMEMBER

- **Three business days.** Notice to cancel resale condominium contract
- **Seven days.** Notice required for week-to-week tenancy at will
- **Ten days.** Notice to cancel time-share contract
- **15 days.** Notice required to cancel month-to-month tenancy at will
- **15 days.** Notice to cancel condominium contract with developer

Titles, Deeds, and Ownership Restrictions (Chapter 9)

■ KEY TERM REVIEW

Abstract of title is summary report of what a title search found in the public record.

Acknowledgment is the formal declaration before a notary public by the grantor that his or her signing is a free act.

Actual notice is direct knowledge acquired in the course of a transaction, such as having actually seen the deed instrument or heard that there is a lien on the property.

Adverse possession arises when the true owner of record fails to maintain possession and the property is seized by another.

Alienation is the act of transferring ownership, title, or an interest in real property.

Chain of title is the complete successive record of a property's ownership.

Construction lien is a statutory right of material supplies or laborers to place a lien on property that has been improved by their supplies and/or labor.

Constructive notice is accomplished by recording the information in the public records.

Deed is a written instrument used to convey title to real property through sale or gift that must be in writing, and signed by a competent grantor and two witnesses.

Deed restrictions are a part of the deed and affect a particular property's future use.

Easement is the right to enter and use an owner's land for a specific use.

Easement appurtenant benefits an adjacent parcel of land.

Easement by necessity is created through a court of law if a property is landlocked.

Easement by prescription is created through a court of law after longtime uninterrupted use.

Easement in gross benefits an individual or business entity and is not related to a specific adjacent parcel, for example, utility easement.

Eminent domain gives government the power to take land from an owner through a legal process known as *condemnation*.

Encroachment is the unauthorized use of another person's property created when an improvement crosses over a boundary line.

Equitable title is the beneficial interest in real estate that implies that an individual will receive legal title at a future date.

Escheat provides for the State of Florida to take the property of an owner who dies intestate and without any known heirs.

Further assurance is a promise in a general warranty deed that guarantees the grantor will sign and deliver any legal instrument that might be required.

General lien is not restricted to one property but may affect all properties of a debtor.

General warranty deed is the most common type of deed for conveying real estate and it contains all the covenants and warranties available to give the most complete protection.

Grantee is the person(s) receiving title to property in a deed.

Granting clause is a clause in a deed that contains the premises or the words of conveyance.

Grantor is the person(s) giving title to property in a deed.

Gross lease is an agreement for the tenant to pay a fixed (base) rent and the landlord pays all of the expenses associated with the property.

Ground lease is an agreement for the tenant to lease the land only and erect a building on the land.

Habendum clause describes the type of estate being conveyed and starts with the words "to have and to hold."

Intestate is to die without leaving a will.

Lender's policy is title insurance issued for the amount of mortgage debt to protect the lender (mortgagee).

Lien is a written document that states that a person is owed money and establishes that the party may foreclose on the property if the debt is not satisfied; the right to have property sold to satisfy the debt.

Lis pendens is a notice of pending legal action; it is filed before initiating a lawsuit.

Net lease is an agreement for the tenant to pay fixed rent plus property costs such as taxes, insurance, and utilities.

Opinion of title is executed by an attorney after studying the abstract of title.

Owner's policy is title insurance issued for the total purchase price of the property to protect the property owner (mortgagor).

Percentage lease is an agreement for the tenant to pay rent based on the gross sales received by doing business on the leased property.

Police power represents the broadest power of the government to limit or regulate the rights of property owners in order to protect the health, safety, and welfare of the public.

Quiet enjoyment is a promise in a general warranty deed that guarantees peaceful possession undisturbed by claim of title.

Quitclaim deed releases the grantor of any rights in the property he or she may have and is used to clear clouds on the title and to cure title defects.

Restrictive covenants are recorded along with the subdivision plat and usually affect the entire subdivision.

Seisin is the clause in a deed that is a promise that the grantor has the right to convey title (a statement of ownership).

Specific liens apply only to a certain specified property.

Testate is to die with a will.

Title insurance is a contract that protects the policyholder from losses arising from a defect in the title.

Title search is an examination of all the public records to determine whether any defects exist in the chain of title.

Variable lease is an agreement for the tenant to pay specified rent increases based on a predetermined index (CPI) at set future dates.

Warranty forever is a promise in a general warranty deed that guarantees the grantor will forever warrant and defend the grantee's title against all unlawful claims.

Will is a legal instrument used to convey title to real and personal property after the person's death.

■ KEY CONCEPTS IN CHAPTER 9

- **Alienation is the act of transferring ownership, title, or an interest in real property from one person to another** and may be
  - Voluntary (with the owner's control and content)
  - Involuntary (without control and consent of the owner)

- **Types of voluntary alienation**
  - Deed
  - Will (testate)

- **Types of involuntary alienation**
  - Descent (intestate)
  - Escheat
  - Adverse possession
  - Eminent domain

- **Alienation by adverse possession (HOT CAN)**
  - **H** Hostile possession
  - **O** Open possession
  - **T** Taxes paid by *adverse possessor*
  - **C** Claim of title
  - **A** Adverse possession continues for *seven or more years*
  - **N** Notorious public possession

- **Two types of notice**
  - *Actual notice* is direct knowledge acquired in the course of a transaction
  - *Constructive notice* is accomplished by recording a document in the public records

- **Title insurance protects the policyholder from title defects**
  - Owner's policy issued for total purchase price and is *not* transferable
  - Lender's (mortgagee's) policy is issued for mortgage amount and is transferable (assignable)

- **Parties to a deed**

  — *Grantor* (owner giving title who must be mentally competent)

  — *Grantee* (person receiving title)

- **Elements of a deed (CEDDING)**

  — **C**   Consideration (valuable or good)

  — **E**   Execution (signed by a competent grantor and two witnesses)

  — **D**   Description of the property

  — **D**   Delivery and acceptance (voluntary)

  — **I**   Interest being conveyed (habendum clause)

  — **N**   Names of the grantee and grantor

  — **G**   Granting clause and other clauses

- **Clauses in a deed**

  — *Granting* (includes premises and words of conveyance)

  — *Habendum* (type of estate conveyed)

  — *Seisin* (grantor has right to convey)

  — *Covenant against encumbrances* (property is free from liens and other encumbrances)

- **General warranty deed includes four clauses above and three special covenants**

  — Quiet enjoyment

  — Further assurance

  — Warranty forever

- **Government restrictions on ownership (PET)**

  — **P**   Police power

  — **E**   Eminent domain

  — **T**   Taxation

- **Private restrictions on ownership**

  — Deed restrictions

  — Easements

  — Leases

  — Liens

- **Easement is a right to use an owner's land for a specific use**

  — *Easement appurtenant* benefits an adjacent parcel of land; it allows an owner the use of a neighbor's property, such as the right to cross parcel A to reach parcel B

  — *Easement in gross* benefits an individual or a business entity and is not related to a specific adjacent parcel, such as utility easements

- — *Easement by necessity* is created through a court of law to allow property owners to enter and exit their landlocked property

- — *Easement by prescription* is created by a court of law after longtime usage

- **Types of leases**

  - — Gross lease

  - — Net lease

  - — Percentage lease

  - — Variable lease

  - — Ground lease

- **Specific liens** apply only to certain specific property

  - — Property tax and special assessment liens become liens as soon as assessment is made

  - — Mortgage lien pledges real property as collateral (priority is based on date of recording)

  - — Vendor's lien is created when a purchase-money mortgage is recorded by seller (priority is established by date of recording)

  - — Construction lien must be filed within 90 days after last work is done and assumes priority over mortgage liens created after first work was done

■ IMPORTANT DATES AND TIME PERIODS TO REMEMBER

- **90 days.** Number of days to file a construction lien (retroactive to the date of the first delivery of material or the first day of work)

- **Seven years.** Number of years of hostile possession to claim adverse possession

- **20 years.** Minimum time period of uninterrupted use to create an easement by prescription

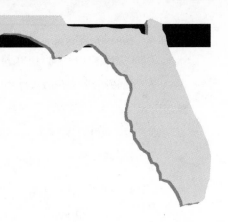

Real Estate Contracts
(Chapter 11)

■ KEY TERM REVIEW

Assignment refers to a transfer of rights and duties under a contract.

Bilateral contract obligates both parties to perform in accordance with the terms of the contract.

Buyer brokerage agreement is an employment contract with a buyer.

Competent parties have the legal capacity to contract, and no mental defects, and are of legal age to contract.

Contract is an agreement between two or more parties to do a legal act for a consideration, which creates certain rights and obligations.

Enforceable contract is a legally binding contract that the law will recognize.

Exclusive-agency listing is given to one broker but the seller reserves the right to sell the property without paying a commission.

Exclusive-right-of-sale listing is a listing given to one broker who is assured of a commission no matter who sells (best from broker's standpoint).

Good consideration is a promise that cannot be measured in terms of money, such as love and affection.

Liquidated damages is the amount specified in the contract (usually the earnest money deposit) to be paid to the seller in case of default by the buyer.

Meeting of the minds is reaching an agreement on all terms in a contract.

Mutual assent is the making and acceptance of an offer (agreement).

Net listing is created when a seller agrees to sell a property for a stated acceptable minimum amount.

Novation is the substitution of a new party for the original one.

Open listing is a listing given to any number of brokers (least preferred by brokers).

Option contract is a unilateral contract (only optionor must perform) to keep open for a specified period of time an offer to sell or lease real property.

Parol contract is an oral agreement.

Statute of frauds requires that certain contracts must be in writing and signed to be enforceable (contracts conveying an interest in real property).

Statute of limitations designates the period of time during which the terms of a contract may be enforced.

Unenforceable means a contract would not stand up in a court of law because it does not meet the requirements of the statute of frauds or it runs beyond the statute of limitations.

Unilateral contract obligates only one party to perform.

Valid contracts have four essentials.

Valuable consideration is the money or a promise of something that can be measured in terms of money.

Vendee is the buyer.

Vendor is the seller.

Void contract does not meet all of the required elements of a valid contract and has no legal effect.

Voidable contract is a contract but one of the parties is allowed to avoid his or her contractual duties such as when one party is a minor or a party is mentally incompetent.

■ KEY CONCEPTS IN CHAPTER 11

■ **Four types of contracts real estate licensees may prepare**

— Listing agreement

— Buyer brokerage agreement

— Sale and purchase contract

— Option contract

■ **Licensees may *not* draw**

— Deeds

— Mortgages

— Promissory notes

— Leases

■ **Licensees may fill in the blanks on Florida Supreme Court preapproved lease instruments for lease periods that do not exceed one year**

■ **Statute of frauds requires written contracts that convey an interest in real property**

— Purchase and sale contracts

— Option contracts

— Lease agreements for more than one year

— Listing agreements for more than one year

■ **Two exceptions to the "in writing" provision in the statute of frauds**

— When the buyer has paid part of the purchase price and then has either taken possession of the property or made some improvements to the property

— If both parties have fully performed as promised

- ■ **Statute of limitations**
  - — Written contracts: five years
  - — Oral (parol) contracts: four years
- ■ **Contracts** are agreements between two or more parties to do or not to do certain things, supported by a sufficient consideration
- ■ **A valid contract has four essentials**
  - — Contractual capacity of the parties (Competent parties)
  - — Offer and acceptance (mutual assent)
  - — Legal purpose
  - — Consideration
- ■ **Contracts** may be in writing or oral with the *exception* of real estate contracts, which must be in writing
- ■ **Two types of consideration**
  - — Valuable (money)
  - — Good (the promises each party agrees to)
- ■ **Elements of a valid and enforceable real estate contract (COLIC)**
  - — **C**   Contractual capacity (*competent*)
  - — **O**   Offer and acceptance (*meeting of the minds*)
  - — **L**   Legal purpose
  - — **I**   In writing and signed (statute of frauds)
  - — **C**   Consideration (*valuable* or *good*)
- ■ **Real estate contracts** are *not* required to be witnessed or notarized
- ■ **Formal and informal contracts**
  - — *Formal contract* is written and under seal
  - — *Informal (parol)* contract is oral
- ■ **Bilateral and unilateral contracts**
  - — *Bilateral* obligates both parties (sale contract)
  - — *Unilateral* obligates only one party (option contract)
- ■ **Express or implied contracts**
  - — *Express contract* exists when all of the terms and conditions have been spelled out and a meeting of the minds is reached
  - — *Implied contract* exists when some of the conditions may be reasonably implied
- ■ **Executory and executed contracts**
  - — *Executory contracts* are not yet fully performed
  - — *Executed contracts* have been completely performed

■ **Ways to terminate an offer (WILD CARD)**

— **W**   Withdrawal by offeror

— **I**   Insanity

— **L**   Lapse of time

— **D**   Death

— **C**   Counteroffer

— **A**   Acceptance

— **R**   Rejection

— **D**   Destruction of the property

■ **Letters and telegraphic communication** can be part of a valid sale contract

■ **Parties to a contract**

— *Offeror* (person making offer)

— *Offeree* (person receiving offer)

— Note: Parties switch roles when there is a *counteroffer*

■ **A contract is created when three events occur**

— Offer is made by the offeror

— Offer is accepted by the offeree

— Acceptance is communicated back to the offeror

■ **Ways to terminate a contract**

— Performance

— Mutual rescission

— Impossibility of performance

— Operation of law

— Bankruptcy

— Breach

■ **Assignment does NOT terminate a contract**

■ **Remedies for breach**

— Specific performance (relief in equity)

— Liquidated damages

— Rescission on breach of contract

— Compensatory damages

- **Types of listings**
  - Open listing
  - Exclusive-agency listing
  - Exclusive-right-of-sale listing
  - Net listing
- **Contract disclosures**
  - Material defects disclosure—sellers of residential real property must disclose material defects
  - Radon gas disclosure—consists of explaining what radon is
  - Lead-based paint disclosure—applies if the home was built prior to 1978
  - Energy efficient brochure—informs buyers, before signing the sale contract, of the option for an energy-efficiency rating on the building
  - Homeowners' association disclosure—requires sellers of property subject to a homeowners' association to provide buyers with a disclosure summary
  - Property tax disclosure—concerns ad valorem (property) taxes
  - Building code violation disclosure—applies if a seller has been cited for a building code violation and is the subject of a pending enforcement proceeding

■ IMPORTANT DATES AND TIME PERIODS TO REMEMBER

- **Four years.** Time period to enforce oral contracts under the statue of limitations
- **Five years.** Time period to enforce written contracts under the statue of limitations

Planning and Zoning
(Chapter 20)

■ KEY TERM REVIEW

Base industries are those industries that attract outside money to an area.

Buffer zone is a strip of land separating one land use from another (for example, a landscaped park can be used to screen a residential area from nonresidential areas).

Building codes protect the public health and safety from inferior construction practices.

Certificate of occupancy is an occupancy permit issued by the local government after construction is completed and the final inspection is approved.

Concurrency provision in Florida's Growth Management Act mandates that the infrastructure, such as roads, water, and waste treatment facilities needed to support additional population, be in place before new development is allowed.

Economic base studies analyze the effect of base-industry employment in an area.

Health ordinances regulate maintenance and sanitation of public spaces.

Nonconforming use is permission to continue a use in spite of a newly enacted zoning ordinance.

Planned unit development (PUD) is a self-contained development planned under special zoning ordinances that allow maximum use of open space by reducing lot sizes and street sizes.

Service industries are business establishments such as grocery stores, barbershops, and retail stores, whose customers are primarily local residents.

Special exception is permission to build or to use property in apparent conflict with existing zoning ordinances.

Variances allow property owners to vary from strict compliance with all or part of a zoning code because to comply would force an undue hardship on the property owner.

Zoning ordinances authorize the segmentation (dividing) of a community into districts or zones in keeping with the character of the land and structures and with their suitability for particular uses to protect the property owners from undesirable land uses on neighboring property.

■ KEY CONCEPTS IN CHAPTER 20

- **■ Planning commission**
  - — Commission is composed of laypersons who are a representative sample of the community
  - — Appointed (not elected)
  - — Not paid to serve on the planning commission—voluntary

- **■ Planning commission authority**
  - — Subdivision plat approval
  - — Site plan approval
  - — Sign control

- **■ Basic background studies used by planners**
  - — *Population study* (most basic and important; concerns population characteristics)
  - — *Economic base study* (want diverse industries; both basic industry and service industry)
  - — *Existing land-use study* (inventory of private and public land)
  - — *Physiographic study* (concerns soil type, drainage, and so forth)
  - — *Recreation and community facilities study* (types and location of community facilities)
  - — *Thoroughfare study* (transportation study)

- **■ Zoning laws**
  - — Exercise of police power
  - — To protect property values
  - — Each zone is assigned a specific land-use classification

- **■ Building code**
  - — Protect against inferior construction practices
  - — Set minimum standards for materials and quality of workmanship
  - — Issue a building permit before construction begins
  - — Periodic building inspections
  - — Final *certificate of occupancy* is issued

- **■ Zoning classifications**
  - — Residential (regulates *density* of units per acre)
  - — Commercial (regulates *intensity* of use, types, and traffic volume)
  - — Industrial (regulates *intensity* of use, environmental concerns)
  - — Agricultural
  - — Special use

■ **Variance** allows a property owner to vary from strict compliance of a zoning ordinance

— Property owner must show that a *hardship* exists or will be created

— Property owner did nothing to create the hardship

■ **Special exceptions** are used to control the location of a particular land use

— A departure from the zoning ordinance

— Must demonstrate that the special exception will benefit the surrounding property owners

■ **Legal nonconforming uses**

— The use is grandfathered in

— Property owner is allowed to continue a use even though zoning ordinances have changed that would no longer allow the use if being constructed today

— The government may not use eminent domain via condemnation just because a property no longer conforms to code

■ **Developments of regional impact**

— Required for large projects that impact more than one county

— Concerned with air quality, water quality, waste treatment, public school classroom space, and roads

■ **Planned unit development (PUD)**

— Allows a mix of land uses along with a high density of residential units

— Clustering of residential units to allow for open spaces

— Reduced lot sizes and street sizes to allow maximum use of open space

— A self-contained development

■ **Environmental impact statement** concerns the environmental impact on waste-disposal systems, air quality, roads, employment, and so forth as the result of large development

■ IMPORTANT FORMULAS TO REMEMBER

■ **Calculate number of potential lots in a subdivision**

1. Calculate number of square feet available for development

2. Determine the potential number of lots per acre

3. Potential number of lots × number of acres = total number of lots in subdivision

Example: A parcel contains 40 acres. Fifteen percent of land must be set aside for common areas plus another 600 feet by 30 feet is allocated for a street. Each lot must contain at least 10,000 square feet.

(Note: *Memorize* 43,560 square feet in one acre.)

40 acres × 43,560 = 1,742,400 total square feet

Deduct square feet for road and common areas

1,742,400 × .15	= 261,360 square feet for common areas
600 × 30	= 18,000 square feet for street
261,360 + 18,000	= 279,360 total square feet unusable for lots
1,742,400 − 279,360	= 1,463,040 square feet for lots

Calculate number of potential (possible) lots

1,463,040 ÷ 10,000	= 146.304 (round to) 146 lots

■ **Calculate cost per front foot**

Total cost ÷ front feet = cost per front foot

Example: A parcel's dimensions are 400' by 600'. Total cost is $260,000.

$260,000 ÷ 400 = $650 per front foot

■ **Calculate the number of acres in a parcel given the cost and price per square foot**

1.   Calculate total square feet

2.   Total square feet ÷ 43,560 = number of acres in parcel

Example: The lot cost $10 per square foot for a total cost of $250,000. (Round to two decimal places)

$250,000 ÷ $10	= 25,000 square feet
25,000 ÷ 43,560	= .5739 (or approximately) .57 acres

REAL ESTATE PRINCIPLES AND PRACTICES
The Real Estate Business (Chapter 1)

■ KEY TERM REVIEW

Absentee owners are owners who do not reside on the property and who usually rely on a property manager to supervise the real estate.

Agricultural property is defined in Florida license law to mean agricultural property of more than ten acres.

Appraisal is the process of estimating the value of real property; a supported, defended estimate of the value of real property as of a specific date.

Business brokers are real estate licensees who engage in the sale, purchase, or lease of businesses.

Business opportunity brokerage is real estate activity dealing in the sale, purchase, or lease of businesses (going concern operations).

Comparative market analysis (CMA) refers to a marketing tool and may not be referred to or represented as an appraisal; CMAs are developed by reviewing the real estate activity in the area, including recent sales of similar properties, properties currently offered for sale, and recently expired listings to indicate what a subject property might be worth based on current market activity.

Counselors provide advice to individuals and firms regarding the purchase and use of real estate investments; counseling involves analyzing existing or potential problems and recommending a course of action.

Dedication is the gift of land by an owner to a government body for a public use.

Deed restrictions are placed by an owner who has created a restriction on future owners of the parcel of real estate.

Farm area refers to a selected and limited geographic area to which a sales associate devotes special attention and study.

Follow-up is what a sales associate does for buyers and sellers after the sale (closing) to promote customer loyalty.

Property management is real estate activity devoted to leasing, managing, marketing, and overall maintenance of property for others.

Real estate business is the industry or occupation whose activities involve real property transactions handled by licensed real estate professionals.

Residential real estate is defined in the Florida license law to mean four or fewer residential units, vacant land zoned for four or fewer residential units, or agricultural property of ten or fewer acres.

Restrictive covenants impose limitations on the use of land in an entire subdivision. They affect how the land can be used and establish criteria such as minimum square footage, and so forth, to ensure that homes built in that subdivision are designed to protect and maintain the value and integrity of the neighborhood.

Subdivision plat map refers to a plan of a tract of subdivided land that is submitted by the developer to the government planning agency showing the size and location of individual lots, planned amenities, streets, and utilities.

■ KEY CONCEPTS IN CHAPTER 1

■ **Real estate brokerage** (also known as *functions of brokerage*) is the day-to-day real estate activity with the public and includes

— Sales and leasing

— Property management

— Appraising

— Financing

— Counseling

■ **Sales and leasing** includes the specialty areas of

— Residential

— Commercial

— Industrial

— Agricultural (farms)

— Businesses

■ **Property management** involves maintenance and directing operations, such as leasing, managing, and marketing of real estate owned by others

— Absentee ownership is responsible for need for property management services

— An *absentee owner* is a property owner who does not reside on the property and who often relies on a professional property manager to manage the owner's investment

— The property manager ensures that the property produces income

— Primary objective is to produce the highest net income for the owner

■ **Appraisal** is the process of estimating value

— A CMA is a marketing tool used by licensees to secure listings—it is *not* an appraisal

— A CMA may *not* be referred to as an appraisal

— Real estate licensees may prepare appraisals *except* when a federally related transaction is involved (a licensee may also *not* conduct an appraisal for the purpose of procuring a listing)

— Appraisal reports involving a federally related transaction must be prepared by a state-certified or licensed appraiser

— When preparing appraisals, real estate licensees must abide by the Uniform Standards of Professional Appraisal Practice (USPAP)

■ **Development and construction** includes three phases

— Land acquisition

— Subdivision (dividing land into lots or tracts) and development

— Construction

■ **Subdivision plat map**

— To protect consumers, most local governments require that developers submit a subdivision plat map of a new development

— A subdivision plat map is an engineer's plan for land use superimposed on a map of the land to be developed

— Plat maps indicate the size and location of individual lots, streets, and public utilities, including water and sewer lines

■ **Three types of residential construction**

— *Spec homes* involves purchasing one or more lots and constructing homes without securing a buyer in advance of construction—construction without a presale

— *Custom homes* refers to constructing homes under contract with a buyer using building plans provided by an architect or the buyer—building according to the owner's plans and specifications

— *Tract homes* is a type of speculative building involving model homes that are used to promote construction of new homes on lots in a subdivision

■ **National Association of REALTORS® (NAR)** is the largest real estate trade organization

— REALTORS® must subscribe to the Code of Ethics

— The term REALTOR® can only be used by members of the NAR

— REALTOR® is a copyrighted designation

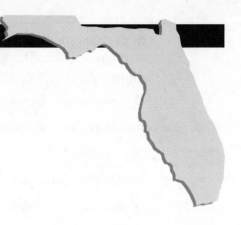

Legal Descriptions
(Chapter 10)

■ KEY TERM REVIEW

Base lines are imaginary lines running east and west that are used as reference lines in the government survey system; they are used to identify the numbering system townships (or tiers) north and south of the base line.

Check is formed when two guide meridians and two correction lines intersect to form a 24-by-24-mile square.

Government survey system is used in Florida and other states except the original 13 states and Kentucky, West Virginia, Tennessee, and Texas.

Legal description is a series of boundary lines on the earth's surface to identify the boundaries of a parcel of land.

Lot and block method of legal description is used to identify lots within a recorded subdivision plat map.

Metes-and-bounds description is the most accurate method of land description that is used to describe both regular and irregular shaped parcels.

Monument is a fixed object (marker) used to identify the POB and the corners of a parcel.

Patent is a certificate issued by the federal or a state government that transfers land to a private individual.

Point of beginning (POB) is the starting reference point in the metes-and-bounds method of legal description.

Principal meridians are imaginary lines running north and south that are used as reference lines in the government survey system; they are used to identify the numbering system of ranges east and west of the principal meridian.

Range is a six-mile-wide vertical (north/south) strip enclosed between two range lines.

Section is one mile square.

Township (or tier) is an east/west strip of land on either side of a base line (think of a tiered wedding cake); *township* also refers to the square formed by the intersection of two range lines and two township lines.

Township lines are six miles apart, run east and west, and are parallel to the base line.

■ KEY CONCEPTS IN CHAPTER 10

- ■ **Methods of legal description**
  - — Metes-and-bounds
  - — Government survey
  - — Lot and block

- ■ **Metes-and-bounds description**
  - — Most accurate method of land description
  - — Used for regular and irregular shaped parcels
  - — *Metes* refers to distance (think meters)
  - — *Bounds* refers to direction
  - — Starting reference point is the point of beginning (POB)
  - — First direction (primary reference direction) is always North or South—due North and due South are both zero degrees
  - — Second direction is always East or West—due East and due West are both 90 degrees
  - — Maximum number of degrees one can move is 90 degrees

- ■ **Government survey system**
  - — Grid system used in Florida and most of United States except original 13 colonies
  - — Based on north-south lines and east-west lines
  - — Florida's principal meridian is a north-south line that runs through a monument located in the city of Tallahassee
  - — Florida's base line is an east-west line that runs through a monument located in the city of Tallahassee
  - — Range lines are north-south lines every six miles
  - — First range west of the principal meridian is R1W
  - — First range east of the principal meridian is R1E
  - — Township lines are east-west lines every six miles
  - — Range lines and township lines intersect to form six mile squares called *townships*

- ■ **Township**
  - — 6 mile square (six miles on each side)
  - — 36 square miles
  - — 36 sections
  - — Note that term is also used to describe an east-west strip of land on either side of the base line

— First township tier north of the base line is T1N

— First township tier south of the base line is T1S

■ **Section**

— 1 mile square (one mile on each side)

— Contains 640 acres

— Sections are numbered within a township right to left, left to right, right to left (like oxen pulling a plow)

■ **Measures and terms** associated with the Government Survey system

— *Check* is a square 24 miles on each side created by intersecting guide meridians and correction lines; used to adjust the grid pattern of squares because of the curvature of the earth

— *Township* is a square 6 miles on each side (6 miles square) containing 36 square miles (36 sections); also an east-west strip of land north and south of a baseline (called a tier)

— *Section* is a square 1 mile on each side (1 mile square) containing 1 square mile (or 640 acres)

— *Quarter section* is 160 acres; historically, it was the area of land originally granted to a homesteader; used today to establish the limits of homesteaded property outside the boundaries of a municipality

— *Government lot* is a fractional piece of land less than a full quarter section located along the banks of lakes and streams

■ IMPORTANT FORMULAS TO REMEMBER

■ **Calculate the acres in a Government Survey legal description**

Multiply the denominators of each fraction together and then divide 640 by the result

Example: NW ¼ of the NE ¼

$$4 \times 4 = 16$$

$$640 \div 16 = 40 \text{ acres}$$

Alternative method: Working backward from the 640-acre section, divide 640 by the denominator of each fraction

Example: N ½ of the NE ¼ of the SW ¼ of section 12

$$640 \div 2 \div 4 \div 4 = 20 \text{ acres}$$

(Note: Either method will result in the same answer. *Memorize* the method that is easiest for you to calculate.)

■ **Calculate the acres in a Government Survey legal description with *and* in the description**

1. Multiply the denominators that immediately precede the *and*

2. Multiply the denominators that follow the *and*

3. Find the acreage of each

4. Sum the two acreages

Example: SE ¼ of the N ½ *and* the SW ¼ of the NE ¼

$$4 \times 2 = 8$$

$$4 \times 4 = 16$$

$$640 \div 8 = 80 \text{ acres}$$

$$640 \div 16 = 40 \text{ acres}$$

$$80 \text{ acres} + 40 \text{ acres} = 120 \text{ acres}$$

Alternative Solution:

$$640 \div 4 \div 2 = 80 \text{ acres}$$

$$640 \div 4 \div 4 = 40 \text{ acres}$$

$$80 \text{ acres} + 40 \text{ acres} = 120 \text{ acres}$$

Note to Readers

For a more complete description of math as it specifically applies to real estate, see the author's *Real Estate Math: What You Need to Know,* Sixth Edition, Dearborn™ Real Estate Education. This self-study book covers the basics of math and provides practice opportunities in all areas. Step-by-step solutions to the math problems are included in *Real Estate Math: What You Need to Know.*

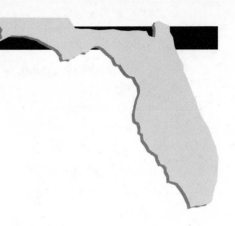

Real Estate Finance
(Chapter 12)

■ KEY TERM REVIEW

Acceleration clause authorizes the mortgagee to accelerate or advance the due date of the entire unpaid balance and call the entire debt due and payable if the mortgagor defaults.

Adjustable-rate mortgage (ARM) is a financing technique in which the lender can raise or lower the interest rate according to a set index.

Amortized mortgage is a financing technique in which the debt is gradually and systematically killed or extinguished by equal regular period payments; the entire loan is paid off at the end of the loan term.

Assignment of mortgage is a legal instrument that states that the mortgagee assigns (transfers) the mortgage and promissory note to the purchaser.

Balloon payment is a single large final payment, including accrued interest and all unpaid principal due at maturity of a partially amortized mortgage.

Biweekly mortgage is a mortgage loan amortized the same way as other loans with monthly payments, except that the borrower makes a payment every two weeks.

Blanket mortgage covers a number of parcels, usually building lots.

Contract for deed (or land contract) is a financing method in which the title to the real property remains with the seller until the loan is repaid.

Deed in lieu of foreclosure is a friendly foreclosure (a nonjudicial procedure) in which the mortgagor gives title to the mortgagee.

Defeasance clause provides that the conveyance of title by the borrower to the lender is defeated when the borrower meets all of the terms and conditions of the mortgage.

Due-on-sale clause allows the mortgagee to call due the outstanding loan balance plus accrued interest thereby preventing the loan assumption; loan is due upon sale of the property.

Equity of redemption allows the mortgagor to prevent foreclosure from occurring by paying the mortgagee the principal and interest due plus any expenses the lender has incurred in attempting to collect the debt.

Estoppel certificate is signed by the borrower verifying the amount of the unpaid balance, the rate of interest, and the date to which the interest has been paid prior to assignment.

Home equity loans are loans secured by the borrower's residence to finance consumer purchases, consolidate existing credit card debt, and pay for other expenses.

Hypothecation refers to the pledging of property as security for payment of a loan without surrendering possession of the property.

Interest rate is the price individuals pay to borrow money.

Loan-to-value ratio (LTV) is the relationship between the amount borrowed and the appraised value (or sometimes purchase price).

Mortgage is a security instrument signed by the mortgagor to voluntarily pledge the property as collateral for the debt.

Mortgagee is the lender.

Mortgage insurance premium (MIP) is a premium for mortgage insurance on FHA mortgages.

Mortgagor is the borrower.

Note is the legal instrument that represents the evidence of a debt and a promise to repay the debt.

Novation is the exchange or substitution of a new debt for an existing debt by mutual agreement.

Package mortgage includes both real and personal property as security for the debt.

Partial release clause stipulates the conditions under which the mortgagee will grant a release of lots, free and clear of the mortgage.

Prepayment clause allows the borrower to pay off part or all of the mortgage debt, without penalty or other fees, prior to maturity.

Purchase-money mortgage (PMM) is a new mortgage accepted by the seller as part of the purchase price.

Receivership clause requires the income from the property to be used to make mortgage payments in the event of default.

Satisfaction of mortgage or *release of mortgage* is executed by the lender once the mortgage debt is paid in full.

Subordination clause provides that the lender voluntarily will allow a subsequent mortgage to take priority over the lender's otherwise superior mortgage (the act of yielding priority).

Wraparound mortgage envelops an existing mortgage and is subordinate (junior) to it; the existing mortgage stays on the property and the new mortgage *wraps* around it.

■ KEY CONCEPTS IN CHAPTER 12

- ■ **Two legal theories**
  - — *Title theory* requires borrower to transfer title to the property to the lender until the mortgage debt is paid in full—borrower retains equitable title
  - — *Lien theory* states protect the lender with a lien against the property but title remains with the borrower

- ■ **Promissory note**
  - — Note must accompany all mortgages
  - — Acknowledgement of the debt and a promise to repay
  - — Makes borrower personally liable
  - — Includes terms of the agreement

- **Mortgage**
  - Pledges the property as security (collateral) for a debt
  - Represents the voluntary lien on real estate
  - *Hypothecation* is the pledging of property as security for the mortgage debt without surrendering possession
  - Parties to mortgage are the mortgagor (borrower) and mortgagee (lender)

- **Assignment**
  - Occurs when ownership of a mortgage is transferred from one company or individual to another
  - Execution of an assignment of mortgage
  - Person or company purchasing the mortgage receives an estoppel certificate verifying the amount of the unpaid loan balance

- **Satisfaction of mortgage**
  - Mortgagee records the satisfaction, which releases the lien

- **Foreclosure**
  - Judicial process that requires a foreclosure auction after court process
  - *Deed in lieu of foreclosure* is a nonjudicial procedure involving transfer of title from the defaulting borrower to the mortgagee

- **Mortgage clauses**
  - Promise to repay
  - Promise to pay property taxes, assessments, and so forth
  - Promise to pay property insurance
  - Occupy as a principal residence
  - Maintenance and covenant of good repair
  - *Due-on-sale clause* provides that upon sale the loan is due and payable
  - *Acceleration clause* provides that upon default the entire debt is due
  - Right to reinstate
  - *Release clause* provides that upon payment in full, the mortgage lien is released
  - *Prepayment clause* provides conditions to repay debt in advance of due date
  - *Prepayment penalty clause* allows an extra charge if any amount of the loan is paid off early

- **FHA government-insured mortgage loan**
  - FHA is a government agency within HUD
  - Insures mortgages made by approved lenders
  - Borrower pays up front mortgage insurance premium (UFMIP) at closing

— Borrower pays monthly mortgage insurance premium (MIP)

— Maximum mortgage amount on sale price (or appraised value) of $50,000 or less: 98.75 percent

— Maximum mortgage amount on sale price (or appraised value) of more than $50,000: 97.75 percent

— Borrower must make a minimum cash investment of at least 3 percent

■ **VA mortgage loan**

— Veterans, surviving spouse of veterans, and active military are eligible

— VA does not set loan limits

— Borrower pays a funding fee or user's fee

— VA guarantees

— No mortgage insurance premiums

— Down payments are not required

■ **Conventional mortgage**

— Require larger down payment than FHA-insured mortgages

— Private mortgage insurance (PMI) is required for loan amount that exceeds 80 percent of value

■ **Partially amortized mortgage**

— Regular payments do not completely pay off the loan at end of term

— Single final balloon payment for unpaid balance

■ **Amortized mortgage**

— Regular payments each month of principal and interest

— *Level payment plan* (payment is constant but amount applied to principal increases each month and amount applied to interest decreases each month)

■ **Biweekly mortgage**

— Borrower makes a payment every two weeks

— Amount paid is one-half the normal monthly payment

— Borrower makes 26 biweekly payments which is the equivalent of an extra month's payment each year

■ **Ways to purchase mortgaged property**

— Cash

— Subject to the mortgage

— Assumption of an existing mortgage

— Novation

■ **Adjustable-rate mortgage (ARM)**

— Interest rate is tied to an index

— Negative amortization results when the payments are less than required to pay all the costs and the difference is *added* to the loan balance

— Teaser rate is an artificially low initial interest rate

■ **Reverse-annuity mortgage**

— Used by elderly homeowners who have built up equity in home

— Borrower receives monthly income in exchange for the equity in their home

■ IMPORTANT FORMULAS TO REMEMBER

■ **Calculate the loan-to-value ratio**

Loan amount ÷ Price = LTV ratio

Example: Purchase price is $116,000. Loan amount is $92,800.

$92,800 ÷ $116,000 = .80 or 80% LTV

■ **Calculate the loan-to-value ratio when given down payment**

1. Price – down payment = loan amount

2. Loan amount ÷ Price = LTV ratio

Example: Purchase price is $250,000. Down payment is $25,000.

$250,000 – $25,000 = $225,000

$225,000 ÷ $250,000 = .90 or 90% LTV

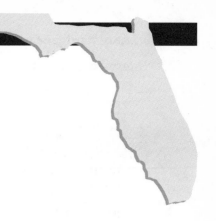

The Mortgage Market
(Chapter 13)

■ KEY TERM REVIEW

Demand deposits are checking accounts.

Discount points are an extra upfront fee charged by lenders to increase the real yield or the APR.

Discount rate is the interest rate charged member banks for borrowing money from the Fed.

Disintermediation is the removal of intermediaries; buyers bypass the middlemen.

Intermediation financial institutions serve as intermediaries between depositors and borrowers.

Monetary policy refers to the actions undertaken by the Fed to influence the availability and cost of money and credit.

Mortgage banker (mortgage lender) originates loans with either their own funds or with money borrowed from financial institutions.

Mortgage broker is an agent who submits loan applications from prospective borrowers to various lenders.

Office of thrift supervision (OTS) charters and regulates member federal savings associations.

Open market operations involve the purchase and sale of U.S. Treasury and federal agency securities.

Primary market is the market where securities are created.

Reserve requirements are the amount of funds that an institution must hold in reserve against deposit liabilities.

Secondary market is an investor market that buys and sells already existing securities.

■ KEY CONCEPTS IN CHAPTER 13

■ **Three economic tools the Federal Reserve System uses**

— Open-market operations

— Discount rate

— Reserve requirement

- **Primary mortgage market consists of lenders who originate new mortgages**

- **Intermediation and disintermediation**

  — Financial institutions serve as *intermediaries* between depositors and borrowers—financial institutions act as financial intermediaries (middlemen) for depositors and borrowers

  — *Disintermediation* occurs when funds are withdrawn from intermediary financial institutions and invested in instruments yielding a higher return—process of bypassing the intermediary financial institutions

- **Commercial banks**

  — National banks are chartered by the federal government

  — *National* or *NA* in name

  — Members of the Federal Reserve System

  — Deposits insured by FDIC

- **Savings Associations**

  — Federally chartered has *Federal* or *FA* in name

  — Savings Association Insurance Fund (SAIF) insures deposits

  — Federal SAs are members of Federal Home Loan Mortgage Bank System (FHLBS)

  — Office of Thrift Supervision (OTS) charters and regulates member federal savings associations

- **Secondary market is where existing mortgages are purchased and sold**

- **Secondary market participants**

  — Fannie Mae

  — Freddie Mac

  — Ginnie Mae

- **Fannie Mae (FNMA)**

  — A quasi-governmental agency (government regulated)

  — Private corporation that issues common stock

  — Deals in conventional, FHA, and VA loans

  — *Conforming loans* meet FNMA guidelines

  — FNMA issues mortgage-backed securities in exchange for pools of mortgages

- **Freddie Mac (FHLMC)**

  — Government regulated

  — Private corporation that issues common stock

  — Primarily a secondary market for conventional loans

- **Ginnie Mae (GNMA)**

    — Government agency under HUD

    — Administers special-assistance programs

    — Only agency to issue mortgage-backed securities that carry full faith and credit guarantee of the federal government

- **Discount points**

    — Upfront charge paid at closing (prepaid interest) to increase lender's yield

    — One discount point is equal to 1 percent of the loan amount

    — Each discount point increases the yield by about ⅛ of one percent

■ IMPORTANT FORMULAS TO REMEMBER

- **Calculate the cost of points**

    Loan amount × number points × .01 = cost of points

    Example: Loan amount is $95,000. Lender charges 3 points

    $95,000 × .03 = $2,850

- **Calculate the lender's yield**

    (Note: *Memorize* that each point increases the yield by ⅛ of one percent)

    (Number of points × ⅛) + interest rate = lender's approximate yield

    Example: The interest rate is 6 percent plus 2 points.

    2 × ⅛ = ²⁄₈ + 6 = 6²⁄₈ reduced to 6¼% yield

- **Calculate the lender's yield and report in decimal form**

    Convert a fraction to a decimal: ⅛ = 1 ÷ 8 = .125

    Example: The interest rate is 5 percent plus 3 points.

    3 × ⅛ = ³⁄₈

    3 ÷ 8 = .375 + 5 = 5.375%

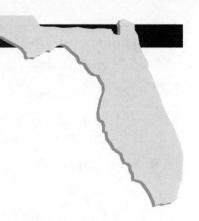

Estimating Real Property Value
(Chapter 15)

■ KEY TERM REVIEW

Appraisal is a supported, defended *estimate* of the value of property rights as of a specified date.

Assemblage is the combining of two or more adjoining properties into one tract; the *process* of consolidating properties.

Cost-depreciation approach estimates value by taking cost minus depreciation plus site value, based on the theory that a knowledgeable purchaser will pay no more for a property than the cost of acquiring a similar site and constructing an acceptable substitute structure.

Curable if correction of a defect would result in as much added value as the cost to correct.

Depreciation is loss in value for any reason.

Economic life or *useful life* is the total estimated time in years that an improvement will add value.

Effective age is the age indicated by a structure's condition and utility.

Effective gross income (EGI) is the result of deducting vacancy and collection losses from annual potential gross income plus adding any income from miscellaneous sources.

Goodwill is an intangible asset arising from the reputation of a business and is often reflected in the sale price; may be considered in a market value appraisal if specifically identified in the report.

Gross income multiplier (GIM) can include income from sources other than rental income (based on annual income); the ratio between a property's gross annual income and its selling price.

Gross rent multiplier (GRM) is the ratio between a property's gross monthly rental income and its selling price.

Highest and best use is the most profitable use to which a property may be put.

Income capitalization approach develops an estimated market value based on the present worth of future income from the subject property.

Incurable defect is one in which the cost of curing the defect is greater than the value added by the cure.

Investment value is the value of a property to a particular investor based on his or her desired rate of return, risk tolerance, and so forth.

Market value is the most probable price a property should bring in a competitive and open market with the buyer and seller each acting prudently and knowledgeably, and assuming the price is not affected by undue stimulus.

Net operating income (NOI) is the income remaining after subtracting all relevant operating expenses from EGI.

Overimprovement occurs when an owner invests more money in a structure than he or she may reasonably expect to recapture.

Plottage is the *added value* as a result of assembling (combining) two or more properties into one large parcel.

Potential gross income (PGI) is total annual income a property would produce if it were fully rented and no collections losses were incurred.

Principle of substitution means that a prudent buyer or investor will pay no more for a property than the cost of acquiring an equally desirable substitute property.

Progression is the principle that states that the value of an inferior property is enhanced by its association with superior properties of the same type.

Reconciliation is a process of weighted averaging used in the sales comparison approach to bring the adjusted values of several comparable properties into a single estimate of value.

Regression is the principle that states that the value of a superior property is negatively affected by its association with an inferior property of the same type.

Replacement cost is the amount of money required to replace a structure having the same use and functional utility as the subject property, but using modern, available, or updated materials.

Reproduction cost is the amount of money required to build an exact duplicate of the structure.

Sales comparison approach is a method for estimating value by comparing similar properties with the subject property based on the theory that a knowledgeable purchaser will pay no more for a property than the cost of acquiring an equally acceptable substitute property.

Situs refers to people's preferences, both physical and economic, for a certain location owing to factors such as weather, job opportunities, and transportation facilities.

Subject property is the property being appraised.

Vacancy and collection losses consist of the expected income loss that will result from occasional turnover of tenants and periodic vacancies as well as the likelihood that not all of the rental income will be collected.

■ KEY CONCEPTS IN CHAPTER 15

- ■ Federally related transaction
  - — Real estate-related transaction that requires an appraisal and involves a federally insured financial institution in which real estate is pledged as security for a loan with a loan value greater than $250,000
  - — Fannie Mae, Freddie Mac, HUD, and the VA require the use of state-certified and licensed appraisers regardless of whether the loan value is greater than the minimum valuation threshold of $250,000
  - — Appraisals of property concerning federally related transactions must be conducted by a state-certified or licensed appraiser

■ **Real estate licensees may prepare appraisal reports**

— Provided *not* a federally related transaction

— Must abide by the Uniform Standards of Professional Appraisal Practice (USPAP)

— May *not* refer to a CMA as an appraisal

— May *not* hold themselves out to be an appraiser

■ **Types of value**

— *Assessed value* is the value used as a basis for property taxation

— *Insurance value* is an estimate of the amount of money required to replace a structure

— *Investment value* is the price an investor would pay, given his or her own financing requirements and income tax situation

— *Liquidation value* is the value associated with a rapid sale

— *Going-concern value* is the value of an income-producing property characterized by a significant operating history

— *Market value* is the most probable price that a property should bring in a competitive and open market under all conditions requisite to a fair sale, the buyer and seller each acting prudently and knowledgeably, and assuming the price is not affected by undue stimulus

■ **Value, price, and cost**

— *Value* is determined by a commodity's ability to command other goods in exchange

— *Price* is the amount of money paid

— *Cost* is the total expenditure to create an improvement

■ **Characteristics of value (DUST)**

— **D** Demand

— **U** Utility

— **S** Scarcity

— **T** Transferability

■ **Highest and best use**

— Most profitable use to which a property may be put

— Use must be legally permissible, physically possible, and financially feasible

— Highest and best use is a *residual concept* (use with highest value after considering costs)

■ **Sales comparison approach**

— Used primarily for single-family residential and vacant land

— Value is estimated by studying the sale prices of similar (*comparable*) properties

— Sale prices of the comps are adjusted to infer value of the subject property

— If a comparable is superior to the subject, adjust comp *down* (subtract)

— If a comparable is inferior to the subject, adjust comp *up* (add)

— Adjusted sale prices of comparables are reconciled into an estimated value of the subject property

■ **Steps in cost-depreciation approach**

— Estimate the reproduction cost of the improvements (can use replacement cost)

— Estimate amount of accrued depreciation

— Estimate the value of the site

— Add land value to the depreciated cost of the structure

■ **Three types of depreciation in cost approach**

— *Physical deterioration* is ordinary wear and tear caused by use

— *Functional obsolescence* is poor design, obsolete equipment, and so forth

— *External obsolescence* is caused by neighborhood influences *external* to the property

■ **Income capitalization approach**

— Measures a flow of income projected into the future

— Principal of anticipation (value is created by the expectation of an income stream into the future)

■ **Steps in the income approach**

— Estimate annual potential gross income (PGI)

— Deduct vacancy and collection loss to derive effective gross income (EGI)

— Deduct operating expenses (fixed, variable, and reserves) to derive net operating income (NOI)

— Compare net operating incomes of properties similar to the subject property and divide each NOI by the property's sale price to derive a capitalization rate

— Apply the cap rate to the subject property's projected annual net income to estimate value

■ IMPORTANT FORMULAS TO REMEMBER

■ **Calculate average price per square foot and apply to estimate land value**

1. Estimate the square footage of each comparable lot

2. Sale price ÷ total square feet = price per square foot

3. Average the price per square foot of the comparables

4. Subject property square feet × average price per square foot = estimated value of subject lot

Example:

Sale	Sale Price	Dimensions
1	$25,000	100' × 120'
2	$28,500	110' × 120'
3	$29,000	100' × 140'

1	100' × 120' = 12,000 square feet
2	110' × 120' = 13,200 square feet
3	100' × 140' = 14,000 square feet

1	$25,000 ÷ 12,000 = $2.08 (rounded to dollars and cents) per square foot
2	$28,500 ÷ 13,200 = $2.16
3	$29,000 ÷ 14,000 = $2.07

$2.08 + $2.16 + $2.07 = $6.31 ÷ 3 sales = $2.10 average price per square foot

Assume subject lot is 115' × 130' and there are no other adjustments required:

115' × 130' = 14,950 sq feet × $2.10 = $31,395 estimated market value or $31,400 (rounded)

■ **Calculate the estimated market value of the subject property using the sales comparison approach**

1. Comp is *inferior add* value **(CIA)**

2. Comp is *better subtract* value **(CBS)**

Example: Subject property is a three bedroom, two bath, two-car garage home with a pool.

A comparable property is a four bedroom, two bath, two-car garage home with no pool but it has a screened in porch.

The appraiser estimates that the fourth bedroom adds $15,000 value, a pool adds $12,000 value, and a screened-in porch adds $2,000 value. The comparable sold for $165,000. Calculate the estimated market value of the subject property based on this information only.

Feature	Subject	Comparable	Value Adjustment
Bedrooms	3	4	($15,000)
Pool	Yes	No	+ $12,000
Porch	No	Yes	($2,000)
Net adjustment			($5,000)

$165,000 − $5,000 net adjustment = $160,000 estimated market value of subject property

■ **Calculate accrued depreciation using effective age and total economic life**

(Effective age ÷ total economic life) × reproduction cost new = accrued depreciation

Example:　　The effective age of a structure is five years old. Total economic life is estimated at 60 years. Reproduction cost new is $250,000.

$(5 ÷ 60)$　　　　　　= .0833 (rounded to four decimal places)

$.0833 × \$250,000$　　= $20,825 accrued depreciation

■ **Calculate estimated property value using the cost approach**

Reproduction new cost of the building – accrued depreciation = building value

Building value + site value = depreciated value of the property

Example:　　A house has a living area of 2,200 square feet and a garage area of 420 square feet. The cost to construct living area today is $90 per square foot and $55 per square foot for the garage area. The home is five years old and has a useful life of 50 years. The lot is appraised at $32,000.

$2,200 × \$90$　　　　= $198,000 reproduction cost new of the living area

$420 × \$55$　　　　　= $23,100 reproduction cost new garage area

$\$198,000 + \$23,100$　= $221,100 reproduction cost new of structure

$(5 ÷ 50) × \$221,100$　=

$.10 × \$221,100$　　　= $22,110 accrued depreciation

$221,100 – $22,110 depreciation + $32,000 land =
$230,990 depreciated value of the property using the cost approach

■ **Calculate estimated property value using the income approach**

NOI ÷ cap rate = value

Example:　　The net operating income of a rental property is $80,000, and the capitalization rate is 8 percent.

$\$80,000 ÷ .08 = \$1,000,000$ value using income approach

■ **Calculate the capitalization rate using the income approach**

NOI ÷ value = cap rate

Example:　　The net operating income of a retail store is $66,000 and the store recently sold for $550,000.

$\$66,000 ÷ \$550,000 = .12$ or 12% cap rate

■ **Calculate the NOI using the income approach**

Value × cap rate = NOI

Example:　　You invest $335,000 in a property that should produce a 9 percent rate of return.

$\$335,000 × .09 = \$30,150$ NOI

■ **Calculate estimated property value using the gross rent multiplier**

Sale price ÷ monthly rent = GRM

GRM × monthly rent = property value

Example:

Sale	Sale Price	Monthly Rent
1	$93,600	$650
2	$95,500	$675
3	$82,000	$565

(Round to nearest whole number):

$93,600 ÷ $650 = 144 GRM

$95,500 ÷ $675 = 141 GRM

$82,000 ÷ $565 = 145 GRM

144 + 141 + 145 = 430 ÷ 3 = 143 market GRM

Subject property has a market rent of $625:

$625 × 143 = $89,375 value

■ **Calculate GIM using the gross income multiplier**

Sale price ÷ annual income = GIM

Example: If the annual income of a commercial property is $120,000 and the sale price is $900,000, what is the GIM?

$900,000 ÷ $120,000 = 7.5 GIM

Product Knowledge
(Chapter 16)

■ KEY TERM REVIEW

Corner lot is bounded with streets on two sides (intersecting).

Cul-de-sac lots occur where a street is open at one end only and the street has a circular turnaround at the other end.

Dormer is a projection that extends out of the roof to provide additional light and ventilation.

Double-hung windows open by sliding the bottom half of the window up or sliding the top half down.

Flag lots are characterized by a long access road or driveway leading back to the main part of the lot.

Flat roofs (or built-up roofs) are nearly flat and are constructed in layers of tar and gravel.

Gable roofs use a single truss design in which the roof peaks at the center ridge and extends downward on two opposite sides.

Gambrel roofs are also known as the American barn-style roof.

Hip roofs peak at the center ride and extend downward on four opposite sides.

Interior lots are bounded on either side by another lot (lots in the middle of the block—not on the corner).

Key lots are generally long skinny lots similar to the shaft of a key that are often bounded by as many as five or six lots (The term also refers to a lot that has added value because of its strategic location).

Mansard roofs have shingles extending down over the top floor.

R-value refers to the effectiveness of insulation and is measured by its resistance to heat flow.

Single-hung windows have a lower sash that moves up and down.

T-intersection lots are interior lots that suffer from their location at the end of a T-intersection (a street ends in front of the lot).

■ KEY CONCEPTS IN CHAPTER 16

■ Lot types

— Corner

— Interior

- — T-intersection
- — Cul-de-sac
- — Flag
- — Key

■ **Two basic residential foundations**

- — Pier (raises floor above ground level)
- — Slab-on-grade

■ **Common types of framing**

- — Platform
- — Balloon
- — Post-and-beam

■ **The pitch of a roof is its slope**

- — Height (*rise*) is divided by distance (*span* or *run*)
- — A roof that rises five inches in height for one-foot of distance has a pitch of 5/12

■ **Roof styles**

- — Gable
- — Hip
- — Saltbox
- — Shed
- — Flat
- — Gambrel
- — Mansard

■ **Insulation is material applied to exterior walls and ceilings to protect the interior from heat loss**

■ **Insulation efficiency is measured by R-value**

■ **Window types**

- — Fixed
- — Awning
- — Casement
- — Jalousie
- — Sliding
- — Hopper
- — Center pivot
- — Double-hung
- — Single-hung

Real Estate Investment Analysis and Business Opportunity Brokerage (Chapter 17)

■ KEY TERM REVIEW

Appreciation is an increase in the worth or value of property.

Asset is anything of value.

Balance sheet shows the company's financial position at a stated moment in time.

Cash flow is the total amount of money generated from an investment after expenses have been paid.

Equity is an investor's own funds in a real estate investment property (the interest that an owner has in property over and above any indebtedness).

Going concern value is the value of an established business property compared with the value of just the physical assets of a business not yet established.

Goodwill is the intangible asset attributed to a business's reputation and the expectation of continued customer loyalty.

Income statement is a concise summary of all income and expenses of a business for a stated period of time.

Investment value is the worth of a property to an individual investor based on that investor's individual standards for achieving a goal (such as risk tolerance).

Leverage is the use of borrowed funds to finance the purchase of an asset.

Liquidity refers to the ability to sell an investment quickly without loss of one's investment.

REIT (or *real estate investment trust*) offers investors the opportunity to invest in a pool of income-producing properties under professional management.

Replacement cost is the cost that would result with materials of the same *utility* but *not* identical.

Reproduction cost is the cost to duplicate *exactly* the business or building being appraised.

Risk is the chance of losing all or part of an investment.

■ KEY CONCEPTS IN CHAPTER 17

- ■ **Advantages of real estate as an investment**
  - — Good rate of return

- — Tax advantages
- — Hedge against inflation
- — Leverage
- — Equity buildup

■ **Disadvantages of investing in real estate**

- — Illiquidity
- — Local market
- — Need for expert help
- — Management
- — Risk

■ **Destination properties** include service industries that support the needs of a local community

■ **Origin properties**

- — Produce a product to seek out an income stream
- — Involved in export activities

■ **Risks associated with general business conditions**

- — *Business risk* (or *operating business risk*) is the degree of variance between budgeted (projected) income and expenses and actual income and expenses
- — *Financial risk* (or *operating financial risk*) is associated with the ability of a property to pay operating expenses from operations, borrowing, and equity
- — *Purchasing-power risk* is related to inflation
- — *Interest-rate risk* is the risk of rising interest rates

■ **Risks that affect return**

- — *Liquidity risk* is the possible loss that may be incurred if the investment has to be converted quickly into cash
- — *Safety risk* is composed of market risk and risk of default

■ **Static risk** is risk that can be transferred to an insurer such as risk of vandalism, fire, and so forth

■ **Dynamic risk** is risk that arises from the continuous change that exists in the business or economic environment and therefore is *not* transferable (insurable) risk

■ **Leverage** is the use of borrowed funds to finance the purchase of an asset

- — *Positive leverage* occurs when the benefits exceed the cost of borrowing
- — *Negative leverage* occurs if the borrowed funds cost more than they are producing

■ **Similarities between business brokerage and real estate brokerage**

— Sale of real property or the assignment of a lease (transfer of interest in real property) is an integral part of a business brokerage transaction

— A real estate license is required to deal in business brokerage

■ **Differences between business brokerage and real estate brokerage**

— May involve personal property

— May involve tangible (real property) and intangible assets (goodwill)

— Value of real estate and value of going concern may be different

— Understanding of financial statements, including accounts payable and short-term liabilities

— Larger geographic market for business brokerage

■ **Methods of appraising businesses**

— Comparable sales analysis

— Cost-depreciation

— Income capitalization

— Liquidation analysis

■ IMPORTANT FORMULAS TO REMEMBER

■ **Calculate an investor's equity**

Current market value – mortgage debt = equity

Example: An investor owns a business property with a value of $1,200,000 and a mortgage of $800,000.

$1,200,000 – $800,000 = $400,000 equity

Taxes Affecting Real Estate
(Chapter 18)

■ KEY TERM REVIEW

Adjusted basis is the owner's original cost plus buying expenses plus capital improvements.

Ad valorem means taxed according to value.

Assessed value is the value of a property for property tax purposes.

Boot is additional capital or personal property included in a like-kind exchange.

Capital gain is profit from the sale of property.

Exempt properties include property belonging to churches and nonprofit organizations.

Green Belt Law was designed to protect farmers from having taxes increased just because the land might be in the path of urban growth.

Immune properties are city, county, state, and federal government properties.

Just value is the fair and reasonable value based on objective valuation methods for property tax purposes.

Mill is one one-thousandth of a dollar or one-tenth of a cent.

Partially exempt property is subject to taxation, but the owner is partially relieved of the burden.

Special assessments are one-time taxes levied on properties to help pay for some public improvement that benefits the property.

Taxable value is the nonexempt assessed value that is determined by subtracting the applicable exemptions from the assessed value.

Tax shelter refers to shielding income or gain from payment of income taxes.

■ KEY CONCEPTS IN CHAPTER 18

- ■ Steps in protest procedure
    - — Contact the county property appraiser's office within 25 days to seek an adjustment
    - — Appeal to the Value Adjustment Board
    - — Litigation

- **Property tax exemptions**
  - *Immune* (government)
  - *Exempt* (churches and nonprofits)
  - *Partially exempt* (homesteaded property)

- **Homestead tax exemption**
  - Base deduction of $25,000 from the assessed value
  - First-time applicants must file for homestead by March 1

- **Additional $500 exemptions on homesteaded property**
  - Widows and widowers
  - Legally blind persons
  - Nonveterans who are totally and permanently disabled

- **$5,000 disabled veteran exemption** for veterans who are at least 10 percent disabled by military service-connected injury

- **Green Belt Law**
  - Shields agricultural property from higher tax assessments
  - Designed to protect farmers from having taxes increase just because their land might be suited for development

- **Save Our Home amendment** caps how much the assessed value of homesteaded property may increase each year to 3 percent annually or the CPI, whichever is less

- **Tax rates**
  - Cities, counties, and school boards are capped at 10 mills each
  - One mill is written in decimals as .001
  - Taxable value multiplied by the tax rate equals annual property taxes due

- **Special assessments**
  - A one-time tax on improvements such as sidewalks, street paving, and so forth
  - Calculated on per foot cost of the improvement

- **Nonpayment of property taxes**
  - Property taxes constitute a lien superior to all other liens on real property
  - Property taxes become a lien on January 1 of each year
  - Property taxes for the previous year become delinquent on April 1

- **Principal residence deductions from income taxes**
  - Mortgage interest
  - Property taxes
  - Interest on a home equity loan

— Mortgage origination fees (points)

■ **Three deductions from taxable income on investment property**

— Operating expenses (*not* reserve for replacements)

— Financing expense

— Depreciation (key to sheltering income from taxation)

■ **Straight-line method of depreciation for investment real estate**

— 27½ years for residential rental property

— 39 years for nonresidential income-producing property

— Depreciate structure *only* (never land)

■ IMPORTANT DATES AND TIME PERIODS TO REMEMBER

■ **January 1.** Date each year that property taxes become a lien on real property

■ **March 1.** Last day for first-time applicants to file for homestead exemption

■ **April 1.** Property taxes from the previous year become delinquent

■ **27½ years.** Useful asset life for residential rental property

■ **39 years.** Useful asset life for nonresidential income property

■ IMPORTANT FORMULAS TO REMEMBER

■ **Calculate the tax rate**

(Budget – nonproperty revenue) ÷ (assessed value – exemptions) = tax rate

Example: County budget is $9,500,000. Nonproperty revenue totals 2,500,000. Total assessed valuation is $850,000,000. Exemptions total $125,000,000.

  1. Calculate the budget less the nonproperty revenue

$9,500,000 budget – $2,500,000 revenue = $7,000,000

  2. Calculate the assessed value less exemptions

$850,000,000 – $125,000,000 = $725,000,000

Remaining budget ÷ property revenue

$7,000,000 ÷ $725,000,000 =

(Note: Drop last set of zeros in each number before dividing.)

$7,000 ÷ $725,000 = .0096 or 9.6 mills

■ **Calculate property taxes due**

1. Calculate total mills

2. Calculate total exemptions

3. Assessed value − exemptions = taxable value

4. Taxable value × millage rate = property taxes due

Example: The city tax rate is 8 mills, the county rate is 7.5 mills, and the school board rate is 5 mills. The property is homesteaded and the owner is legally blind. The assessed value is $320,000.

8 + 7.5 + 5	= 20.5 total mills or .0205
$25,000 homestead + $500 blind	= $25,500 total exemptions
$320,000 − $25,500	= $294,500 taxable value
$294,500 × .0205	= $6,037.25 taxes due

■ **Calculate tax savings realized from allowable exemptions**

Homestead exemptions × millage rate = tax savings

Example: Assessed value is $320,000 and allowable exemptions total $25,500. The millage rate is 20.5 mills.

$25,500 × .0205 = $522.75 tax savings

■ **Calculate the cost of a special assessment**

1. Calculate total cost of paving

2. Calculate cost of homeowners' share

3. Divide cost by 2 (*Assume* cost is split with owner across the street)

Example: The lot measures 125′ by 150′. The cost to pave the street is $60 per foot. The city will pay 45 percent of the cost.

125 front feet × $60	= $7,500 total cost of paving
$7,500 × .55	= $4,125 homeowners' share
$4,125 ÷ 2	= $2,062.50

■ **Calculate annual depreciation allowance on residential rental property**

1. Calculate the value of the building without the land

2. Building ÷ 27.5 years = annual depreciation

Example: Property was purchased for $450,000 and the site is valued at 20 percent. Sale occurred in January. (Round depreciation to nearest dollar.)

$450,000 × .80	= $360,000 building
$360,000 ÷ 27.5	= $13,090.91 (round to) $13,091 annual depreciation

■ **Calculate annual depreciation allowance on nonresidential income property**

1. Calculate the value of the building without the land

2. Building ÷ 39 years = annual depreciation

Example: Income property was purchased for $450,000 and the site is valued at 20 percent. Sale occurred in January. (Round depreciation to nearest dollar.)

$450,000 × .80   = $360,000 building

$360,000 ÷ 39   = $9,230.77 (round to) $9,231 annual depreciation

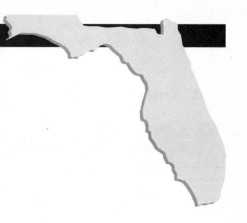

The Real Estate Market
(Chapter 19)

■ KEY TERM REVIEW

Buyer's market occurs when the supply and demand equilibrium is upset by excess supply; more supply available than buyers (supply exceeds demand).

Demand has to do with the desire and ability to purchase or rent goods and services.

Household is any person or group of persons occupying a separate housing space.

Seller's market occurs when the supply and demand equilibrium is upset with excess demand; more buyers competing for a limited supply (demand exceeds supply).

Supply is the amount and type of real estate available for sale or rent at differing price levels in a given real estate market.

Vacancy rate is the percentage of rental units that are not occupied.

■ KEY CONCEPTS IN CHAPTER 19

■ Real estate market characteristics

— *Immobility* (the geographic location is fixed and therefore its value is largely influenced by the surrounding area)

— The market is slow to respond to change in supply and demand

— Land is *indestructible*; however, the physical structures (improvements) on the land deteriorate and become obsolete over time

— Real estate is *unique*; there is no standard product (the uniqueness of land is also called *heterogeneity*); no two parcels are identical for they are at least in different locations

— Government controls influence the market through zoning, building codes, taxes, and so forth

■ Variables that influence supply

— Availability of skilled labor

— Availability of construction loans and financing

- — Availability of land
- — Availability of materials
- **Variables that influence demand**
  - — Price of real estate
  - — Population numbers and household composition
  - — Income of consumers
  - — Availability of mortgage credit
  - — Consumer taste or preferences
- **Demand is *inversely* related to price**
  - — When prices *rise* demand goes *down*
  - — When prices *decrease* demand goes *up*
- **Buyer's market**
  - — Excess supply
  - — Supply exceeds demand
  - — Prices go down
- **Seller's market**
  - — Excess demand
  - — Demand exceeds supply
  - — Prices go up
- **Interpreting market conditions**
  - — Price levels
  - — Vacancy rates
  - — Sales volume

Computations and Title Closing
(Chapter 14)

■ KEY TERM REVIEW

Arrears means paid at the end of the period for which payment is due.

Credit means to be reimbursed for an expense.

Debit means to be charged for an expense.

Level-payment plan is a mortgage in which the monthly payments are a fixed amount (payment does not change) but the amount applied to principal increases each month and the amount applied to interest decreases each month.

Preclosing inspection is a final walk-through with the sales associate to verify that repairs have been completed and that the property is left in good condition.

Principal is the unpaid balance of the debt.

Profit is how much one makes over and above cost.

Prorate means to divide various debits (charges) and credits between buyer and seller; a proration is a *shared expense* between the buyer and seller.

■ KEY CONCEPTS IN CHAPTER 14

■ **Sale commission is the typical method of compensating licensees**

— Simple commission based on sale price

— Graduated commission

— Net

■ **Profit is how much you make over and above cost and may be expressed as a dollar amount or as a percent of cost**

■ **Three facts needed to calculate a mortgage amortization**

— The outstanding amount of the debt (principal)

— The rate of interest

— The amount of the payment (principal and interest "PI" *only*)

■ **Prorating expenses**

— Debit to one party and a credit to the other party

— Dollar amount of the debit and credit are the same

— Some prorations are based on the 30-day method or 360-day method (each month is counted as 30 days—even February and 31-day months)

— Some prorations are based on 365-day method (based on actual number of days in each month)

■ **State transfer taxes**

— Documentary stamp tax on deeds is paid on full purchase price: $.70 ($.60 in Dade County) per $100 or fraction thereof

— Documentary stamp tax on notes is paid on amount of debt: $.35 per $100 or fraction thereof

— Intangible tax is paid on new debt: $.002 per $1 of new debt

■ **Closing statement items**

— Total purchase price is entered as a credit to seller and a debit to buyer

— New purchase money mortgages and assumed mortgage loans are entered as a credit to buyer and a debit to seller

— New mortgages from nonseller sources and the binder deposit are entered as a credit to the buyer (no entry on seller's side)

— Unpaid property tax proration entered as a credit to buyer and debit to seller

— Use seller days to prorate items paid in arrears

— Use buyer days to prorate items paid in advance

— Expenses are debited to party paying the expense

■ IMPORTANT FORMULAS TO REMEMBER

■ **Calculate simple sale commission**

Purchase price × percent of commission = commission

Example: Purchase price is $80,000. Commission rate is 6 percent

$80,000 × .06 = $4,800 total commission due

■ **Calculate the net to the seller**

Sale price × (100% − commission rate)

Example: Sale price is $85,000 and commission rate is 8 percent

$85,000 (100% − 8%)

$85,000 × .92 = $78,200 net to seller

■ **Calculate sale price given the amount seller wants to net and the mortgage amount**

(Seller's net + mortgage amount) ÷ (100% − commission rate)

Example: The seller wants to net $100,000. There is an existing mortgage of $45,000 and the broker wants to earn 7 percent commission

($100,000 + $45,000) ÷ (100% − 7%)

$145,000 ÷ .93 = $155,913.98 (round to $155,914) sale price

■ **Calculate a graduated commission**

Sale price portion × first rate = commission due

Sale price portion × second rate = commission due

Sum the two commissions

Example: The broker agrees to 8 percent on the first $500,000 of sale price and 10 percent on the balance. The property sells for $820,000.

$500,000 × .08	= $40,000
$320,000 × .10	= $32,000
$40,000 + $32,000	= $72,000

■ **Calculate broker's share of commission**

Full commission × broker's split = commission due broker

Example: The broker agreed to pay the sales associate 55 percent of the total commission. The property sold for $200,000. Commission rate was 8 percent.

$200,000 × .08	= $16,000
100% − .55	= .45
$16,000 × .45	= $7,200 broker's split

■ **Calculate percentage of profit**

1. Calculate total cost

2. Calculate amount made on sale

3. Amount made on sale ÷ total cost = percentage of profit

Example: Investor purchased two lots for $25,000 each. He subdivided them into five lots and sold them for $12,000 each.

2 × $25,000	= $50,000 total cost
5 × $12,000 = $60,000 − $50,000	= $10,000 amount made on sale
$10,000 ÷ $50,000	= .20 or 20%

■ **Calculate percentage of profit given lot dimensions and cost per front foot**

1. The first dimension is always front feet

2. Front feet × cost per front foot = total cost

Example: Developer purchased four lots each 100' × 150' at $250 per front foot. He subdivided the lots into six lots and sold them for $25,000 each.

100' × $250 × 4 lots	= $100,000 total cost
6 × $25,000 = $150,000 – $100,000	= $50,000 amount made on sale
$50,000 ÷ $100,000	= .50 or 50%

■ Calculate a mortgage amortization

1. Principal balance × annual interest ÷ 12 = first month's interest

2. Monthly mortgage payment – 1st mo. interest = principal payment

3. Beginning loan balance – principal paid = new principal balance

Example: What is the principal balance on a $100,000 mortgage at 4 percent interest after two monthly payments of $477.40? (Note: Round to dollars and cents.)

Month 1:

$100,000 × .04 ÷ 12	= $333.33 first month's interest
$477.40 – $333.33	= $144.07 principal paid month 1
$100,000 – $144.07	= $99,855.93 new principal balance after one payment

Month 2:

$99,855.93 × .04 ÷ 12	= $332.85 second month's interest
$477.40 – $332.85	= $144.55 principal paid month 2
$99,855.93 – $144.55	= $99,711.38 principal balance after two payments

■ Calculate total interest paid on a mortgage loan over an extended period of time

1. Calculate number of payments paid to date

2. Calculate the total amount paid to date

3. Amount borrowed × percent paid off = principal paid to date

4. Total paid to date – principal repaid = total interest paid to date

Example: Monthly mortgage payments of $365.49 have been paid for ten years. The original amount borrowed was $40,000. After ten years 35 percent of the loan has been paid.

10 years × 12 payment a year	= 120 payments to date
$365.49 × 120	= $43,858.80 total paid to date
$40,000 × .35	= $14,000 principal paid to date
$43,858.80 – $14,000	= $29,858.80 interest paid to date

■ Calculate a rent proration

1. Rent is paid in *advance* (usually at the 1st of the month) therefore the unused portion of advance rent belongs to the buyer

2. Monthly rent ÷ days in month = rent per day

3.   Rent per day × days owed buyer = amount of proration (credit buyer, debit seller)

Note: Prorations are calculated using either 30 days for each month (360-day method) or using the actual number of days in each month (365-day method).

Example: The scheduled date for closing a duplex is October 12. Total rent collected on the first of the month was $875. Day of closing belongs to buyer. Use actual number of days method.

$875 ÷ 31 = $28.2258 per day (rounded to four decimal places)

$28.2258 × 20 days = $564.516 or $564.52 (rounded)

Debit seller (seller already received entire month's rent) $564.52

Credit buyer (buyer is due rent for day of closing through remainder of month) $564.52

■ Calculate a property tax proration

1.   Property taxes are paid *in arrears* (due November 30th); therefore the seller has usually not paid the property taxes at time of closing

2.   Calculate number of days the seller *owes* for the calendar year

Example: Property taxes are $1,250. Closing date is March 10. Day of closing belongs to seller. Use 365-day method.

Total days charged seller:

31 January + 28 February + 10 March = 69 days

$1,250 ÷ 365 = $3.4246575

$3.4246575 × 69 days = $236.30137 or $236.30 rounded

Debit seller (seller has not paid the property taxes) $236.30

Credit buyer (buyer will pay entire tax bill in November) $236.30

■ Calculate a mortgage interest proration on an assumed mortgage

1.   Mortgage payments are normally paid monthly

2.   Mortgage interest is usually paid *in arrears*

3.   Proration is based on monthly *interest* not monthly payment of principal and interest

4.   Calculate daily interest charge

Example: Closing day is May 8. Buyer is assuming mortgage with an outstanding balance of $93,600 at 6 percent interest. Seller paid interest on the mortgage through April 30th. Day of closing is charged to the buyer. Use 360-day method.

Seller owes interest for seven days (May 1 through midnight May 7)

$93,600 × .06   = $5,616 annual interest ÷ 360 = $15.60 daily interest

$15.60 × 7 days   = $109.20 *debit seller* (because seller has not paid May interest)

                       = $109.20 *credit buyer* (because buyer will pay entire month's interest when it becomes due on May 30th)

- ■ **Calculate documentary tax on deeds**
    1. Tax is paid on full purchase price
    2. Rate is $.70 per hundred dollar increments ($.60 in Dade County)
    3. If not an even $100 increment round *up* to next even $100 increment
    4. Typically seller pays the tax on the deed (entered as a *debit* to seller)

    Example: Sale price is $175,000.

    $175,000 ÷ $100 = 1,750 × $.70 = $1,225 doc stamps on deed

- ■ **Calculate documentary tax on notes**
    1. Tax is paid on note amount of *new* and *assumed* mortgage notes
    2. Rate is $.35 per hundred dollar increments
    3. Typically buyer pays doc stamps on notes (entered as a *debit* to buyer)

    Example: Buyer assumes the existing first mortgage of $85,530 and the seller takes back a purchase money mortgage in the amount of $15,000.

    Doc stamps on assumed mortgage:

    $85,530 ÷ $100 = 855.3 round up to 856 × $.35 = $299.60 doc stamps on assumed note

    Doc stamps on purchase money (2nd) mortgage:

    $15,000 ÷ $100 = 150 × $.35 = $52.50 doc stamps on new note

- ■ **Calculate intangible tax on new debt (note)**
    1. Taxed on new debt only
    2. Rate is 2 mills ($.002) per dollar of new debt
    3. Typically buyer pays intangible tax (entered as a *debit* to buyer)

    Example: Calculate intangible tax on purchase money mortgage of $15,000

    $15,000 × $.002 = $30 intangible tax

Note to Readers

For a more complete description of math as it specifically applies to real estate, see the author's *Real Estate Math: What You Need to Know*, Sixth Edition, Dearborn™ Real Estate Education. This self-study book covers the basics of math and provides practice opportunities in all areas. Step-by-step solutions to the math problems are included in *Real Estate Math: What You Need to Know*.

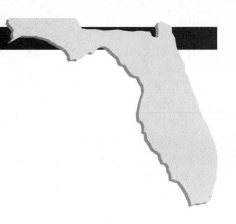

Florida Real Estate License Law Chapters

■ LICENSE LAW AND QUALIFICATIONS FOR LICENSURE (CHAPTER 2) FLORIDA REAL ESTATE BROKER'S GUIDE (CHAPTER 1)

1. An individual does not intend to engage in real estate activity. However, he does plan to be an officer of a real estate brokerage corporation. Which status best describes this situation?
   A. Active sales associate license
   B. Active broker license
   C. Registered with the FREC
   D. Inactive sales associate license

2. An individual who has fulfilled all of the academic and experience requirements for real estate brokers but who operates as a sales associate in the employ of a supervising broker is classified as an
   A. active sales associate.
   B. active broker.
   C. inactive broker.
   D. active broker associate.

3. When purchasing a commercial property from a seller without the services of a real estate professional, a buyer would be well advised to carefully verify information conveyed regarding the property. This is sometimes referred to as
   A. constructive notice.
   B. eminent domain.
   C. caveat emptor.
   D. lis pendens.

4. A nonresident wishing to become a Florida real estate licensee must, among other requirements, complete a notarized irrevocable consent to service. This means that the applicant agrees to
   A. consent, once licensed, to having all documents notarized that become part of future real estate transactions in which he or she is involved.
   B. permit legal action to be initiated against the licensee in Florida.
   C. become a Florida resident within the initial license period.
   D. accept permanent revocation of his or her license should any violation of the real estate license law be upheld.

5. A broker changed his legal residency from Panama City, Florida, to Gulfport, Mississippi. Within how many days must the licensee comply with all nonresident requirements?
   A. 10
   B. 30
   C. 60
   D. 90

6. Which activity is NOT one of the real estate services?
   A. Mortgaging real property
   B. Advertising real property
   C. Renting real property
   D. Auctioning real property

7. Which statement is FALSE regarding mutual recognition agreements?
   A. The agreements are intended to recognize the education and experience that real estate licensees have acquired in other states or nations.
   B. Mutual recognition applicants are required to take an examination on Florida real estate laws.
   C. Mutual recognition applicants may be Florida residents or nonresidents.
   D. Mutual agreements allow Florida real estate licensees to have an equal opportunity for licensure in jurisdictions with which agreements are concluded.

8. Sales associate Joshua sells real estate on the weekend for Weekend Getaways Realty. He also works as a sales associate for Real Estate Inc. Which statement applies to this situation?
   A. As long as the broker for Weekend Getaways is also an owner-developer, this is an acceptable arrangement.
   B. Joshua is in violation of Chapter 475, F.S.
   C. Joshua must register both employers with the Commission.
   D. This is legal, provided Joshua is issued a multiple license.

9. Which of the criteria listed below is NOT required to hold a Florida real estate license?
   A. U.S. citizenship
   B. 18 years of age or older
   C. High school diploma or GED
   D. Be honest and of good character

10. Mr. Plenty owned two farms, a home, and two restaurants when he died intestate. The court appointed Mr. Goss to dispose of any portions of Mr. Plenty's estate that might be subject to estate taxes and debts of the deceased. Mr. Goss
    A. must have the clerk of the circuit court auction any property sold.
    B. must register with the DRE if he expects to be paid for his work.
    C. may advertise, negotiate, and sell the property and be compensated for his work without registering with the DRE.
    D. must dispose of all real property through an active real estate broker.

11. Richard is on the board of directors of Able Realty. He is also the owner and broker of Richard Realty. Which statement is true?
    A. Richard is in violation of Chapter 475, F.S.
    B. Richard must request a multiple license.
    C. Richard may serve in a nonbrokerage capacity for Able Realty and be the active broker for Richard Realty.
    D. Both B and C apply.

12. A license applicant has completed the 63-hour sales associate pre license course. Within what period of time after being issued a course completion slip for the pre license course must the applicant pass the state license exam?
    A. Indefinitely
    B. Two years
    C. One year
    D. Six months

13. What type of evidence unless refuted by evidence to the contrary will prove a case?
    A. Prima facie
    B. Notarized
    C. Case law
    D. Enforceable

◼ LICENSE LAW AND ADMINISTRATION (CHAPTER 3)

14. Florida Statutes prohibit members from serving on the Commission for more than
    A. one two-year term.
    B. one four-year term.
    C. two consecutive four-year terms.
    D. three consecutive two-year terms.

15. The Commission's authority to promulgate administrative rules is part of its
    A. judicial powers.
    B. executive powers.
    C. quasi-judicial powers.
    D. quasi-legislative powers.

16. The Florida Real Estate Commission is obligated to notify which agency when it takes disciplinary action against any licensees of that agency?
    A. Division of Time Share
    B. Department of Business and Professional Regulation
    C. Division of Florida Land Sales, Condominiums and Mobile Homes
    D. Division of Professions

17. The Commission is obligated to report any criminal violation of Chapter 475, F.S., when knowledgeable of such violations, to the
    A. state's attorney having jurisdiction.
    B. secretary of the DBPR.
    C. local police.
    D. Division of Professions.

18. The Commission is NOT empowered to impose which disciplinary action against a licensee?
    A. Suspend a license
    B. Revoke a license
    C. Impose an administrative fine
    D. Sentence a licensee to six months' imprisonment

19. The licensee status that results when a license is not renewed at the end of the license period is referred to as
    A. canceled.
    B. delinquent.
    C. involuntary inactive.
    D. voluntary inactive.

20. Mrs. Imma Winner, an active broker, accompanies her husband when he goes on active military duty in Ohio for five years. Mrs. Winner is not active in real estate in Ohio. To obtain a current Florida broker's license within six months of Lt. Winner's discharge, Mrs. Winner
    A. must first complete seven hours of continuing education for each inactive year.
    B. must first complete 14 hours of continuing education.
    C. must first complete 35 hours of activation education.
    D. need not complete any continuing education or activation education for those five years.

21. An active sales associate became involved in a second job to the extent that he allowed his license to expire. What must this sales associate do to obtain another active license after five years have lapsed?
    A. Complete 35 hours of continuing education
    B. Complete FREC Course I and pass the license exam
    C. Complete 35 hours of activation education
    D. Complete the post-licensing and continuing education requirements

22. Al Amnesia, the only active general partner in a real estate partnership, did not account properly for his escrowed funds. His license was suspended. All of Al's sales associates' licenses are
    A. suspended.
    B. canceled.
    C. placed in involuntary inactive status.
    D. not affected.

23. Broker Tom wishes to be issued several broker licenses for business reasons. Tom may
    A. only be issued one broker license.
    B. be issued one broker license only, but have several broker associate licenses.
    C. be issued a group license.
    D. hold multiple licenses.

24. Broker Tom changes his business address and notifies the Commission. The licenses of Tom's sales associates
    A. are canceled.
    B. remain effective and in force.
    C. are null and void.
    D. are ineffective.

25. John decides to relocate his real estate brokerage office. John notifies the Commission of the change in business address. He also informs the Commission of the names of three sales associates who are no longer associated with his brokerage. The sales associates' licenses will be
    A. suspended until they find new employment.
    B. placed in involuntary inactive status.
    C. null and void.
    D. canceled.

■ BROKERAGE RELATIONSHIPS AND ETHICS (CHAPTER 4) FLORIDA REAL ESTATE BROKER'S GUIDE (CHAPTER 10)

26. A contract for sale and purchase is executed and the sales associate prepares the property file for the office. In the file she places a copy of the sale contract, the transaction broker notice, a photocopy of the earnest money deposit, and other miscellaneous information associated with the transaction. Prior to closing the deal falls through because the buyer was unable to secure financing according to the terms of the contract. How long must the real estate firm retain the property file and its contents?
    A. It may be destroyed.
    B. It must be retained for five years.
    C. It must be retained for two years.
    D. It must be retained for one year.

27. A real estate broker is typically authorized by a principal to act as a
    A. universal agent.
    B. special agent.
    C. general agent.
    D. nonagent.

28. Which transaction is exempt from the requirements concerning brokerage relationship disclosures?
    A. A contract to purchase ten acres of agricultural land
    B. A contract to purchase a duplex
    C. A contract to purchase a new condominium from the builder
    D. A contract to purchase an undeveloped site zoned residential

29. The property owner of a listed property has instructed the broker not to show the property when the owner is out of town. A potential buyer asks the sales associate to show the listed property, however, the owner is out of town. How should the sales associate handle the situation?
    A. Show the buyer the property because the owner will not find out.
    B. Explain to the buyer that the sales associate cannot show the property until the owner returns.
    C. The sales associate can show the property anytime unless the owner put his instructions in writing.
    D. Show the buyer the property provided the buyer has been prequalified and is a serious buyer.

30. A sales associate has been told by her real estate broker to commit an unlawful act. The sales associate should
    A. indicate her concern but comply with her employing broker.
    B. notify the FREC.
    C. refuse and withdraw from the relationship.
    D. comply because of the fiduciary obligation involved.

31. The seller informs the broker that he wants single agency representation. The broker must
    A. give the seller the no brokerage relationship notice.
    B. have the seller sign that he or she was informed of all the agency relationship options.
    C. have the seller sign the transition to single agent notice.
    D. give the seller the single agent notice.

32. A sales associate or broker associate owes fiduciary duties
    A. only to his or her broker if working as an employer of the broker.
    B. to the principal as does his or her broker, including those situations where the sales associate, for tax purposes, is an independent contractor.
    C. to the buyer when working for a transaction broker.
    D. to all of the above.

33. The buyer's or seller's signature is required on which brokerage relationship disclosure before the licensee may continue?
    A. No brokerage relationship notice
    B. Single agent notice
    C. Consent to transition to transaction broker notice
    D. Transaction broker notice

34. The brokerage relationship disclosure requirements in Section 475.278, F.S., do NOT apply to
    A. agricultural property of ten acres or less.
    B. an agreement to lease a residential condominium.
    C. improved residential property of no more than four units.
    D. an unimproved site intended for development as a residential duplex.

35. In Florida which brokerage relationship is NOT legal?
    A. Nonrepresentation—facilitator
    B. Single agent
    C. Transaction broker
    D. Dual agent in a residential transaction

36. A transaction broker may disclose, without exception
    A. to the buyer, that the seller will accept a price less than the listed price.
    B. the motivation of the other party for buying or selling the property.
    C. to the buyer, the listed price and physical characteristics of the home.
    D. all of the above information.

37. A transaction broker of residential property has which duty(ies) and responsibility(ies)?
    A. Undivided loyalty to both the buyer and seller
    B. Full disclosure between buyer and seller
    C. To disclose any latent defects to the buyer
    D. A transaction broker has all of the above duties.

38. Which statement applies to designated sales associates?
    A. Designated sales associates have the duties of a single agent.
    B. Designated sales associates work as nonrepresentatives in transactions involving commercial property.
    C. Designated sales associates are sales associates working under a broker who has been issued multiple licenses.
    D. Designated sales associates have earned a designation awarded by a professional organization.

39. Duties owed by a transaction broker include
    A. loyalty.
    B. accounting for all funds.
    C. confidentiality.
    D. fiduciary.

■ REAL ESTATE BROKERAGE OPERATIONS (CHAPTER 5) FLORIDA REAL ESTATE BROKER'S GUIDE (CHAPTERS 2 AND 4)

40. Real property ads and yard signs of a licensed broker must include the name of the
    A. broker associate who obtained the listing.
    B. broker only.
    C. seller or broker's principal.
    D. brokerage firm.

41. Any broker who places money or other valuables in an escrow account must
    A. be a signatory on any such account.
    B. file with the FREC the name of persons authorized to sign checks on the account.
    C. file a signature card with the DRE for each person authorized to sign checks on the account.
    D. appoint one officer, or representative, of the bank, trust company, or SA as custodian of the account during the broker's absence.

42. A broker associate is ordering business cards. May she put "broker" on the card instead of "broker associate"?
    A. Yes, because she is broker-qualified.
    B. Yes, with the consent of her broker.
    C. No, she must use the title, "broker associate."
    D. This is a matter of personal taste.

43. A sales associate is selling her own property "by owner." Which statement is TRUE regarding advertising the property for sale?
    A. The licensee must disclose in the ad that she is a real estate licensee.
    B. The licensee must include the name of her broker in the ad.
    C. The property must be listed with the sale associate's broker.
    D. The licensee should disclose to a buyer prospect the fact that she holds a real estate license at the first point of meaningful negotiation.

44. Commingling occurs when a broker
    A. deposits earnest money in a personal account.
    B. employs unlicensed persons to obtain listings and sales.
    C. attempts to channel persons of a particular race to a certain neighborhood.
    D. deposits up to $1,000 of his or her own personal funds in a sales escrow account.

45. Rebecca K. Sammis, broker of Executive Homes Inc., is ordering the sign for her new office. She is NOT required to have what information on her sign?
    A. Licensed Real Estate Broker
    B. Executive Homes Inc.
    C. 1000 N. Gulf to Bay Blvd.
    D. Rebecca K. Sammis

46. The term *immediately* as it applies to brokers and the deposit of escrow funds is defined to mean
    A. not later than the end of the next business day.
    B. not later than the end of the third business day.
    C. not later than the end of the third calendar day.
    D. within 24 hours.

47. If both buyer and seller claim the earnest money deposit in a broker's escrow account, how much time after the last claim received does the broker have to notify the FREC in writing?
    A. 5 calendar days
    B. 15 business days
    C. 7 calendar days
    D. 30 business days

48. An escrow account may NOT be in a(n)
    A. Florida-based title company having trust powers.
    B. credit union located in Florida.
    C. qualified Florida attorney's trust account if designated in the contract.
    D. insurance company located in Florida.

49. Which statement is FALSE regarding unearned fees?
    A. Payment of an unearned fee is also called a kickback.
    B. Real estate licensees are prohibited from sharing part of their commission with the buyer or seller in a real estate contract unless the buyer or seller is a real estate licensee.
    C. Payment of an unearned fee must not violate RESPA.
    D. An owner of an apartment complex may pay a finder's fee of up to $50 to an unlicensed person who is tenant of the apartment complex for the referral of a prospect who decides to rent an apartment in the complex.

50. The Federal telemarketing law restricts telephone solicitation calls to what hours?
    A. 8:00 AM to 5:00 PM
    B. 8:00 AM to 6:00 PM
    C. 8:00 AM to 9:00 PM
    D. 9:00 AM to 8:00 PM

51. A dispute over escrowed funds arises between the buyer and seller. The broker notifies the FREC of the conflicting demands and requests that the Commission issue an escrow disbursement order; however, the FREC declines. The following alternative methods can resolve the matter EXCEPT
    A. petition for review or appeal.
    B. mediation.
    C. arbitration.
    D. litigation.

52. A broker of a large office hired a certified public account (CPA) and a full-time bookkeeper to manage the escrow account. Which statement is TRUE regarding this situation?
    A. The broker is relieved of liability in the event there is an escrow violation because a certified CPA has been hired to manage the escrow account.
    B. Both the CPA and the bookkeeper must also hold a real estate license if they are going to write checks on the escrow account.
    C. The broker is required to personally prepare the monthly escrow account reconciliation statement.
    D. The broker must be a signatory on the escrow account.

53. Broker Dan has an agreement with a local rental car agency. The agreement stipulates that Dan will pay a $25 referral fee to the rental car agency for each prospective buyer referred to Dan. Which applies?
    A. This is a legal kickback or rebate.
    B. This is legal, provided Broker Dan informs each prospect of the agreement.
    C. Florida Real Estate Law prohibits all kickbacks and rebates.
    D. Broker Dan is in violation of Chapter 475, F.S., because he has promised to compensate an unlicensed person for the referral of real estate business.

54. In which situation is the broker NOT exempt from the notice requirements regarding conflicting demands?
    A. A sale of HUD-owned property that utilizes a HUD sale contract
    B. A dispute over escrow funds related to a property inspection
    C. A buyer's cancellation of a residential condominium purchase agreement within the allowable time period for review
    D. A buyer's inability to secure financing for the purchase according to the terms of the contract

55. Kathy was recently transferred to Jacksonville. She was not familiar with the city so she purchased a rental list for $100 from a local real estate company. Kathy referred to the list while looking for an apartment but was unable to locate a suitable unit. Kathy has requested a refund of her $100. Which applies?
    A. Kathy is entitled to a refund of her $100 if requested in writing within 30 days.
    B. Kathy is entitled to a refund of $75 if requested either verbally or in writing within 30 days.
    C. Kathy is not entitled to a refund because there was nothing wrong with the list.
    D. The broker is guilty of a first degree misdemeanor.

56. If an owner-principal of residential property refuses to pay a sale commission after a listing broker has fully performed his or her contractual obligations, the broker may
    A. file a suit against the owner.
    B. record a complaint with the Commission.
    C. record a lien against the property.
    D. file a notice of encumbrance against the property.

57. Which statement is true regarding kickbacks?
    A. Kickbacks are illegal without exception.
    B. They are legal, provided the amount of the kickback does not exceed $200.
    C. They are legal, unless specifically prohibited by law, provided the broker, prior to payment and receipt of the kickback, fully advises the principal and all affected parties in the transaction of the arrangement.
    D. Anyone who accepts a kickback is guilty of a misdemeanor of the first degree.

58. May escrow funds be moved from a noninterest bearing account to an interest bearing account?
    A. No, to do so would be a violation of Chapter 475, F.S.
    B. No, funds may not be removed from the noninterest bearing account until title closing.
    C. Yes, the broker is free to move the funds from one escrow account to another escrow account.
    D. Yes, provided the broker secures the written permission of all interested parties to the contract before moving the funds.

59. A real estate sales associate might lawfully accept an extra commission for a difficult sale from
    A. an appreciative seller.
    B. a thankful buyer.
    C. the broker-employer.
    D. the mortgage lender.

60. If a licensee accepts a postdated check as down payment on real property, which applies?
    A. The FREC must be notified within 24 hours.
    B. The seller's approval must first be obtained.
    C. The sales associate must get approval from his or her employing broker.
    D. The postdated check may not be drawn on an out-of-state bank account.

61. Before leaving the employ of Broker Bernhardt for whom she has worked for three years, Sales Associate Sarah takes the original records of all her own listings. Sarah can be charged with
    A. larceny.
    B. fraud.
    C. concealment.
    D. misrepresentation.

62. In Florida, if a real estate broker registers as a foreign corporation, it means the business entity is chartered
    A. outside the State of Florida.
    B. outside the continental United States only.
    C. outside the 50 states.
    D. in a foreign country.

63. A real estate broker maintains an escrow account for sales transactions and a separate property management escrow account. The broker is allowed to deposit his own funds in the two accounts up to a maximum of
    A. $6,000.
    B. $5,000.
    C. $2,000.
    D. $1,000.

64. Which business entity would obligate all principals as personally liable for organization-incurred debts?
    A. General partnerships
    B. Limited partnerships
    C. Limited liability companies
    D. Corporations for profit

65. The legal term that applies when two real estate brokers share office space in such a manner that the public is deceived into believing that a partnership exists is referred to as a
    A. quasi-partnership.
    B. limited partnership.
    C. quasi-corporation.
    D. quasi-joint venture.

66. A licensed real estate sales associate and broker desire to open a new real estate brokerage firm as general partners. They may
    A. be registered as a joint venture.
    B. register the partnership with the broker as the required active broker partner and the sales associate as a junior partner.
    C. not register as a partnership; however, they can incorporate and register as a corporation with the sales associate as vice president and the broker as president.
    D. not do so.

67. Which entity is exempt from registering the trade name (if one is used) with the Florida Department of State?
    A. Brokerage corporation
    B. Brokerage partnership
    C. Real estate broker
    D. Limited liability brokerage corporation

68. A joint venture usually is created to
    A. simplify appraisals.
    B. carry out a single project.
    C. quiet title.
    D. take advantage of business opportunities.

69. On July 1 a broker received conflicting demands from a buyer and seller regarding a good faith deposit. Twelve business days later the broker is unable to resolve the conflict between the parties and notifies the FREC. Within how many days does this broker have to implement a settlement procedure?
    A. 10 business days
    B. 15 business days
    C. 18 business days
    D. 30 business days

■ COMPLAINTS, VIOLATIONS, AND PENALTIES (CHAPTER 6) FLORIDA REAL ESTATE BROKER'S GUIDE (CHAPTER 5)

70. Mary was issued a sales associate's license by mistake. She has been informed that the license has been revoked. Which applies?
    A. This action is referred to as "revocation without prejudice."
    B. Mary is not allowed to reapply for a sales associate's license for one year.
    C. Mary has been disciplined for a violation of Chapter 475, F.S.
    D. Revocation means that Mary may not be licensed in Florida for five years.

71. The DBPR is empowered to demand information from and issue subpoenas to
    A. real estate licensees only.
    B. DBPR licensees only.
    C. anyone, provided the information relates to a case already before the FREC.
    D. anyone thought to possess information relevant to the case at hand.

72. If a legally sufficient complaint has been filed, investigated, and found valid, the next step in the complaint process is
    A. an informal proceeding.
    B. a formal hearing.
    C. probable cause determination.
    D. final order issuance.

73. False advertising concerning real estate information incurs what type of penalty?
    A. Administrative penalty
    B. Third-degree felony
    C. First-degree misdemeanor
    D. Second degree misdemeanor

74. During its regular monthly meeting, the Commission modified several license fees and broker advertising requirements. These actions will be reflected formally in changes to
    A. F.S. 455.
    B. F.S. 475.
    C. Rule 61J2.
    D. Rule 22I.

75. A sales associate was issued a citation for failing to timely notify the Commission of her change of address. How many days does the licensee have to either pay the citation or file an objection to the alleged violation?
    A. 30
    B. 45
    C. 60
    D. 90

76. As a result of the step-by-step complaint process, an administrative law judge discovered evidence that the current practices of a large property management brokerage firm were an immediate danger to the public welfare and to the economic welfare of its principals. The FREC chairperson convened a special session to conduct a hearing prior to a summary suspension being issued. Upon conclusion of the hearing, the FREC issued a final order for summary suspension of the

brokerage firm's license. Why will this suspension be illegal and invalid?
A. The summary suspension final order was not accompanied by a formal suspension order.
B. Only the DBPR Secretary or a legally appointed representative may issue a final order of summary suspension.
C. A summary suspension order may not be issued until three days after a respondent has been notified of the pending action.
D. A review of the summary suspension final order must be conducted by the DBPR before it can be valid and effective.

77. Upon completion of the entire complaint process, Broker Badder was convicted of three violations of Chapter 475, F.S. The FREC does NOT have the power and authority to
A. revoke or suspend Badder's license.
B. reprimand Broker Badder.
C. fine Badder $15,000.
D. sentence Badder to 60 days in jail.

78. A DBPR investigator is authorized, in cases that involve a first-time offense of a minor violation, to issue a(n)
A. cease and desist order.
B. notice of noncompliance.
C. letter of guidance.
D. administrative fine.

79. The FREC is empowered to revoke the license of any licensee found guilty of
A. violation of the motor vehicle laws.
B. drunkenness in a public place.
C. representation of facts.
D. conversion of escrowed funds.

80. A broker followed the instructions in an escrow disbursement order, but he was the victim of a civil court judgment that resulted in a payment of $10,000 from the Recovery Fund due to his actions. As a consequence, the FREC
A. will take no action against the broker.
B. will probably suspend the broker's license.
C. will probably revoke the broker's license.
D. is required to suspend the broker's license.

81. A real estate broker has an inactive license. May the broker sue a customer for a commission?
A. Yes, but the broker will have to reactivate his license first.
B. No, any agreement between the broker and the customer is invalid.
C. The broker may sue the customer for consulting services but not call them real estate services.
D. Yes, provided the broker performed according to the terms of a listing or buyer brokerage agreement.

82. Does a licensee who is convicted of a misdemeanor offense have a duty to report the conviction to the FREC?
A. A licensee is required to disclose misdemeanor convictions within 30 days.
B. Licensees must disclose all convictions to the FREC.
C. Licensees are required to disclose felony convictions but not misdemeanor convictions.
D. The licensee is required to disclose the misdemeanor conviction unless the licensee pleads nolo contendere.

83. Which statement is FALSE regarding the probable-cause panel?
    A. At least one member must be a professional member.
    B. A former Commissioner with an inactive real estate license may serve on the panel.
    C. A consumer member may serve on probable-cause.
    D. The FREC chairperson appoints the probable-cause panel.

84. A licensee has been issued an administrative complaint. The licensee has signed the election of rights indicating that he does not dispute the allegations of fact and he requests an informal hearing. How much prior notice of a hearing must be given to the licensee-respondent?
    A. 14 days
    B. 15 days
    C. 30 days
    D. 45 days

General Real Estate Law Chapters

■ **FEDERAL AND STATE HOUSING LAWS (CHAPTER 7) FLORIDA REAL ESTATE BROKER'S GUIDE (CHAPTERS 2, 12, AND 18)**

85. The United States Supreme Court ruling in *Jones v. Mayer,* as it pertains to real property, focuses on
    A. discrimination.
    B. truth-in-lending.
    C. informing buyers of latent defects.
    D. misrepresentation by land developers.

86. The Civil Rights Act of 1968 made discrimination illegal if based on any of these criteria EXCEPT
    A. age.
    B. race.
    C. sex.
    D. religion.

87. The Fair Housing Act of 1968 was part of the
    A. National Housing Act.
    B. Interstate Land Sales Full Disclosure Act.
    C. Truth-in-Lending Act.
    D. Civil Rights Act.

88. The act of inducing homeowners to sell by stating that minority persons might move into a neighborhood is called
    A. blockbusting.
    B. redlining.
    C. steering.
    D. ethnic zoning.

89. The act of refusing to make mortgage loans or stating different mortgage terms or conditions based on racial groups is called
    A. blockbusting.
    B. redlining.
    C. steering.
    D. overwriting.

90. The act of channeling buyers to a particular area either to maintain or to change the character of a neighborhood is called
    A. blockbusting.
    B. redlining.
    C. steering.
    D. riparian right.

91. The law that makes it illegal to deny credit on the basis of age is the
    A. Equal Credit Opportunity Act.
    B. Consumer Credit Protection Act.
    C. Fair Housing Act.
    D. Civil Rights Act of 1968.

92. A developer selling lots in a 100-lot subdivision that is nationally promoted through advertising must provide potential buyers, prior to their signing a purchase contract, with a
    A. Statement of Record.
    B. Uniform Settlement Statement.
    C. copy of Regulation Z.
    D. Property Report.

93. The Truth-in-Lending Act of 1969, enacted to protect the consumer, is implemented by
    A. Regulation Z.
    B. RESPA.
    C. Regulation D.
    D. a Property Report.

94. The most important objectives of the federal Truth-in-Lending Act are to ensure disclosure of finance charges and
    A. to inform buyers of probable closing expenses where known.
    B. the use of a uniform settlement statement by closing agents.
    C. the annual percentage rate.
    D. to provide borrowers with a copy of HUD's special information booklet.

95. The Real Estate Settlement Procedures Act does NOT require that
    A. buyers be informed of all known closing costs prior to the closing.
    B. a uniform settlement statement be used for closing a construction loan unless intended for conversion to a permanent loan.
    C. lenders provide prospective borrowers with a HUD special information booklet.
    D. lenders give borrowers, who are to pay closing costs, an estimate of the lender's closing agent's charges.

96. Under which circumstance may a real estate licensee lawfully refuse to show a listed property to a member of a protected class who has specifically requested to see the property?
    A. Never
    B. When the owner is out-of-town and has instructed the broker not to show the listed property when the owner is away on business
    C. When the owner has expressed his intent in writing to exercise his exemption under the Fair Housing Act
    D. When the licensee believes that showing the property to the prospective buyer will be considered steering

97. Which real estate loan transaction is exempt from the provisions of RESPA?
    A. Purchase of a home for personal use with FHA financing
    B. Purchase of a 120-acre farm
    C. Purchase of a four-unit apartment building
    D. Purchase of a condominium with VA financing

98. When a security deposit or advance rent is required by a landlord, the landlord may
    A. commingle such funds with his or her own funds.
    B. post a surety bond in the total amount of security deposits/advance rents or $50,000, whichever is less, and pay the tenant 5 percent per year simple interest.
    C. deposit such funds in a separate interest-bearing account, and pay the tenant at least 50 percent of the annualized average interest.
    D. do either A or C.

99. Stu Student was required to pay $1,200 as advance rent and security deposit in order to move into his new apartment. He received a form receipt for the $1,200. Three weeks later, the landlord passed along to Stu by phone the mandatory information concerning his deposit of the funds. During the next 13 months, Stu had no contact with the landlord—he paid his monthly rent on time by mail. Why has the landlord violated F.S. 83?
    A. The landlord failed to notify Stu in writing of the bank name, address, and other information concerning the $1,200 deposited.
    B. The landlord collected advance rent and/or a security deposit exceeding legal limits.
    C. The landlord failed to notify Stu within 15 days of the manner in which his funds were held.
    D. Advance rent and security deposit of $1,200 is an "unconscionable agreement or provision."

100. If a tenant vacates rented premises at the end of a lease, how many days does the landlord have by law to notify the tenant if the landlord intends to claim a part of the tenant's security deposit?
    A. 3
    B. 7
    C. 15
    D. 30

101. Authority to physically evict a delinquent tenant from rented property is vested in
    A. the Commission.
    B. the landlord.
    C. a court of law.
    D. the sheriff.

102. Any legal remedy sought by a tenant or a landlord under the Florida Residential Landlord and Tenant Act must be through the
    A. civil courts.
    B. criminal courts.
    C. Division of Florida Land Sales, Condominiums and Mobile Homes.
    D. Division of Real Estate.

103. On June 20, after several weeks of litigation, a landlord obtained a final judgment to evict a tenant. At 9:00 AM on June 21, a writ of possession was delivered to the sheriff requesting immediate service of the writ. At 2:00 PM that same day, the sheriff was stopped from evicting the tenant by the tenant's attorney. What grounds did the tenant's attorney have for stopping the eviction?
    A. The tenant had not been served the writ of possession.
    B. The tenant must be given copies of the final judgment and writ of possession prior to eviction.
    C. The landlord had not given the tenant three days' notice that there was to be a physical eviction.
    D. The sheriff must give the tenant 24 hours' notice to surrender the premises before physical eviction can begin.

PROPERTY RIGHTS: ESTATES, TENANCIES, AND MULTIPLE OWNERSHIP INTERESTS (CHAPTER 8)

104. Real property includes any interest or estate in
    A. business opportunities.
    B. mineral rights.
    C. land and improvements.
    D. all of the interests listed above.

105. The rights of an owner of land that abuts water are referred to as
    A. subsurface rights.
    B. navigational rights.
    C. riparian rights.
    D. reliction rights.

106. A tree growing near the corner of a lot is ordinarily considered to be
    A. real property.
    B. personal property.
    C. a fixture.
    D. chattel.

107. Real property can be converted into personal property by
    A. severance.
    B. substitution.
    C. accretion.
    D. attachment.

108. Chuck owns an automobile parts business. He rents space in a commercial shopping center. Chuck has installed shelving and display racks for his inventory. The shelving is bolted to the floors and the racks are attached to the walls. The racks and shelving are considered to be
    A. real property.
    B. trade fixtures.
    C. property of the landlord.
    D. accretion.

109. How many days' notice is required to terminate a month-to-month tenancy at will?
    A. 3
    B. 7
    C. 15
    D. 30

110. Any estate or interest in real property that can be measured by the lifetime of an individual is a(n)
    A. fee simple estate.
    B. estate by the entireties.
    C. freehold estate.
    D. estate for years.

111. David Dunn and his daughter Denise bought a commercially zoned tract for cash. The property was deeded to them "with full and legal rights of survivorship." David and Denise are
    A. tenants by the entireties.
    B. tenants in common.
    C. joint tenants.
    D. tenants in severalty.

112. A widow who owns a condominium unit holds a
    A. proprietary lease.
    B. proprietary estate.
    C. freehold estate.
    D. tenancy by the entireties.

113. If two or more persons have an undivided interest in real property, which estate MAY NOT be created unless specific wording in the deed provides for the right of survivorship?
    A. Joint tenancy
    B. Tenancy in common
    C. Tenancy by the entireties
    D. Tenancy at will

114. Columbia, Bradford, and Union were co-owners of a parcel of real property. Bradford died, and his ownership passed, according to his will, to become part of his estate. Bradford was a
    A. tenant by the entirety.
    B. joint tenant.
    C. tenant in common.
    D. tenant at will.

115. Rebecca and Joshua are brother and sister. They both are married. Brother and sister want to go into business together and are purchasing a parcel on which to build a restaurant. To protect each of their families, how should they take title?
    A. Joint tenancy
    B. Tenancy in common
    C. Estate for years
    D. Life estate

116. The ownership right that permits an owner of real property to sell, mortgage, dedicate, or otherwise dispose of all or any portion of the property is referred to as the right of
    A. use and control.
    B. disposition.
    C. exclusion.
    D. possession.

117. EXCEPT for husband-and-wife ownership, the most frequently used form of co-ownership of property is
    A. tenancy by the entirety.
    B. tenancy in common.
    C. joint tenancy.
    D. tenancy at will.

118. Two single persons are joint tenants. This tenancy would become a tenancy in common if one of them
    A. married.
    B. died.
    C. sold the interest to the other.
    D. sold the interest to a third party.

119. A man and a woman each own real property in their own names. The couple gets married. After the wedding it is which type of property?
    A. Community
    B. Marital
    C. Separate
    D. Estate by entireties

120. Kim and Kelly bought a three-story building and took title as legal joint tenants. Kelly died testate. Kim now owns the building
    A. as a tenant by the entirety.
    B. in severalty.
    C. in absolute ownership under the law of descent.
    D. subject to the terms of Kelly's will.

121. Lee bought half-interest in an office building on Monday. Polk purchased the other half-interest of the same property the following Saturday. Lee and Polk own the building as
    A. tenants in common.
    B. joint tenants.
    C. tenants in severalty.
    D. tenants in equity.

122. An interest in real property that exists for a designated period, created by a properly executed lease agreement, is a(n)
    A. freehold estate.
    B. estate for years.
    C. tenancy at will.
    D. fee simple estate.

123. By definition, an estate for years
    A. must last for one or more years.
    B. must be for at least two years.
    C. is for a fixed term, whether for a week, a month, a year, or longer.
    D. requires a written document.

124. A father deeded a beachfront villa to his daughter who suffered from a terminal illness. The deed specified that the property was to return to the father or his heirs when the daughter died. The estate owned by the father, or his heirs, is a(n)
    A. life estate.
    B. fee simple estate.
    C. estate for years.
    D. estate in reversion.

125. Jenny sells time-share units for a large owner-developer in Ft. Myers, Florida. Jenny is a salaried employee. Each Christmas Jenny receives a year-end bonus based on her sales production for the year. Must Jenny be licensed as a real estate sales associate?
    A. No, Jenny is exempt from a real estate license because she works for an owner-developer.
    B. Yes, Jenny must be licensed as a real estate sales associate because part of her compensation is based on real estate sales production.
    C. No, Jenny is exempt from a real estate license because she must hold a time-share license.
    D. Yes, Jenny must be licensed as a real estate sales associate because she sells real estate for an owner-developer.

126. In which document will a condominium owner find the rules and regulations?
    A. Bylaws
    B. Declaration
    C. Frequently Asked Questions and Answers sheet
    D. Master deed

127. A tenant rents a condominium at the beach from July 1 to August 31. This is known as a tenancy
    A. for years.
    B. in common.
    C. at will.
    D. at sufferance.

128. The estate in real property with the least bundle of rights is the
    A. tenancy at will.
    B. tenancy at sufferance.
    C. fee simple estate.
    D. estate for years.

129. The Florida Constitution allows a base tax exemption from assessed property value in the amount of
    A. $10,000.
    B. $20,000.
    C. $25,000.
    D. $26,500.

130. Which right is NOT included in the bundle of rights under the allodial system?
    A. Possession
    B. Control
    C. Inheritance
    D. Enjoyment

131. Lucy lives in Tall Towers Condominiums. She enjoys swimming in the condominium's pool each morning before going to work. The pool is referred to as
    A. chattel.
    B. proprietary rights.
    C. common elements.
    D. community property.

132. If I lease my lake front property to you for an indefinite period of time, your interest in real property would be a(n)
    A. estate for years.
    B. tenancy by the entireties.
    C. tenancy at will.
    D. tenancy at sufferance.

133. A condominium is created by
    A. recording a declaration in the public records.
    B. forming a corporation and filing the articles of incorporation with the Florida Department of State.
    C. filing a copy of the bylaws with the county property assessor's office.
    D. filing the building plans with the county.

134. The legal document that allows a purchaser of a cooperative to occupy a particular unit is referred to as a(n)
    A. estate for years.
    B. proprietary lease.
    C. declaration of intent to occupy.
    D. declaration of possession.

135. The statutory creation of a condominium building requires certain basic items of legal documentation, one of which is NOT the
    A. declaration.
    B. articles of incorporation.
    C. common elements agreement.
    D. bylaws.

136. The process of land buildup from water-borne rock, sand, and soil is
    A. accretion.
    B. alluvion.
    C. erosion.
    D. reliction.

137. Which condominium document is required to be given to prospective buyers ONLY for new residential construction of 20 or more units?
    A. Frequently Asked Questions and Answers
    B. Bylaws
    C. Articles of Incorporation
    D. Prospectus

■ TITLES, DEEDS, AND OWNERSHIP RESTRICTIONS (CHAPTER 9)

138. A legal instrument that is used to give constructive notice of pending legal action is referred to as
    A. estoppel.
    B. novation.
    C. lis pendens.
    D. escheat.

139. All of the following represent a transfer of real property that takes place on the death of the owner EXCEPT
   A. transfer by devise.
   B. transfer by domain.
   C. transfer by descent.
   D. escheat to the state.

140. Abbott owns a parcel of property. Costello takes possession of the land after obtaining Abbott's permission. Costello's possession continues for 15 years. Thereafter, Costello brings suit to obtain title to the property. Costello will be
   A. successful because he possessed the property for 15 continuous years.
   B. successful because he satisfied all of the requirements of eminent domain.
   C. unsuccessful because he may not obtain title through possession for only 15 years.
   D. unsuccessful because not all of the requirements for adverse possession have been satisfied.

141. Lenny Luckman inherits his uncle's 1,150-acre cattle ranch. The legal term for Luckman in this situation is
   A. personal representative.
   B. devisee.
   C. administrator.
   D. trustee.

142. When a real property owner fails to occupy his or her property and the land is occupied by someone else for seven years, the basis for a title claim may be created by use of the legal principle of
   A. escheat.
   B. estoppel.
   C. adverse interest.
   D. adverse possession.

143. The purpose of recording a deed is to
   A. give the world actual notice of ownership.
   B. give the world constructive notice of ownership.
   C. establish a future right of redemption.
   D. bring the county records up to date as to ownership.

144. Legal title always passes from the seller to the buyer
   A. on the date of the execution of the deed.
   B. when the closing statement has been signed.
   C. when the deed is placed in escrow.
   D. when the deed is voluntarily delivered and voluntarily accepted.

145. The term *acknowledgment* refers to
   A. the stamp indicating delivery to the clerk of the court.
   B. public acknowledgment of true ownership by giving actual notice.
   C. a signer's formal declaration before an authorized official that he or she is executing the instrument as a free act and deed.
   D. the act of recording a legal document.

146. Each of these is a method of acquiring legal title to real property EXCEPT
   A. descent.
   B. quitclaim deed.
   C. eminent domain.
   D. novation.

147. The terms in each pair are synonymous EXCEPT
   A. vendee—purchaser.
   B. mortgagee—lender.
   C. lessor—landlord.
   D. grantee—seller.

148. Which statement does NOT describe an owner's title insurance policy?
    A. The premium is paid once only—at time of issue.
    B. The policy may not be transferred from one owner to another owner.
    C. Damages are paid for any defect in the title not listed as an exception.
    D. The policy is issued for an amount equal to the unpaid balance of the mortgage loan.

149. Mr. Sumter sold his home to Mr. and Mrs. Lake and gave them a warranty deed. The Lakes moved into the home but did not record the deed. Two days later, Mr. Sumter died, and his heirs in another state sold the property without any knowledge of the previous sale. The heirs conveyed title to Mr. and Mrs. Flagler, who did record the deed. Who owns the property?
    A. Mr. and Mrs. Lake
    B. Mr. and Mrs. Flagler
    C. Mr. Sumter's heirs
    D. The Flaglers and Lakes as joint tenants

150. Which description is NOT an essential element of a deed?
    A. Consideration
    B. Under seal
    C. Witnessed
    D. Delivered

151. The clause in a deed that contains the words "bargains and sells" or similar words is the
    A. granting clause.
    B. habendum clause.
    C. encumbrances clause.
    D. seisin clause.

152. The clause in a deed that specifies the type of estate being transferred is the
    A. premises clause.
    B. seisin clause.
    C. habendum clause.
    D. granting clause.

153. Can a property owner give a sales associate power of attorney to draft a lease?
    A. Only brokers may act as a power of attorney.
    B. Yes, provided the power of attorney authorizes a licensee to perform such an act.
    C. No, only attorneys may draft leases for others.
    D. Yes, with the broker's consent.

154. Buyer and seller are discussing the type of deed that is to be conveyed. The buyers are requiring a guarantee that the seller owns the property and has a legal right to sell. This guarantee is part of which clause in the deed?
    A. Seisin
    B. Habendum
    C. Premises
    D. Encumbrance

155. A type of deed that contains the words "remise and release" or similar words is the
    A. special warranty deed.
    B. quitclaim deed.
    C. bargain and sale deed.
    D. personal representative's deed.

156. Private restrictions on ownership of real property include which restriction?
    A. Police power
    B. Deed restrictions
    C. Eminent domain
    D. Escheat

157. The covenant in a general warranty deed that promises that the grantor will obtain and deliver any legal instrument that might be required to make the title good in the future is the covenant of
    A. further assurance.
    B. quiet enjoyment.
    C. warranty forever.
    D. habendum et tinendum.

158. Compensation often follows a court action related to
    A. quiet title.
    B. police power.
    C. condemnation.
    D. writ of escheat.

159. Which pair does NOT belong together?
    A. Fee simple—Absolute
    B. Escheat—Testate
    C. Tenancy in common—No right of survivorship
    D. Joint tenancy—Undivided interest

160. The key difference between police power and eminent domain is whether
    A. the action was by a governmental agency.
    B. any compensation was paid to an affected owner.
    C. the owner's use was affected.
    D. the improvements are to be destroyed.

161. Against his will, Farmer Fallen's farm was taken in order that a municipal water supply could be built. The legal principle justifying this action is called
    A. police power.
    B. eminent domain.
    C. escheat to the state.
    D. estoppel.

162. If you have an acknowledged right to use a small portion of your neighbor's property for a basketball backboard, you have a(n)
    A. lien.
    B. easement.
    C. life estate.
    D. encroachment.

163. Sad Sam dies intestate. The principle of law applying to disposition of Sam's real property is
    A. escheat.
    B. estoppel.
    C. easement.
    D. eminent domain.

164. An easement created by court order to allow the right of ingress and egress over another person's property to landlocked property is which type of easement?
    A. Easement by prescription
    B. Easement by condemnation
    C. Easement by necessity
    D. Easement by adverse possession

165. All of the following are necessary parts of a lease EXCEPT
    A. parties to the lease.
    B. term of the lease.
    C. option to purchase.
    D. valuable consideration.

166. When leased property is sold, the lease
    A. has to be renewed.
    B. is binding on the new owner.
    C. creates a tenancy from month to month.
    D. is considered void.

167. If a tenant legally subrogates or subordinates his or her rental space, it means that he or she has
    A. assigned the lease.
    B. given up the lease.
    C. terminated the lease.
    D. subleased the lease.

168. Which type of statutory deed is typically used to clear clouds on the title?
    A. Quitclaim
    B. Bargain and sale
    C. General warranty
    D. Special warranty

169. Billy Bob builds a bridge across a stream he owns, but the footing on the other side extends onto his neighbor's property. The legal term for this action is
    A. easement.
    B. implied easement.
    C. encroachment.
    D. subrogation of space.

170. Mike Meany succeeds in gaining legal use of Nancy Nice's property by open and notorious possession of the land for over 20 years. The legal term for this result is
    A. encroachment.
    B. easement by prescription.
    C. accretion.
    D. adverse possession.

171. An instrument that transfers possession of real property but does not transfer ownership is a(n)
    A. deed.
    B. easement.
    C. mortgage.
    D. lease.

172. An oral agreement between a lessor and lessee is legally
    A. a valid tenancy for years.
    B. unenforceable due to the statute of frauds.
    C. a valid tenancy at will.
    D. unenforceable due to the statute of limitations.

173. A type of contractual agreement having all essential elements of a contract plus a property description and a definite term of tenancy specified creates which type of interest in real property?
    A. Tenancy at will
    B. Leasehold
    C. Fee simple estate
    D. Life estate

174. All these terms apply to leasing EXCEPT
    A. eviction.
    B. assignment.
    C. subrogation.
    D. title.

175. Which government restriction on ownership represents the broadest power of government to limit the rights of property owners?
    A. Eminent domain
    B. Police power
    C. Escheat
    D. Government liens

176. Which statement is TRUE?
    A. All liens are encumbrances.
    B. All encumbrances are liens.
    C. Specific liens affect all personal property of the debtor.
    D. A property tax lien is a type of general lien.

177. A valid lease, in writing and witnessed by two people, is
    A. a contract.
    B. an interest in real property.
    C. neither a contract nor an interest in real property.
    D. both a contract and an interest in real property.

178. Which encumbrance is NOT a lien?
    A. Mortgage
    B. Deed restriction
    C. Attachment
    D. Property taxes

179. Which statement is TRUE with respect to the assignment of a lease?
    A. The original lessee is not liable for the payment of the rent.
    B. It is the same as a sublease.
    C. The original lessee would still retain a right to use the property for a limited time.
    D. The entire leasehold is transferred.

180. A sublease will result in a lease of
    A. the entire premises by a new tenant.
    B. a portion of the leased rights and interests.
    C. the entire premises located below ground level.
    D. all of the leased premises for the full duration of the remainder of the original lease.

181. Which lien is NOT a specific lien?
    A. Mortgage lien
    B. Construction lien
    C. Property tax lien
    D. Income tax lien

182. A railroad company may use which method to acquire land?
    A. Escheat
    B. Police power
    C. Eminent domain
    D. Auction

183. Which encumbrance constitutes a lien on real property?
    A. Easement
    B. Encroachment
    C. Restriction
    D. Mortgage

184. Normally, the priority of a mortgage lien is determined by
    A. the order in which other liens are filed or recorded.
    B. the order in which the cause of action arose.
    C. the size of the claim.
    D. a court of law.

185. Unless a written agreement exists to change the usual order of priority, the mortgage with the highest priority is the
    A. construction loan mortgage.
    B. mortgage that was recorded first.
    C. mortgage for the greatest amount.
    D. mortgage containing the subordination clause.

186. A real property tax is an example of a
    A. specific voluntary lien.
    B. specific involuntary lien.
    C. general voluntary lien.
    D. general involuntary lien.

187. A recorded notice of a current lawsuit involving title to real property is called a(n)
    A. lis pendens.
    B. writ of mandamus.
    C. injunction.
    D. attachment.

188. A lawsuit against Owner Olson is pending. The court rules that his vegetable farm be seized and held as security in case of a judgment against Olson. This legal action is called
    A. lis pendens.
    B. adverse possession.
    C. attachment.
    D. assignment.

189. A type of lien that results when a seller accepts a mortgage as part of the purchase price for a home is a
    A. general lien.
    B. vendor's lien.
    C. construction lien.
    D. home equity lien.

190. Which term describes the beneficial interest in real estate that implies that an individual will receive legal title at a future date?
    A. Legal title
    B. Equitable title
    C. Cloud on title
    D. Marketable title

■ REAL ESTATE CONTRACTS (CHAPTER 11)
FLORIDA REAL ESTATE BROKER'S GUIDE (CHAPTER 11)

191. Mr. Good and Ms. Best make an oral agreement regarding the sale of Ms. Best's grapefruit grove. This contract normally would be unenforceable in a court of law based on the
    A. laws of agency.
    B. statute of frauds.
    C. statute of limitations.
    D. real estate licensing laws.

192. Essential elements of a real estate contract include all EXCEPT
    A. consideration.
    B. offer and acceptance.
    C. in writing and signed.
    D. recordation.

193. To be valid, a real estate sale contract must contain
    A. an earnest money deposit.
    B. an offer and acceptance.
    C. evidence of two witnesses' signatures.
    D. a notary's seal.

194. A properly executed contract that has as its purpose an illegal objective is
    A. valid and enforceable.
    B. valid but not enforceable.
    C. legal but depends on voluntary performance.
    D. void and unenforceable.

195. A real estate contract that is signed by a minor is
    A. enforceable.
    B. valid.
    C. terminated.
    D. voidable.

196. A real estate sale contract becomes valid or in effect when it has been signed by the
    A. broker and buyer.
    B. buyer and spouse.
    C. seller and broker.
    D. buyer and seller.

197. A broker promises to give a $20,000 bonus to the first sales associate who sells 20 homes. Which type of contract is this?
    A. Unilateral contract
    B. Bilateral contract
    C. Executed contract
    D. Implied contract

198. John orally agrees to purchase Sandi's home. John gives Sandi a cash down payment of $20,000 and moves into the property. Is this contract enforceable under the statute of frauds?
    A. No, the statute of frauds requires all contracts involving the sale of real property to be in writing without exception.
    B. Yes, because the buyer has paid part of the purchase price and has taken physical possess of the property.
    C. No, because the buyer has not made any improvements to the property.
    D. Yes, a written contract is not necessary because both parties are honest and trustworthy.

199. A contract stating that a property owner grants another party the right to buy property at a fixed price any time during a specified period is a(n)
    A. option.
    B. contractual right of first refusal.
    C. exclusive-agency listing.
    D. property escrow agreement.

200. If a buyer makes an offer under certain terms and the seller makes a counteroffer, the buyer
    A. is bound by the original offer.
    B. must accept the counteroffer.
    C. is relieved of the original offer.
    D. remains the offeror.

201. When a real estate sale contract has been signed by the purchaser and given to the seller's broker along with an earnest money check
    A. this transaction constitutes a valid contract in the eyes of the law.
    B. the purchaser can sue the seller for specific performance.
    C. this transaction is considered an offer.
    D. the earnest money will be returned if the buyer defaults.

202. Lake signs a contract to purchase Land's home for $170,000. The listing broker submits the contract to Land, but Land insists on the listed price of $180,000. The broker prepares a new contract for $180,000 that Lake refuses to sign. Land then instructs the broker to take Lake's original offer of $170,000 back to Lake because Land has decided to accept the offer. Lake has changed his mind and refuses to accept the contract. The result is
    A. no valid contract exists.
    B. an enforceable contract exists.
    C. the buyer, having refused the contract, must pay the broker's commission.
    D. the seller owes the broker a sales commission.

203. A buyer made an offer at less than the asking price. The seller then made a counteroffer, but the buyer would not accept the counteroffer. If the seller then agreed to accept the first offer, which statement is true?
    A. The buyer is legally bound to complete the deal.
    B. The broker has earned the commission.
    C. The buyer was released from the offer when the seller made a counteroffer.
    D. The broker is liable if the contract is unenforceable.

204. When an offeror withdraws an offer before acceptance, this is called
    A. abandonment.
    B. renunciation.
    C. revocation.
    D. breach.

205. The best way for a real estate broker to terminate a contract is by
    A. assignment.
    B. renunciation.
    C. performance.
    D. lapse of time.

206. The phrase "time is of the essence" means
    A. the buyer wants to take possession quickly.
    B. the seller wants to close quickly.
    C. actions are required by dates set forth in the agreement.
    D. a specified period of time must lapse before the contract can legally be concluded.

207. Rowan and Martin enter into a contract in which Rowan agrees to sell his house to Martin. Later, Rowan changes his mind and defaults. Martin then sues Rowan to force him to go through with the contract. This action is known as a suit for
    A. specific performance.
    B. damages.
    C. unliquidated damages.
    D. declaratory judgment.

208. Which method is NOT a legal means for terminating an offer made via a real estate contract?
    A. Counteroffer
    B. Acceptance
    C. Rejection
    D. Breach

209. The concept that requires an injured party to bring an action within a specific period of time after the injury is derived from the statute of
    A. obligations.
    B. limitations.
    C. fraud.
    D. specific enforcement.

210. A written instrument authorizing a person to act for and on behalf of another person is called a(n)
    A. attorney-in-fact.
    B. acknowledgment.
    C. option.
    D. power of attorney.

211. If a broker is given the right to sign a real estate sale contract that will be binding on his principal, the broker is
    A. an attorney-in-fact.
    B. given general power of attorney.
    C. a special agent trustee.
    D. the attorney of record.

212. A real estate licensee is NOT authorized to draw which contract?
    A. Option
    B. Buyer-brokerage
    C. Lease
    D. Sale and purchase

213. A listing to sell property and obtain a specified amount for the owner-principal is called a(n)
    A. open listing.
    B. exclusive right-to-sell listing.
    C. implied listing.
    D. net listing.

214. The term *procuring cause* is most significant in which type of listing?
    A. Open
    B. Exclusive-agency
    C. Exclusive right-to-sell
    D. Net

215. If an option contract is duly executed by the seller and the buyer, which statement is TRUE?
    A. The property owner reserves an option to either sell or not sell.
    B. The buyer must buy.
    C. The property owner must sell, but the buyer need not buy.
    D. It is specifically enforceable by both parties.

216. In a valid option contract to purchase real estate, the optionee
    A. is the prospective seller of the property.
    B. must purchase the property within the option period.
    C. has no obligation to purchase the property.
    D. is limited to a refund of the option consideration if the option is exercised.

217. Any contract that obligates both parties to perform in accordance with the terms of the contract is a(n)
    A. unenforceable contract.
    B. unilateral contract.
    C. bilateral contract.
    D. voidable contract.

218. A broker mailed a signed purchase offer to a property owner. Instead of signing the purchase offer contract, the owner sent the broker a telegram accepting the offer. Which is correct?
    A. There has been a valid offer but not a legal acceptance.
    B. There is a valid contract between the buyer and seller.
    C. There has been a valid offer and a telegraphic acceptance but not an enforceable contract.
    D. To be enforceable, a contract must contain the offer and acceptance within the same instrument.

219. Jacob is a 17-year-old high school student who has entered into a contract to purchase Able's 1957 Crown Victoria. This is a(n)
    A. void contract.
    B. illegal contract.
    C. option contract.
    D. voidable contract.

220. Seller Stacey and Buyer Linda negotiated the sale and purchase of Stacey's condominium over a two-week period. Finally, they reached a meeting of the minds regarding the purchase price and terms of the sale. What type of contract exists at this point?
    A. Implied contract
    B. Express contract
    C. Executed contract
    D. Option contract

221. A broker must give a copy of the written listing agreement to the seller
    A. at the time of acceptance.
    B. by the end of the next business day.
    C. within 24 hours after the seller signs the agreement.
    D. by the end of the third business day.

222. A contract may be terminated by any of these actions EXCEPT
    A. rejection.
    B. performance.
    C. mutual rescission.
    D. impossibility of performance.

223. In case of breach by the buyer, most real estate sale contracts include a provision that the earnest money be regarded as
    A. liquidated damages to the broker.
    B. liquidated damages to the seller.
    C. unliquidated damages to the seller.
    D. unliquidated damages in escrow.

224. A seller who wishes to recover monetary damages equal to the extent of loss suffered in excess of the earnest money deposit may
    A. sue for specific performance.
    B. sue for compensatory damages.
    C. seek compensation from the Real Estate Recovery Fund.
    D. sue the broker for breach of duty to perform.

225. Which reason below would NOT make a valid contract to purchase and sell real estate unenforceable?
    A. It violates the statute of frauds.
    B. The time frame extends beyond the statute of limitations.
    C. The property is destroyed.
    D. No earnest money was pledged.

■ PLANNING AND ZONING (CHAPTER 20) FLORIDA REAL ESTATE BROKER'S GUIDE (CHAPTER 16)

226. The state law requirement that local governments provide public facilities and services at the same time as the impact of each phase of development is called the
    A. community impact provision.
    B. infrastructure provision.
    C. concurrency provision.
    D. Florida building code.

227. A strip of land that separates one type of land use from another is a(n)
    A. nonconforming use.
    B. buffer zone.
    C. boundary.
    D. easement.

228. Which study is designed to determine whether there is adequate diversification regarding employment within a community?
    A. Population background
    B. Economic base
    C. Existing land-use
    D. Community facilities

229. Zone R-1A probably refers to
    A. rural areas.
    B. railroad yards.
    C. single-family dwellings.
    D. light industry.

230. Government regulations that establish construction requirements are termed
    A. health ordinances.
    B. building codes.
    C. master plans.
    D. zoning regulations.

231. An example of a previously granted variance could be a
    A. house whose owner established a business in his home that is zoned single-family residence.
    B. business in an area that has been rezoned residential.
    C. house next to a service station.
    D. shopping center that has fewer than the number of parking spaces required per square foot of rentable space.

232. To extend the side of your house beyond the setback boundary, you must first obtain
    A. a variance.
    B. a special exception.
    C. a nonconforming use.
    D. site plan approval.

233. A grandfather clause in a zoning ordinance probably would allow an owner to
    A. reshingle the roof of a structure that is a nonconforming use.
    B. enlarge a building that is a nonconforming use.
    C. rebuild a structure 60 percent destroyed by fire that is a nonconforming use.
    D. convert a three-room structure into two large rooms.

234. Which procedure is NOT used by a local municipality to enforce building codes?
    A. Issue certificates of occupancy
    B. Issue building permits
    C. Conduct building inspections
    D. Conduct condemnation proceedings

235. A new office center complex is being planned that will have a substantial effect on the health, safety, and welfare of the citizens of two adjoining counties. What review process is mandated by the state to evaluate every aspect from air quality to schools prior to the start of construction?
    A. Planned unit development
    B. Environmental impact statement
    C. Zoning board of adjustment review
    D. Economic base study

236. Which statement describes a planned unit development?
    A. A mix of land uses along with a high density of residential units
    B. Single-family dwelling units predominate
    C. Shopping areas included, but not professional offices
    D. Organized rejuvenation of depressed urban areas

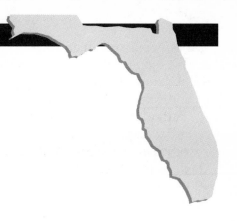

Real Estate Principles and Practices Chapters

■ THE REAL ESTATE BUSINESS (CHAPTER 1)

237. Business brokers
  A. must be licensed as real estate licensees.
  B. are not required to qualify as real estate licensees.
  C. must hold a business brokerage license.
  D. are required to be licensed as a real estate broker only if the sale of a business involves the sale of real property.

238. The term *dedication* refers to
  A. the initial stage of subdivision development ("ceremonial start-up").
  B. the transfer of certain subdivision areas from private to public ownership.
  C. recordation of a subdivision plat at the county courthouse.
  D. a covenant placed in the deeds to all subdivision lots.

239. The practice of using five or six model homes to sell houses in a subdivision is associated with
  A. speculative (spec) building.
  B. tract building.
  C. custom building.
  D. mass market building.

240. A property manager
  A. is limited to collection of rent, maintenance, and repair.
  B. is synonymous with rental agent.
  C. is responsible for leasing, managing, marketing, and overall maintenance of property.
  D. is no longer in demand because of increased absentee ownership.

241. Follow-up refers to which activity?
  A. Making sure all of the inspections are completed prior to closing
  B. Returning all phone calls to the buyer and seller in a timely manner
  C. Keeping in touch with the new homeowner who purchased the home through the sales associate
  D. Attending the title closing and collecting the commission check

242. A licensed real estate broker may
  A. NOT appraise real property unless he or she is a licensed appraiser.
  B. prepare CMAs only in the scope of listing property.
  C. NOT charge for a comparative market analysis (CMA).
  D. NOT appraise property that involves a federally related transaction unless he or she is also a licensed or state-certified appraiser.

243. A subdivision plat map
    A. is a map provided to prospective buyers by local real estate offices.
    B. indicates the size and location of individual lots, streets, and utilities.
    C. is developed by the tax assessor's office for tax assessment purposes.
    D. depicts the side and front elevations of structures.

244. A property owner who does NOT reside on the property and who often relies on a professional property management company to manage the investment is a(n)
    A. property manager.
    B. absentee owner.
    C. real estate licensee.
    D. nonresident owner.

■ LEGAL DESCRIPTIONS (CHAPTER 10)

245. The legal description method that uses direction, distance, and a POB is the
    A. metes-and-bounds method.
    B. government survey method.
    C. rectangular method.
    D. lot-and-block numbers method.

246. The section number located due west of Section 6 is
    A. 7.
    B. 5.
    C. 3.
    D. 1.

247. Which description is most nearly due north?
    A. N 89° 30′ E
    B. N 0° 45′ E
    C. N 0° 30′ W
    D. N 1° 15′ W

248. The compass direction that is the straight-line opposite of S 45° E is
    A. N 45° E.
    B. N 45° W.
    C. S 45° W.
    D. S 45° E.

249. In Florida, the principal meridian and base line intersect in Tallahassee because
    A. the state government is located there.
    B. the governor in office in 1831 decreed that it be there.
    C. Florida State University is located there.
    D. it is the basic reference point selected by the federal government.

250. Which statement is FALSE concerning townships?
    A. Each township is composed of 36 sections.
    B. A township is six miles square.
    C. There are 640 acres in a township.
    D. Townships are located by referring to principal meridians and base lines.

251. The SW ¼ of the SE ¼ of the NW ¼, of Section 10, Township 3 South, Range 5 East, describes a tract of
    A. .125 acre.
    B. .5 acre.
    C. 10 acres.
    D. 64 acres.

252. In Florida, Range 2 East is closest to
    A. Tallahassee.
    B. Jacksonville.
    C. Miami.
    D. Pensacola.

253. What is the shortest distance between the closest borders of Section 1 and Section 36 of the same township?
    A. 3 miles
    B. 4 miles
    C. 5 miles
    D. 6 miles

254. A range is numbered to the
    A. north or south of a principal meridian.
    B. east or west of a principal meridian.
    C. north or south of a base line.
    D. east or west of a township or tier.

255. Which statement is true about the sections in a township?
    A. Section 13 lies to the north of Section 24.
    B. Section 1 is, by law, set aside for school purposes.
    C. Section 31 lies in the southeast corner of the township.
    D. Section 7 lies to the east of Section 8.

256. Which type of legal description is used only in developed subdivisions?
    A. Government survey
    B. Metes-and-bounds
    C. Lot and block
    D. Tax assessor's map

257. How many acres are contained in a parcel described as the SE¼ of the NW¼ and the S½ of the NE¼ of a certain section?
    A. 5
    B. 40
    C. 80
    D. 120

■ REAL ESTATE FINANCE (CHAPTER 12) FLORIDA REAL ESTATE BROKER'S GUIDE (CHAPTER 12)

258. Which method involves a conveyance of the title to the lender to avoid foreclosure?
    A. Judicial foreclosure
    B. Deed in lieu of foreclosure
    C. Satisfaction of mortgage
    D. Quasi judicial procedure

259. When a promissory note is executed, it becomes
    A. security for the debt.
    B. evidence of the debt.
    C. a legal obligation of the creditor.
    D. a conveyance of interest in real property.

260. A mortgage clause (in title theory states that provides for the transfer of title to real property to the borrower once the mortgage debt has been repaid is the
    A. defeasance clause.
    B. novation.
    C. exculpatory clause.
    D. hold harmless clause.

261. Which legal instrument would contain the interest rate, loan amount, maturity date, and payment schedule?
    A. Deed
    B. Closing statement
    C. Lease
    D. Note

262. The mortgagor is the person who
    A. holds the property as security for the loan.
    B. lends the money.
    C. signs the note.
    D. receives the monthly payments.

263. Upon satisfaction of the existing mortgage, the property may be conveyed
    A. free and clear.
    B. subject to the mortgage.
    C. upon reassumption of the mortgage.
    D. as encumbered property.

264. Which statement is FALSE regarding actions that can be taken in the case of default by a mortgagor in Florida?
    A. The mortgagee may bring suit on the basis of the note or the mortgage, or both.
    B. The legal action may be initiated anywhere in the nation if based on the note.
    C. The legal action may be initiated only in the county in which the property is located if based on the mortgage.
    D. The mortgagee may take title or possession during foreclosure proceedings.

265. Which mortgage clause legally allows the lender to declare the entire unpaid sum due when the debtor defaults?
    A. Acceleration clause
    B. Escalator clause
    C. Exculpatory clause
    D. Prepayment penalty clause

266. One mortgage clause NOT normally found in a VA or FHA mortgage is the
    A. subordination clause.
    B. redemption clause.
    C. acceleration clause.
    D. prepayment penalty clause.

267. Which information is the best indicator of a loan applicant's willingness to repay debt?
    A. Housing expense ratio
    B. Credit score
    C. W-2 income data
    D. Total obligations ratio

268. Which mortgage clause allows a mortgagee to have a third party appointed to collect income and manage the property?
    A. Personal representative's clause
    B. Administrator's clause
    C. Redemption clause
    D. Receivership clause

269. By paying his or her debt prior to a foreclosure sale, a borrower has the right to regain the property through
    A. redemption.
    B. reversion.
    C. recovery.
    D. receivership.

270. A mortgage clause that states that a first mortgagee's rights will be allowed to become junior to a subsequent mortgage is called a(n)
    A. redemption clause.
    B. subordination clause.
    C. release clause.
    D. escalator clause.

271. The clause in a mortgage in which a lender waives the right to a deficiency judgment against the borrower and the borrower is relieved of personal liability to repay the loan is the
    A. exculpatory clause.
    B. subordination clause.
    C. defeasance clause.
    D. release clause.

272. A due-on-sale clause has which of these features?
    A. It allows the mortgagee to call the outstanding loan balance plus accrued interest due.
    B. The lender initiates the clause if all or part of the property is sold or transferred without the lender's prior consent.
    C. The clause prevents another party from assuming the mortgage and requires the mortgage debt to be paid in full when the property is sold.
    D. A due-on-sale clause has all of the features described above.

273. When a loan is paid off in a lien theory state such as Florida, the lender should give the borrower a(n)
    A. deed of reconveyance.
    B. certificate of title.
    C. satisfaction of mortgage.
    D. opinion of title.

274. Complete Title Services is preparing for a closing. The closing agent wants to verify the balance of an existing mortgage before cutting a check to pay the lender in full at closing. Which document verifies this information?
    A. Broker's reconciliation statement
    B. Due on sale clause
    C. Estoppel certificate
    D. Novation

275. Which statement is true concerning VA loans?
    A. A down payment is required on all VA loans.
    B. Veteran borrowers are charged mortgage insurance premiums (MIP).
    C. The VA has the authority to partially guarantee mortgage loans made to veterans by private lenders.
    D. The veteran must secure an estoppel certificate from the VA to begin the loan process.

276. The VA loan guarantee is referred to as the
    A. maximum entitlement.
    B. certificate of guarantee.
    C. certificate of reasonable value.
    D. minimum cash investment.

277. FHA calls the amount of money it insists a homebuyer pay in cash or its equivalent the borrower's
    A. down payment.
    B. initial investment.
    C. earnest money deposit.
    D. minimum cash investment.

278. Which statement is true regarding FHA loans?
    A. New FHA home mortgages are available to qualified investors.
    B. FHA makes loans to qualified borrowers.
    C. FHA insures mortgage loans.
    D. Down payments are not required on FHA loans.

279. FHA requires borrowers to pay
    A. a funding fee.
    B. one-twelfth of the estimated property taxes with each monthly payment.
    C. discount points.
    D. a user's fee.

280. The amount of a loan expressed as a percentage of the value of real property offered as security is the
    A. loan-to-value ratio.
    B. amortization schedule.
    C. leverage ratio.
    D. debt-service coverage ratio.

281. All home loans have four components
    A. principal, interest, taxes, and insurance (PITI).
    B. principal amount, interest rate, property taxes, and loan term.
    C. principal amount, interest rate, loan term, and monthly payment.
    D. principal, interest, insurance, and down payment.

282. A loan amortization schedule shows monthly payments of
    A. principal.
    B. interest.
    C. principal and interest.
    D. principal, interest, taxes, and insurance.

283. Which pair of terms does NOT belong together?
    A. FHA—mortgage insurance premium
    B. VA—minimum cash investment
    C. Conventional—PMI more than 80%
    D. VA—funding fee

284. Assume that a buyer is making fully amortized payments of $700 per month on a purchase-money mortgage. Which applies?
    A. The amount applying to principal decreases each month.
    B. The interest payment remains constant.
    C. Interest and principal remain constant.
    D. The amount applying to interest decreases each month.

285. Mortgage loan payments made in regular installments of interest only with the full principal amount plus accrued interest paid at one time at the end of the loan period describes a(n)
    A. blanket mortgage.
    B. package mortgage.
    C. term mortgage.
    D. adjustable-rate mortgage.

286. The basic or standard mortgage used for many years before innovative forms of financing appeared is the
    A. package mortgage with a 30-year term.
    B. adjustable-rate, 20-year to 30-year mortgage.
    C. fixed-rate, 25-year to 30-year mortgage.
    D. term mortgage with a 15-year to 20-year term.

287. The seller has an existing first mortgage. In order to limit exposure to further liability, the seller should find a buyer ready to
    A. take title subject to the mortgage.
    B. subordinate his or her position to the mortgage.
    C. assume the mortgage and note.
    D. obtain his or her own financing.

288. A buyer assumed an existing recorded $82,000 mortgage as part of a real estate purchase. This action will necessitate
    A. a new mortgage instrument.
    B. a new promissory note.
    C. payment of an intangible tax to the state.
    D. the seller remaining primarily liable for the debt.

289. A financing device that grants a buyer "equitable title" without a deed from grantor to grantee is called
    A. a land contract.
    B. an installment sale contract.
    C. a contract for deed.
    D. any of the terms listed above.

290. When an owner obtains a new, larger loan and the seller continues to make regular payments on the old loan, the financing arrangement is known as a
    A. package mortgage.
    B. reverse mortgage.
    C. wraparound mortgage.
    D. purchase-money mortgage.

291. You purchase a home under a contract for deed. Until the contract is paid, you have
    A. legal title to the property.
    B. no legal interest in the property.
    C. a life estate in the property.
    D. equitable title to the property.

292. Legally, lending institutions are permitted to link the interest rate of an ARM loan with any recognized, nonlender-controlled
    A. margin.
    B. index.
    C. cap.
    D. yield.

293. A buydown mortgage typically reduces the
    A. interest rate.
    B. loan duration.
    C. down payment.
    D. sale price.

294. Determining housing objectives and economic capabilities is a process called
    A. loan underwriting.
    B. buyer qualification.
    C. loan qualification.
    D. risk analysis.

■ THE MORTGAGE MARKET (CHAPTER 13)

295. Which parties are most involved in the secondary market?
    A. Mortgage broker and mortgage banker
    B. Mortgagor and mortgagee
    C. Mortgage broker and mortgagee
    D. Fannie Mae and Ginnie Mae

296. Which statement best describes Fannie Mae's function?
    A. It regulates lending terms and policies of member banks.
    B. It absorbs any losses incurred by Ginnie Mae.
    C. It acts as a secondary market in purchases of FHA, VA, and conventional loans.
    D. It insures FHA loans.

297. If the Fed decides to sell securities through open-market bulk trading, the result will be a(n)
    A. increase of money in circulation.
    B. decrease of money in circulation.
    C. relaxing of interest rates.
    D. increase in the discount rate.

298. Fannie Mae does NOT
    A. purchase conventional loans.
    B. sell mortgages to institutions.
    C. buy FHA and VA loans.
    D. originate federal loans.

299. Which entity can be considered both a lender and a middleman?
    A. Commercial bank
    B. Mortgage banker
    C. Mortgage broker
    D. Savings association

300. Which of the following assists agricultural communities with loans and other assistance?
    A. Green belt laws
    B. Agricultural land classification
    C. Federal Housing Administration
    D. Rural Housing Service

301. Freddie Mac is a
    A. part of Ginnie Mae.
    B. subsidiary of Fannie Mae.
    C. secondary market for SAs.
    D. government insurance program.

302. The discount rate is best defined as the
    A. interest rate charged borrowers when the mortgage is discounted.
    B. interest rate charged member banks for borrowing money from the Federal Reserve.
    C. up-front cost charged borrowers to increase the yield on mortgage loans.
    D. interest rate charged on VA loans.

303. Which statement is NOT true regarding savings associations?
    A. If the savings association is federally chartered, the words "Federal" or the initials "FA" must appear in the name.
    B. The Federal Home Loan Bank System (FHLBS) serves the same function as the Federal Reserve Bank System for national banks.
    C. The Office of Thrift Supervision (OTS) charters federal savings associations.
    D. The Federal Deposit Insurance Corporation (FDIC) insures deposits of federally chartered savings associations.

304. All nationally chartered commercial banks must be members of the
     A. Federal National Mortgage Association.
     B. Government National Mortgage Association.
     C. Federal Reserve System.
     D. Federal Home Loan Mortgage Corporation.

305. Which statement most accurately describes mortgage companies that act as mortgage loan correspondents?
     A. They prefer negotiating loans that will be sold on the secondary market.
     B. They are organized under federal laws and are subject to rigorous supervision.
     C. They do not service the loans they originate.
     D. They prefer to represent one large, established lending institution.

306. Rent for the use of money is called
     A. credit.
     B. return.
     C. devise.
     D. interest.

307. To compute the dollar value of a loan discount, each discount point is equal to
     A. 1 percent of the amount loaned.
     B. one-eighth of 1 percent of the amount to be loaned.
     C. 1 percent of the appraised value plus closing costs.
     D. 1 percent of the purchase price.

308. The discount charged by a lender and paid on a VA loan is a percentage of the
     A. sale price.
     B. appraised value.
     C. loan amount.
     D. down payment.

309. Which fee does a lender charge for making a loan to a homebuyer?
     A. Commitment fee
     B. Origination fee
     C. Administrative fee
     D. Transfer fee

■ ESTIMATING REAL PROPERTY VALUE (CHAPTER 15) FLORIDA REAL ESTATE BROKER'S GUIDE (CHAPTERS 6–9)

310. Plottage can best be described as the
     A. recorded instrument that identifies the individual lots in a developed subdivision.
     B. development of raw land.
     C. the process of combining two or more small lots into one large tract to enhance potential development.
     D. the increase in value that results from combining contiguous lots so that the value of the combined properties is greater than the sum of the individual lot values.

311. Both Fannie Mae and Freddie Mac have adopted a definition of market value that reads in part
     A. "the highest price in terms of money a property will bring."
     B. "the most probable price that a property should bring."
     C. "the best estimate of local market value available from recent sales."
     D. "the highest number of dollars a property will bring from informed buyers."

312. Which statement is TRUE regarding the provisions of the USPAP?
    A. Comparative market analyses are exempt from compliance with the USPAP.
    B. Appraisals prepared by real estate sales associates are exempt from compliance with the USPAP.
    C. Only state-certified or licensed appraisers are required to use the USPAP.
    D. The USPAP establishes disciplinary guidelines for USPAP violations.

313. If the capitalization rate remains constant, but net operating income is increased, how will the property value be affected?
    A. Not enough data is provided to answer this question.
    B. Property value remains constant.
    C. Property value decreases.
    D. Property value increases.

314. The amount of dollars spent to create an improvement is called
    A. price.
    B. cost.
    C. retail value.
    D. probable value.

315. Elements that affect real estate value do NOT include
    A. utility.
    B. cost.
    C. transferability.
    D. scarcity.

316. The most suitable appraisal method for a vacant lot in a choice subdivision is the
    A. comparable sales approach.
    B. comparative market analysis.
    C. cost-depreciation approach.
    D. income capitalization approach.

317. Which pair is most appropriate in estimating value?
    A. Apartment building—Cost approach
    B. Hospital—Income approach
    C. Single-family dwelling—Cost approach
    D. Raw land—Market approach

318. A post office of historic value and unique construction is best appraised by which approach to estimating value?
    A. Income approach
    B. Market approach
    C. Cost approach
    D. Comparability approach

319. The top priority approach to appraising an apartment complex would focus on
    A. comparative market analysis.
    B. present value of future income.
    C. cost to reproduce.
    D. comparable sales.

320. If a comparable property is superior in lot size compared with the subject property, the price of the
    A. comparable is adjusted upward.
    B. comparable is adjusted downward.
    C. subject is adjusted downward.
    D. subject is adjusted upward.

321. Land value is obtained separately when using which approach to estimating value?
    A. Income approach
    B. Cost approach
    C. Market approach
    D. Multiplier approach

322. The factor by which annual rent from a commercial property is multiplied to obtain an estimate of the property's value is called the
    A. rental index.
    B. net rent multiplier.
    C. net operating income.
    D. gross income multiplier.

323. Which factor is used in determining gross rent multipliers?
A. Capitalization rate
B. Net income
C. Gross monthly income
D. Net operating income

324. The most common method used by appraisers to estimate building reproduction costs is the
A. quantity survey method.
B. unit comparison method.
C. unit-in-place method.
D. component cost method.

325. When measuring the square footage of a house, use the
A. net rentable area.
B. exterior dimensions.
C. room sizes.
D. interior dimensions, excluding partitions.

326. For real property to be depreciated, it must
A. be free and clear.
B. be owned in fee simple.
C. be in good condition.
D. have improvements.

327. Over which factor of depreciation does a property owner have the least control?
A. Ordinary wear and tear
B. Exterior facade
C. A poorly designed traffic pattern
D. Forces outside the property boundaries

328. When the estimate of value is adjusted because of an outdated kitchen, it is called
A. external obsolescence.
B. functional obsolescence.
C. curable physical deterioration.
D. incurable physical deterioration.

329. Which is NOT a cause of physical deterioration depreciation?
A. Lack of maintenance
B. Wear and tear due to use
C. Layout of the traffic pattern
D. Exposure to the elements

330. Which statement is TRUE concerning loss in value due to depreciation?
A. Extra-large, load-bearing columns in a large but old, one-floor store represent incurable functional obsolescence.
B. An unattractive storefront window represents incurable physical deterioration.
C. An unattractive storefront window represents curable external obsolescence.
D. Extra-large, load-bearing columns in a large but old, one-floor store represent curable functional obsolescence.

331. You have just learned that the nearby airport has obtained government approvals to redirect the flight path of planes over your subdivision. The effect on your subdivision is called
A. functional obsolescence.
B. external obsolescence.
C. physical deterioration.
D. environmental obsolescence.

332. Which characteristic might be classified as functional obsolescence?
A. Exterior needs repainting.
B. Property fronts on a busy expressway.
C. Property has a one-car garage.
D. Neighborhood is 60 years old.

333. Correction of an incurable element of physical deterioration or functional obsolescence results in a value increase that is
A. less than the cost to cure the defect.
B. equal to the cost to cure the defect.
C. greater than the cost to cure the defect.
D. unrelated to the cost to cure the defect.

334. The period of time through which a property gives benefits to its owner is best described as its
    A. investment duration.
    B. physical life.
    C. value duration.
    D. economic life.

335. Which valuation method is least applicable for owner-occupied, single-family residences?
    A. Comparative sales approach
    B. Comparative market analysis
    C. Market approach
    D. Income capitalization approach

336. Given just these steps, what is the correct sequence to arrive at an estimate of value using the income capitalization approach?
    I. Determine effective gross income
    II. Find net operating income
    III. Find operating expenses
    IV. Determine potential gross income
        A. I, II, III, IV
        B. I, III, IV, II
        C. IV, I, III, II
        D. IV, II, I, III

■ PRODUCT KNOWLEDGE (CHAPTER 16)

337. A custom two-story home has flagstone veneer installed along the lower portion of the exterior walls. The type of framing most suited to this situation is
    A. post-and-beam.
    B. platform.
    C. balloon.
    D. pier.

338. Mechanical equipment is sometimes placed on top of which type of roof?
    A. Gable
    B. Hip
    C. Gambrel
    D. Built-up

339. A three-wire electrical system to a home can supply a maximum of how many volts of electricity for large appliances?
    A. 240
    B. 220
    C. 120
    D. 110

340. The purpose of a U-shaped pipe located under the kitchen sink is to
    A. provide space to install a garbage disposal.
    B. form a seal in the plumbing line.
    C. make room for the kitchen sink to be dropped into place.
    D. increase the water pressure inside the pipe.

■ REAL ESTATE INVESTMENT ANALYSIS AND BUSINESS OPPORTUNITY BROKERAGE (CHAPTER 17) FLORIDA REAL ESTATE BROKER'S GUIDE (CHAPTER 15)

341. If an investment property is considered to lack liquidity, this means that the property
    A. is debt-ridden.
    B. has no access to a public water supply.
    C. cannot be sold quickly at full value.
    D. represents a substantial risk to the investor.

342. When associated with real estate finance, the term *leverage* means
    A. the use of a purchaser's funds to gain concessions from a seller.
    B. the use of borrowed funds to minimize the necessity for a borrower to use his or her own money.
    C. a lender's use of current conditions in the mortgage market to obtain the highest interest rate and best terms for each new mortgage.
    D. a prospective borrower's use of various mortgage rates and terms obtained by shopping for a mortgage loan.

343. Which deduction from gross income is NOT allowed when calculating the taxable income?
    A. Operating expenses
    B. Mortgage interest
    C. Depreciation
    D. Advertising and marketing

344. For tax purposes, the installment sale method
    A. relieves the seller of paying tax on a capital gain before it is received.
    B. requires that a capital loss be deferred.
    C. requires that any capital gain or loss be deferred.
    D. requires that a qualified loss be recognized in the year of the final installment payment.

345. A measure of the financial risk associated with lending and borrowing money is the
    A. capitalization rate.
    B. gross rent multiplier.
    C. discount rate.
    D. loan-to-value ratio.

346. The financial report that indicates a firm's financial position at a stated moment in time is the
    A. profit and loss report.
    B. income statement.
    C. balance sheet.
    D. cash flow statement.

347. The intangible advantage a business enjoys over its competitors is known as
    A. liquidity.
    B. leverage.
    C. cash flow.
    D. goodwill.

348. The going concern value of a business
    A. is equal to the value of its real estate holdings.
    B. excludes goodwill.
    C. is the worth of an established business property.
    D. is equal to working capital plus cash flow.

349. The effect of positive leverage is to increase the
    A. borrower's return on equity.
    B. lender's yield.
    C. the loan-to-value ratio.
    D. amount borrowed.

350. Widely accepted appraisal techniques for appraising businesses does NOT include
    A. comparable sales analysis.
    B. reproduction or replacement cost less depreciation analysis.
    C. leverage analysis.
    D. liquidation analysis.

■ TAXES AFFECTING REAL ESTATE (CHAPTER 18) FLORIDA REAL ESTATE BROKER'S GUIDE (CHAPTER 14)

351. Ms. Goodlady, a full-time employee of a government agency, evaluates real property for tax purposes. She is a(n)
    A. appraiser.
    B. tax collector.
    C. notary public.
    D. ad valorem administrator.

352. The Value Adjustment Board is composed of
    A. three county commissioners and two school board members.
    B. two county commissioners and three school board members.
    C. three county commissioners and two MAI-certified property appraisers.
    D. two county commissioners and three MAI-certified property appraisers.

353. Mr. Diaz was upset by the assessed value assigned to his home by the county property appraiser. He decided to protest the assessment and within prescribed time limits appealed to the Value Adjustment Board. Why did the Board refuse to hear Mr. Diaz's appeal?
    A. Such a protest requires that Mr. Diaz seek litigation in the courts.
    B. Mr. Diaz should register his protest with the county property appraiser.
    C. The Board is not authorized to review assessments made by the county property appraiser.
    D. The property must first be reappraised before the Board can determine the validity of the assessment.

354. Mary is a 66-year-old widow who is totally disabled due to a serious heart condition. Her cumulative tax exemption on her homesteaded residence is
    A. $25,500.
    B. $26,000.
    C. $50,500.
    D. nothing, she is totally exempt from taxes.

355. A fast-growing church has just purchased an adjacent apartment building and plans to convert it to a retirement home. Disregarding other factors, property owners in that area probably would be affected by
    A. lower taxes.
    B. higher taxes.
    C. subrogation of space.
    D. increased property values.

356. Which property is neither exempt nor immune from ad valorem property taxes?
    A. County hospital
    B. New church
    C. High school
    D. Undeveloped farmland

357. A lower assessment for land classified as being for agricultural purposes is protected by laws known as
    A. green belt laws.
    B. homestead laws.
    C. constitutional homestead laws.
    D. blue belt laws.

358. The term *mill* is most frequently associated with
    A. mortgages.
    B. interest rates.
    C. tax rates.
    D. listings.

359. In the formula for determining the tax rate for a government taxing unit, the approved budget minus nonproperty tax revenue is divided by
    A. total assessed property valuation.
    B. total assessed property valuation minus exemptions.
    C. property tax revenues from the district.
    D. net proceeds from all taxes levied in the district.

360. When a city or county government in Florida must collect delinquent taxes on a property, it issues a
    A. property tax certificate.
    B. tax lien.
    C. tax deed.
    D. special assessment.

361. The purpose of Florida's Save Our Home amendment is to
    A. limit the amount of increase in assessed value of homesteaded property.
    B. reduce the amount of government sponsored mortgage foreclosures.
    C. provide incentives for revitalization of inner city neighborhoods.
    D. limit the millage rate that may be applied to residential property.

362. Income tax benefits to homeowners are available only if
   A. applied for in the year of purchase.
   B. deductions are itemized annually.
   C. at least one spouse is 55 years of age or older.
   D. applied for within two years before or after selling the former principal residence.

363. Special assessments are
   A. used to help pay for some public improvement that benefits the property.
   B. levied on a calendar year basis.
   C. based on assessed value.
   D. charged to everyone in a specific tax district.

364. Thelma, a single person, bought her home 18 months ago and is now relocating to another city because of a change in employment. Is Thelma entitled to an exclusion of gain from the sale of her home?
   A. Yes, Thelma is entitled to a $500,000 exclusion.
   B. Thelma is entitled to a reduced exclusion because she did not occupy the residence for at least two years.
   C. Yes, Thelma is entitled to a $250,000 exclusion.
   D. Thelma is entitled to an exclusion, provided she purchases another home within 24 months.

365. One result of the current tax law is that, after May 7, 1997, homeowners
   A. pay capital gains tax at an 8 percent lower rate on their home sales.
   B. may use a one-time $500,000 exclusion if they file their taxes jointly.
   C. are not required to reinvest the sale proceeds in a new residence to claim the exclusion.
   D. are permitted to use the $125,000 over-55 exclusion more than once.

366. Tax advantages of homeownership include all EXCEPT
   A. deduction of mortgage interest paid on a second home.
   B. depreciation allowance.
   C. deduction of property taxes on principal residence.
   D. exclusion of up to $250,000 of gain ($500,000 for married couples filing jointly).

367. What number of years has the IRS established as the useful asset life for nonresidential income-producing property for calculating depreciation?
   A. 15
   B. 27.5
   C. 39
   D. 47

■ THE REAL ESTATE MARKET (CHAPTER 19)

368. The sale price of real estate generally is determined by
   A. existing economic conditions.
   B. the marketplace.
   C. sellers and owners.
   D. real estate professionals.

369. The statement that land is heterogeneous refers to which characteristic of the real estate market?
   A. Real estate is immobile.
   B. Land is indestructible.
   C. Real estate is unique.
   D. The market is slow to respond to changes in supply and demand.

370. To better estimate the demand for dwelling space, most experts charged with analysis of populations will use as a basis for their analysis
   A. total population size.
   B. the household.
   C. average family income.
   D. average family size.

371. Which variable influences supply?
    A. Price of real estate
    B. Income of consumers
    C. Availability of labor
    D. Mortgage credit availability

372. When the supply and demand equilibrium is upset by excess demand which market activity results?
    A. Pressure to relax interest rates
    B. Buyer's market develops
    C. Seller's market develops
    D. Drop in housing starts

■ TITLE CLOSING (CHAPTER 14 NARRATIVE) FLORIDA REAL ESTATE BROKER'S GUIDE (CHAPTER 13)

373. The customary method of accounting to parties in a real estate transaction regarding all expenses involved is by
    A. a letter of explanation.
    B. copies of receipted bills paid.
    C. the sale contract.
    D. closing statements.

374. The day of closing
    A. is always charged to the seller.
    B. if belonging to the seller, means that the seller is charged one extra day.
    C. is always charged to the buyer.
    D. if belonging to the seller, means that the seller is charged one less day.

375. When mortgage interest paid in arrears is prorated, the amount up to the day of closing is
    A. debited to the seller, credited to the buyer.
    B. debited to the seller.
    C. debited to the buyer, credited to the seller.
    D. not shown on the closing statement.

376. Which statement is TRUE with respect to composite closing statement entries?
    A. Brokerage commission is usually entered as a debit to seller and a credit to buyer.
    B. The binder deposit is entered as a credit to the buyer.
    C. Title insurance expense, when applicable, is usually entered as a debit to seller and a credit to buyer.
    D. Abstract continuation expense, when applicable, is usually entered as a debit to buyer.

377. After contracting to sell and unless otherwise agreed, the seller is responsible for
    A. existing liens and title insurance.
    B. lis pendens.
    C. existing liens and documentary stamps on the note.
    D. existing liens.

378. When monthly rent paid in advance is prorated, how is the calculated figure entered on the closing statement?
    A. Debit to the seller, credit to the buyer
    B. Debit to the seller
    C. Debit to the buyer, credit to the seller
    D. Credit to the buyer

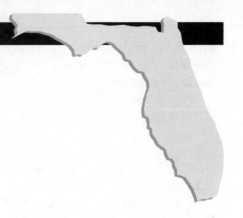

Math Problems

379. What did a new home cost if the state documentary stamp tax on the deed was $546?
    A. $74,500
    B. $78,000
    C. $156,000
    D. $273,000

380. Al Alachua's house was appraised by an FHA appraiser at $142,500. The county property appraiser assigned an assessed value of $117,500, and a homestead exemption has been granted. The total millage rate is 26 mills. Calculate the property taxes.
    A. $2,405
    B. $2,845
    C. $3,055
    D. $3,705

381. Ms. Dake's home has been assessed at $116,000 by the county property appraiser. The property has been granted homestead exemption. The total millage this year is 30 mills. How much is saved by the homestead exemption?
    A. $3,480
    B. $2,730
    C. $1,750
    D. $750

382. A corner lot measures 100' × 125'. Paving costs are $24 per foot. The city has agreed to pay 50 percent of the paving costs. What will be the lot owner's assessment?
    A. $675
    B. $1,250
    C. $1,350
    D. $2,700

383. Your lot is 180' × 225'. The city is assessing all lot owners on your street based on $24 per foot for paving. The city has agreed to pay 30 percent of the paving cost. What will your paving assessment be?
    A. $648
    B. $1,296
    C. $1,512
    D. $3,024

384. A home sold for $108,400. The buyers paid $18,400 down, assumed a recorded mortgage of $72,000, and gave the sellers a new second mortgage in the amount of $18,000. How much will the buyers pay for state taxes resulting from these financial arrangements?
    A. Intangible tax $36; documentary stamp tax $252
    B. Intangible tax $36; documentary stamp tax $315
    C. Intangible tax $144; documentary stamp tax $230.40
    D. Intangible tax $180; documentary stamp tax $63

385. Mr. and Mrs. Stoufer purchased a home for $116,000 and secured a new conventional mortgage with a 30 percent cash down payment. Calculate the intangible taxes due.
  A. $102.20
  B. $162.40
  C. $371.20
  D. $568.40

386. The documentary stamp tax charged for a property is $825.30. Calculate the purchase price.
  A. $57,750
  B. $82,500
  C. $117,900
  D. $195,835

387. The L.M.R. Good Development Corp. purchased 1,600 acres of Florida ranch land from a foreign seller for $5,600,000. Current law requires the buyer to withhold from the seller and pay to the IRS approximately
  A. $560,000.
  B. $840,000.
  C. $1,120,000.
  D. $1,400,000.

388. The N½ of a standard section contains
  A. 80 acres.
  B. 160 acres.
  C. 320 acres.
  D. 640 acres.

389. A multifamily residential investment property is appraised at $235,000. Land value is 20 percent of the total appraised value. Calculate the annual depreciation deduction. (Round to the nearest dollar.)
  A. $6,065
  B. $6,836
  C. $7,581
  D. $8,545

390. Broker Ben paced off a tract by beginning at the extreme northeast corner of a section. He proceeded South zero degrees East 891 feet to a cement monument, thence North 90 degrees West 440 feet to a second marker, thence North zero degrees East 891 feet, thence to the point of beginning. How many acres are contained in the parcel Ben walked around?
  A. 4½
  B. 7¼
  C. 9
  D. 12

391. If a parcel described as the S½ of the SW¼ of Section 21 sold for $4,000 per acre, its sale price was
  A. $160,000.
  B. $280,000.
  C. $320,000.
  D. $640,000.

392. What is the cost per acre of a tract of land that sold for $1,306,800 and is described as follows?

  Beginning at a point on the North side of State Highway 50, exactly 200 feet West of the corner formed by the intersection of the West side of Dillard Street and the North side of State Highway 50; running thence due West 4,000 feet; thence due North 2,000 feet; thence due East 4,000 feet; thence directly to the point of beginning.
  A. $8,712 per acre
  B. $7,116 per acre
  C. $6,246 per acre
  D. $4,356 per acre

393. A lot is 73 feet wide and 120 feet deep. What fraction of an acre is this lot?
  A. ½
  B. ⅓
  C. ¼
  D. ⅕

394. Ms. Jones paid a state intangible tax of $60 on her $55,000 home. What was the mortgage amount and how much was the state documentary stamp tax on the note?
    A. $30,000 mortgage; $105 on the note
    B. $40,000 mortgage; $128 on the note
    C. $40,000 mortgage; $385 on the note
    D. $30,000 mortgage; $96 on the note

395. The sale price on a home is $180,000. The buyer secured a $140,000 loan and paid $3,200 in closing costs and prepaid expenses. What is the loan-to-value ratio? (Round to the nearest whole percentage point.)
    A. 76%
    B. 78%
    C. 79%
    D. 80%

396. The loan-to-value ratio offered by a local financial institution is 75 percent. If a buyer wishes to acquire a property selling for $129,500, she will need to make a down payment of
    A. $1,727.
    B. $5,180.
    C. $25,780.
    D. $32,375.

397. A county has an approved budget for the next year of $12,000,000. Revenue from non-real estate sources is estimated at $750,000. The total assessed valuation of all taxable property in the county is $1,500,000,000 less $50,000,000 in exemptions. What millage rate must be charged to meet the budget?
    A. .008
    B. .009
    C. .010
    D. .100

398. An ARM loan was written for $100,000 at an initial interest rate of 8 percent for 30 years with first-year principal and interest payments of $734 per month. The loan agreement provides for a 15 percent increase in monthly payment amounts at the end of each year during the first three years. If the allowed increases are made, how much will the annual mortgage expense amount to for the third year (rounded down to the nearest cent)?
    A. $13,395.72
    B. $11,648.58
    C. $11,450.40
    D. $10,129.20

399. What is the FHA housing expense ratio for a borrower with monthly housing expenses of $696, total monthly gross income of $2,400, and total monthly obligations of $960?
    A. 29%
    B. 33%
    C. 38%
    D. 40%

400. Ms. Smith purchased a home appraised at $60,000 with closing costs of $2,500. Her loan is for $50,000. If the seller paid a $2,500 discount, how many points were charged by the lender?
    A. 3 points
    B. 4 points
    C. 5 points
    D. 6 points

401. Mr. Vee applied for a 30-year, fixed-rate $105,000 mortgage. The lender will grant the loan if Mr. Vee will pay interest at the rate of 10.5 percent plus three points and a 1 percent loan origination fee. What will the total loan charges be if Mr. Vee decides to take the loan offer?
    A. $525
    B. $1,444
    C. $3,150
    D. $4,200

402. A building was sold for $90,000. The buyer paid 10 percent cash and obtained a loan for the balance. The lending institution charged a 1 percent loan origination fee. The total cash used by the buyer for this purchase was
    A. $9,900.
    B. $9,810.
    C. $9,000.
    D. $810.

403. A 43,560 square-foot lot is to be sub-divided. One-fourth of the lot is made up of a retaining pond, and one-eighth of the lot will be used for a road. How many square feet of usable area are left?
    A. 5,445 sq. ft.
    B. 10,890 sq. ft.
    C. 16,335 sq. ft.
    D. 27,225 sq. ft.

404. The seller wants to net $100,000. If the broker wants to earn 6 percent commission and the seller's closing costs are estimated at $5,000 (not including commission), for what price must the property sell?
    A. $105,000
    B. $111,000
    C. $111,383
    D. $111,702

405. The broker agreed to pay his sales associate 45 percent of the total commission. The property sold for $320,000 and the commission rate was 7 percent. The property was sold "in house." What was the broker's share of the commission?
    A. $22,400
    B. $12,320
    C. $11,200
    D. $10,080

406. A developer purchased five lots each measuring 110′ × 150′. The lots cost $325 per front foot. The developer subdivided the lots into eight lots and then sold them for $28,000 each. How much profit did the developer make on the deal?
    A. 10%
    B. 15%
    C. 20%
    D. 25%

407. If two brokers split the 7 percent commission 50/50 on a property that sold for $98,400, what did each receive?
    A. $3,444
    B. $4,200
    C. $6,888
    D. $8,400

408. Three tracts are 2¾ acres, 3⁵⁄₁₂ acres, and 4⅚ acres in size. Together, they represent
    A. 10 acres.
    B. 10¹⁄₁₂ acres.
    C. 11 acres.
    D. 11½ acres.

409. Monthly mortgage payments of $450 have been paid for 15 years. The original mortgage amount was $45,000. After 15 years 50 percent of the loan has been paid. What is the total amount of interest paid to date?
    A. $6,750
    B. $22,500
    C. $58,500
    D. $60,450

410. A commercial property leases for $200,000 per year. Miscellaneous income derived from the property totals $12,000 per year. The property recently sold for $1,395,000. What is the GIM?
    A. 6.6
    B. 6.8
    C. 7.0
    D. 7.5

411. Some years ago, the Maloneys built their home for $70,000 on a lot that cost them $30,000. If building costs have doubled and lot prices have increased 300 percent, how much has their original investment of $100,000 appreciated?
    A. 130%
    B. 160%
    C. 260%
    D. 500%

412. Mr. Fuqua owns a building that contains five furnished apartments. All are leased for periods varying between two and five years. Over a period of time, Mr. Fuqua found that his gross expenses related to the apartments have invariably averaged about 55 percent of gross income. If one apartment rents for $320 per month, another for $340 per month, and the remaining three for $300 per month each, what are Mr. Fuqua's annual gross and net incomes?
    A. $1,560 gross income; $702 net income
    B. $18,720 gross income; $10,296 net income
    C. $11,520 gross income; $5,184 net income
    D. $18,720 gross income; $8,424 net income

413. If a capitalization rate of 10.5% is used, what is the market value of an investment property assuming a net income of $8,424?
    A. $49,371.43
    B. $80,228.57
    C. $98,057.14
    D. $178,285.71

414. Licensee Anita receives a monthly salary of $700, a 3.5 percent commission on all of her listings that sell, and 2.8 percent commission on all of her property sales. None of the listings she obtained sold last month, but she did receive a total of $8,050 in salary and commissions. What was the value of the properties she sold?
    A. $210,000
    B. $230,000
    C. $262,500
    D. $287,500

415. Mr. and Mrs. Kimbel contract to purchase an $80,000 home and put up earnest money of $2,000. The 7 percent commission is to be paid by the sellers. The Kimbels will get a credit of $325 for the sellers' portion of real estate property taxes. If the Kimbels obtain an 80 percent conventional loan at 13 percent interest with 3 points to be paid by them, how much should they bring to the closing?
    A. $15,595
    B. $15,920
    C. $16,075
    D. $16,245

416. If a home that sold for $80,000 had sold for its asking price of $85,000 and the sale commission was 7 percent, how much additional commission would have been paid in excess of the actual commission?
    A. $5,600
    B. $3,500
    C. $560
    D. $350

417. A developer sold a lot for $36,000. This represented a loss of 10 percent. What was the cost of the lot?
    A. $32,400
    B. $39,600
    C. $40,000
    D. $42,800

418. A real estate office sold 180 homes this year. This was 20 percent more sales than last year. How many homes did the office sell last year?
    A. 140
    B. 144
    C. 150
    D. 154

419. If a $5,600 sale commission is split 60/40 between Broker Bob (the listing broker) and Broker Ben (the selling broker), and each broker splits his share of the commission 50/50 with respective listing and selling sales associates, how much more will Broker Bob earn from the sale than Broker Ben?
    A. $3,360
    B. $2,240
    C. $1,120
    D. $560

420. A buyer has made an earnest money deposit of $10,150 on a house selling for $94,500. A local lender has agreed to lend 85 percent of the selling price at 10½ percent interest for 30 years. If the buyer's closing costs amount to $1,575, how much more cash must the buyer produce at closing?
    A. $5,600
    B. $7,175
    C. $12,889
    D. $14,175

421. Your home is assessed at $190,000. You have qualified for the homestead tax exemption. The millage rate is 28.6 mills. How much do you owe in property taxes?
    A. $576.92
    B. $664.34
    C. $4,719
    D. $5,434

422. Mr. Ross bought half of a quarter-section of land for $160,000. He plans to develop the property into a residential subdivision. Local zoning will require all lots in the community to be not less than 100′ × 120′ in size, and the engineering firm employed by Mr. Ross has informed him that approximately 484,800 square feet of the tract will be required for parks, streets, storm sewers, and other development purposes. The engineering firm has also estimated that total development costs and associated expenses will amount to five times the raw land costs. Mr. Ross wants to make a profit of 10 percent based on total costs. How much must Mr. Ross average per lot to accomplish his profit objective?
    A. $3,200
    B. $3,641
    C. $3,840
    D. $4,224

423. Your principal asks for help with a mortgage problem. His mortgage balance is $20,000 on June 1, and the monthly payments for principal and interest are $161, payable on the last day of each month. What will your principal's mortgage balance be on September 1 if the interest rate is 9 percent?
    A. $19,955.50
    B. $19,966.75
    C. $19,977.92
    D. $19,989

424. Mr. and Mrs. D. Storm have signed a contract to purchase a home for $96,800. A lender has agreed to lend them 75 percent of the purchase price at 10 percent interest with a monthly payment of $849.50 for principal and interest over a period of 30 years. How much of the second month's mortgage payment will be allocated to the payment of the mortgage principal?
    A. $602.96
    B. $246.54
    C. $244.50
    D. $43.19

425. Ms. Cortez, who owns an eight-unit apartment building, spent $2,400 on improvements. How much should the monthly rent on each apartment be increased if this expense is to be recovered by the owner in just one year?
    A. $25
    B. $50
    C. $200
    D. $300

426. A closing date of April 30 is set, with prorations (using the 365-day method) effective at midnight on the day of closing. The property taxes are estimated to be $1,095. On the seller's closing statement would appear a
    A. debit for $360.
    B. debit for $735.
    C. credit for $360.
    D. credit for $735.

427. Mrs. Osceola is selling her ten-unit apartment building. Each apartment rents for $465 per month. The transaction will be closed on June 15 after the June rents have been collected. All prorations become effective at midnight prior to the date of closing. What portion of the June rents will be credited to the buyers? (Use the 30-day month method to prorate.)
    A. $2,170
    B. $2,325
    C. $2,480
    D. $2,550

428. A single-family residence is available for listing. A comparable home recently sold for $140,000. Compared with the subject property, the comparable has a superior location ($12,500), is smaller ($8,000), and is three years older ($5,000). What is the subject property's value based solely on the information given?
    A. $139,500
    B. $140,500
    C. $144,500
    D. $157,500

429. A house cost $89,500 to build. When new, the building was estimated to have a 50-year useful life. Using straight-line depreciation, what is the accumulated depreciation after four years?
    A. $1,790
    B. $7,160
    C. $8,200
    D. $8,741

430. The scheduled date for closing a duplex is June 15. Rent collected on the first of each month is $600 per unit. Day of closing belongs to the buyer. How will the proration be entered on the closing statement?
    A. $320 debit seller; $320 credit buyer
    B. $600 debit seller; $600 credit buyer
    C. $640 debit seller; $640 credit buyer
    D. $640 debit seller; $560 credit buyer

431. Based on the following, what is the estimated market value of a lot 100′ × 110′ in the Cove Hill Subdivision?
    Comparable Sales Data
    Sale 1: lot 100′ × 120′ adjacent to subject lot, sold one week ago for $36,720
    Sale 2: lot 100′ × 100′ located four blocks away, sold three months ago for $29,800
    Sale 3: lot 110′ × 110′ located on same street, four lots removed, sold two weeks ago for $36,800
    Sale 4: lot 90′ × 110′ across the street, sold one month ago for $29,700
    A. $30,130
    B. $32,880
    C. $33,220
    D. $35,400

432. An appraiser has been asked to appraise a building lot in a quality subdivision. His research efforts reveal that five lots have been sold in the past four months in the same neighborhood as the subject lot.

Sale No.	Lot Size	Price	Price per sq. ft.
1.	100' × 130'	$5,600	_____
2.	104' × 132'	$5,800	_____
3.	102' × 130'	$5,600	_____
4.	102' × 130'	$5,600	_____
5.	100' × 132'	$5,400	_____

If the lot being appraised is 110' × 130', what would the total market value be if based on the average price per square foot of the five previous sales, with no adjustments for time or location?
   A. $5,600
   B. $6,023
   C. $24,000
   D. $32,200

433. The Brantleys are asking $72,000 for their 1,800-square-foot home. The asking price per square foot is
   A. $25.
   B. $36.
   C. $40.
   D. $46.

434. A rental house produces $375 per month in gross income. The house costs $48,750. What is the monthly gross rent multiplier?
   A. .00769
   B. 10.83
   C. 130
   D. 375

435. Dr. Marion owns an 1,800-square-foot rental house that she rents for $.24 per square foot per month. If the GRM (monthly) for that property is 120, what is the market value of the property?
   A. $27,777
   B. $43,260
   C. $49,630
   D. $51,840

436. A licensee has been asked to determine the current market value of a six-year-old building with a reproduction cost of $480,000. When new, the economic life of the structure was estimated to be 40 years. If the site value is known to be $100,000, what is the current market value of the entire property?
   A. $493,000
   B. $508,000
   C. $568,000
   D. $580,000

437. A sales associate measured the exterior of a home and found it to be 40' × 60'. Disregarding other factors, what is the cost per square foot if the house sold for $57,000?
   A. $20
   B. $22.50
   C. $23.75
   D. $25.25

438. If a building has an estimated economic life of 20 years, the percentage loss of economic life per year is
   A. 2%.
   B. 4%.
   C. 5%.
   D. 20%.

439. An open office that measures 20' × 40' rents for $840 per month. The annual rent per square foot is
   A. $9.52.
   B. $10.50.
   C. $11.43.
   D. $12.60.

440. Henrietta leases the 12 apartments in Crow Hollow for a total net monthly rental of $4,800. If this figure represents a 12 percent annual return on her investment, what was the original cost of this property?
   A. $240,000
   B. $480,000
   C. $576,000
   D. $720,000

441. An apartment building has eight units, each of which rents for $475 per month. A vacancy rate of 10 percent persists year after year. Total operating expenses average $1,875 per month. If a capitalization rate of 12 percent is found to be appropriate, what is the market value of the property?
   A. $154,500
   B. $192,500
   C. $342,000
   D. $380,000

442. An office building produces an effective gross income of $96,400. Building operating expenses total $36,600, and the monthly mortgage payment is $2,240. What is the building's net operating income?
   A. $32,920
   B. $57,560
   C. $59,800
   D. $69,520

443. A contractor builds a two-story warehouse measuring 120 feet × 150 feet. Ten percent of the space is allocated to elevators and landings. The contractor plans to store bins of construction material that each measure 10 feet × 12 feet. How many bins will the building accommodate?
   A. 120
   B. 220
   C. 250
   D. 270

444. A building is valued at $185,000 when NOI is capitalized at a rate of 8 percent. NOI is 40 percent of effective gross income. Calculate the effective gross income.
   A. $14,800
   B. $24,667
   C. $32,000
   D. $37,000

445. Examination of documentary stamps on recently recorded deeds provided the following sale prices. Data obtained from property managers produced the income figures. Use the information given to determine the correct overall capitalization rate for the comparable apartment properties. (Round all decimals to three numbers before final rounding to two places.)

Comparable Properties	NOI	Sale Prices
Apt. Project 1	$39,400	$345,000
Apt. Project 2	$45,680	$464,000
Apt. Project 3	$36,800	$386,000
Apt. Project 4	$43,790	$424,000

   A. 9.77%
   B. 10.25%
   C. 10.50%
   D. 11.00%

446. What is the loan-to-value ratio for a loan amount of $80,000, a property price or value of $100,000, and a net operating income of $18,400?
   A. 61.6%
   B. 80.0%
   C. 98.4%
   D. 125.0%

447. Nan and Jim paid a cash down payment of $55,000 and applied for a $145,000 loan. What is the LTV ratio?
   A. 27.5%
   B. 37.9%
   C. 72.5%
   D. 80.0%

448. What is the net operating income of a building if the operating expenses are $8,350, the effective gross income is $26,750, and the mortgage payment is $11,100?
   A. $18,400
   B. $11,100
   C. $7,300
   D. $6,900

449. What is the net operating income for a property that produces a potential gross income of $26,750, has fixed operating expenses of $8,350, has a mortgage payment of $11,100, and has a reserve for replacements of $450?
    A. $6,850
    B. $17,950
    C. $18,400
    D. $19,900

450. Which property has the highest assessed value?
    A. Market value $49,500; assessed at 100% of value
    B. Market value $66,900; assessed at 75% of value
    C. Market value $81,400; assessed at 60% of value
    D. Market value $119,600; assessed at 40% of value

451. Mr. Webster sold his home and agreed to a June 16, 20XX, closing date. The last day for which interest was paid on the $105,500 remaining balance of the 8 percent, 30-year conventional mortgage was April 30, 20XX. If the total monthly mortgage payment was $774.14, what amount of prorated mortgage interest would appear on the closing statement as a debit to Mr. Webster? (Use the 365-day method of proration and charge the day of closing to the buyer.)
    A. $1,054.76
    B. $1,063.52
    C. $1,086.64
    D. $1,406.66

452. The Sloans have a combined gross monthly income of $2,350. They have applied for an FHA loan that will require monthly housing expenses of $658. They have other credit obligations of $282 per month. Will they meet the established FHA standards/ratios for housing expenses and total obligations?
    A. No, their housing expense ratio exceeds FHA maximums.
    B. They meet the housing expense ratio standard but not the total obligations ratio standard.
    C. No, they do not meet either standard/ratio.
    D. Yes, they meet the FHA standards for both ratios.

453. A ten-year-old structure has an effective age of eight years. Total economic life is estimated to be 55 years. Reproduction cost new of the structure is $300,000. What is the accrued depreciation for this structure?
    A. $22,450
    B. $35,890
    C. $43,500
    D. $45,500

454. An investor owns a business property with a value of $1,500,000. The market capitalization rate is 8 percent. Operating expenses total 30 percent of potential gross income. The investment is leveraged with a $1,250,000 mortgage. What is the investor's equity?
    A. $100,000
    B. $120,000
    C. $250,000
    D. $450,000

455. ONE SECTION

640 acres

SEC 7, T23S, R27E

Determine proper description *and* acreage for the *numbered areas*.

<u>Description</u>   <u>Acreage</u>

1 = _____   _____

2 = _____   _____

3 = _____   _____

4 = _____   _____

5 = _____   _____

6 = _____   _____

7 = _____   _____

Provide an *alternative* way of describing.

3 = _____   _____

5 = _____   _____

Determine proper description *and* acreage for the *lettered areas*.

<u>Description</u>   <u>Acreage</u>

A = _____   _____

B = _____   _____

C = _____   _____

D = _____   _____

F = _____   _____

G = _____   _____

H = _____   _____

I = _____   _____

J = _____   _____

The acreage for SE¼ of NE¼ and N½ of NE¼ of SE¼ is _____ acres.

Broker Investment Problems

Questions 456 through 470 test mastery of broker math in the *Florida Real Estate Broker's Guide*.

Use the following information to answer problems 456 through 466:

An investor purchased an apartment building in January for $350,000. The contract specified that $300,000 of the purchase price was allocated to the building and $50,000 of the purchase price was for the land. The investor made a down payment of $50,000 and financed the remainder of the purchase with a loan. The mortgage is for 30 years at 7 percent interest with a monthly payment of $1,995.91. The apartment building consists of 12 apartments that each rent for $650 per month. Vacancy and collection losses are estimated at 5 percent. Operating expenses are 30 percent of the effective gross income and include reserves of $10,000.

456. What is the potential gross income for this investment property?
   A. $82,950
   B. $85,700
   C. $93,600
   D. $95,800

457. What is the effective gross income for this investment property?
   A. $78,920
   B. $88,920
   C. $90,750
   D. $93,600

458. What is the dollar amount of the total operating expenses?
   A. $15,875
   B. $16,676
   C. $26,676
   D. $28,080

459. What is the net operating income for this property?
   A. $50,925
   B. $52,244
   C. $60,840
   D. $62,244

460. What is the annual debit service for this property? (Round to nearest dollar.)
   A. $23,951
   B. $23,979
   C. $24,276
   D. $24,500

461. What is the debt service coverage ratio for this property? (Round to two decimal places.)
   A. 1.97
   B. 2.20
   C. 2.55
   D. 2.60

462. What is the before-tax cash flow for this property?
     A. $23,851
     B. $28,935
     C. $36,340
     D. $38,293

463. What is the operating expense ratio for this property?
     A. .28
     B. .29
     C. .30
     D. .32

464. What is the equity dividend rate for this property expressed as a percent?
     A. 24.9%
     B. 35.5%
     C. 48.7%
     D. 76.6%

465. What is the annual IRS depreciation allowance for this property? (Round to nearest dollar.)
     A. $9,677
     B. $10,909
     C. $11,290
     D. $12,727

466. What is the cash break-even ratio expressed as a percent for this property?
     A. 43.4%
     B. 44.9%
     C. 45.7%
     D. 54.1%

467. Sara's home is appraised for $345,000. Her existing first mortgage has a balance of $181,435. She applies for a home equity mortgage loan and the lender agrees to make a loan with a maximum loan-to-value rate overall of 80 percent, including both mortgages. How much more can she borrow?
     A. $94,565
     B. $98,794
     C. $115,435
     D. $118,565

468. Mike buys an office building on a 2-acre site for $995,000. Acquisition costs are: appraisal $4,500, survey $900, title insurance $3,400. The land value represents 20 percent. What is the depreciable basis of Mike's building?
     A. $786,540
     B. $796,000
     C. $800,945
     D. $803,040

469. An office property is purchased for $1,675,000. The building represents 80 percent of the value. What is the typical annual depreciation deduction for this building? (Round to nearest dollar.)
     A. $22,307
     B. $27,454
     C. $34,359
     D. $48,727

470. A retail business rents space in the regional mall under a percentage lease. The store pays a base rent of $3,250 and 5 percent of their monthly sales based on an overage clause. Above what annual sales level does the store pay rent in excess of the base rent?
     A. $65,000
     B. $197,500
     C. $741,000
     D. $780,000

100 Multiple-Choice Question Exam 1

Instructions. Before taking the state license examination prepare by taking the Practice Exams in this book. Doing so will allow you to test your knowledge, to practice your exam-taking strategies, and to reduce your anxiety. Take the practice exam under timed conditions and then review both your right and your wrong answers. This exam is designed as a representative test: Questions are from all major subject areas; they are of the type and in the form used on state exams for sales associates and brokers; and the degree of difficulty is on a par with, or is slightly more difficult than, the typical licensing exam. Thus, successful completion (75 or higher) under simulated exam conditions (three uninterrupted hours using no reference material) should indicate your readiness for the state exam. Darken your answers in the spaces on the Answer Sheet provided on page 197. The correct answers (with textbook chapter number references) for this exam are in the Practice Exam 1 Answer Key at the end of this book, complete with explanations of the correct answers.

1. In Florida, the maximum commission a broker may charge for services rendered is
   A. 7%.
   B. 10%.
   C. any rate agreed on by the broker and the buyer or seller.
   D. set by FREC rules and state usury laws, whichever is less in the transaction involved.

2. Terry is a real estate licensee who is representing a tenant in a commercial rental. Terry wants to share part of her commission with the tenant. Which statement is true regarding this situation?
   A. A licensee may share a commission with a party to a real estate sale and purchase agreement, but not with parties to lease agreements.
   B. Real estate licensees may share commissions with parties to residential lease agreements, but not with parties to commercial lease agreements.
   C. Real estate licensees may share their commission with a party to a lease agreement, provided it is disclosed to all interested parties.
   D. It is illegal for a real estate licensee to share commissions with a party to any real estate transaction unless the party is a real estate licensee.

3. When the value of a business's tangible assets is subtracted from its purchase price, the amount remaining represents the
   A. price paid for goodwill.
   B. accounts payable to the business.
   C. long-term liabilities of the business.
   D. sales tax collected but not yet remitted to the state.

4. Which type of estate in real property is held for a definite number of years?
   A. Fee simple estate
   B. Life estate
   C. Estate for years
   D. Estate by the entireties

5. In the government survey system of legal descriptions, a "check" is subdivided into "townships" that measure
   A. 6 square miles.
   B. 6 miles square.
   C. 640 acres.
   D. 640 square miles.

6. Scott is a buyer's agent. Scott's broker charges a retainer fee in advance of closing for representing the buyer. Which statement is true regarding this arrangement?
   A. The retainer fee is an advanced fee and therefore Scott's broker must comply with advanced fee accounting procedures.
   B. The retainer fee is considered to be a kickback and is illegal.
   C. The retainer fee must be placed into the broker's regular escrow account until closing.
   D. The retainer fee may be deposited into the broker's operating account because it is not a commission.

7. In Dade County, the building, housing, and health codes require landlords to maintain rented premises in good repair, capable of resisting normal forces and loads, and to provide heat during cold weather, running water, and hot water. Ms. Trufare leased a two-bedroom, single-family home from Mr. Si Lagree in June for a one-year period. In November, Ms. Trufare told Mr. Lagree that she had no source of heat and requested he install a heater. Mr. Lagree said he would install the heater, but it would result in a rental increase of $10 per month. Which is most correct?
   A. Mr. Lagree is wrong because the house should be provided with heat to comply with county ordinances, and the rent was established by lease.
   B. Mr. Lagree is entitled to increase the rent because the single-family home is exempt from the Florida Landlord and Tenant Act.
   C. Ms. Trufare is not entitled to any free additions or improvements because she should have inspected the premises prior to signing the lease.
   D. Both B and C are correct.

8. Listing agreements do NOT have which requirement?
   A. Written form
   B. Definite expiration date
   C. Description of the property
   D. Fee or commission charged

9. The "highest and best use as though vacant" is considered to be the use that will result in the greatest amount and longest duration of net income that accrues to the
   A. improvements on a property.
   B. land itself.
   C. lessee of commercial property.
   D. lessor of commercial property.

10. Mark Meany has listed his property with Happy Customers Realty. Mark has informed the sales associate that he will not sell his condominium to college students. Which statement is true regarding this situation?
    A. Mark can refuse to sell to college students, but the real estate licensee cannot refuse college students.
    B. Mark and his sales associate can be fined for violating the Fair Housing Act.
    C. Although this may be a poor business decision, it is not a violation of the Fair Housing Act.
    D. The licensee should withdraw from the listing and report Mr. Meany to the FREC.

11. Teresa is a receptionist at Best Price Realty. A buyer comes into the office and hands Teresa an earnest money deposit on Wednesday (no legal holidays involved). Which statement applies to this situation?
    A. The broker must deposit the check into the escrow account no later than the end of business on Monday of the following week.
    B. Teresa could be charged with providing real estate services without a license.
    C. The broker must deposit the check into the escrow account by the end of business on Friday.
    D. Only a licensed real estate sales associate is allowed to accept an earnest money deposit on behalf of the broker.

12. A broker's principal is away on vacation. The broker receives an offer of $67,000 for the principal's property. Before the principal returns, the broker receives a second offer of $64,000. The broker should
    A. refuse the lower offer.
    B. submit only the best offer when the principal returns.
    C. hold the lower offer until the first offer is accepted or rejected.
    D. submit both offers to the principal.

13. Developer Bob wishes to sell several parcels of vacant land that are encumbered by a blanket mortgage. Broker Sal lists the parcels for $25,000 per lot. A buyer enters into a contract to purchase one of the lots for $24,000. After contacting the lender, Sal learns that in order to release the lot from the blanket mortgage, the lender requires a payment of $30,000. Which statement applies?
    A. Developer Bob must pay the $6,000 difference to the lender prior to closing.
    B. The buyer is liable to the lender for the $6,000 difference because it was an existing lien.
    C. The broker can be charged with fraudulent and dishonest dealing by trick, scheme, or device.
    D. Developer Bob can be charged with conversion.

14. Bob White was a successful licensed real estate broker. He and his wife jointly owned Quail Haven Realty, Inc., a two-person corporation for profit registered with the FREC as an active real estate brokerage firm. Mrs. White was registered as an officer of the corporation but had never qualified to be licensed. Mr. and Mrs. White mutually agreed to a divorce, and the court awarded Mrs. White the profitable real estate brokerage corporation as part of the property settlement. Mrs. White retained her married name, and Bob White organized a new brokerage firm. Which is correct?
    A. As a result of the court's action, Mrs. White may continue operating the brokerage firm if she chooses.
    B. Mrs. White is entitled to the same rights and privileges as full owner of the firm as existed before the divorce.
    C. Mrs. White need only request that her status be changed to active real estate broker.
    D. It is illegal for Mrs. White to continue operating the firm.

15. Mr. Will Taykit called the office of a real estate broker and expressed a desire to see "the property you advertised at 1066 Hickham." The broker made an appointment to show the property to Mr. Taykit that same afternoon. When they meet, the broker must give Mr. Taykit the
    A. single agent notice.
    B. seller's single agent notice.
    C. no brokerage relationship notice.
    D. transaction broker notice.

16. A sales associate has earned a commission of $2,400. The broker for whom she works pays her $2,000 and uses the remainder of her commission to pay office expenses with a promise to pay the remaining $400 when he can afford to do so. The broker is guilty of
    A. nothing illegal.
    B. grand larceny.
    C. culpable negligence.
    D. conversion.

17. The owner of an apartment complex plans to be away for a full year. He arranges for a tenant to take care of his apartment house and to act as his representative during the year's absence. The tenant is to be given a free apartment plus $150 per week for this service. Which is most correct?
    A. The owner has violated Chapter 475, F.S.
    B. The tenant has violated Chapter 475, F.S.
    C. The tenant can perform all the functions the owner would if present.
    D. The tenant can use only legally approved lease forms during the owner's absence.

18. The law that requires at the time of loan application (or within three business days) that the lender provide the borrower with a good-faith estimate of settlement costs is the
    A. Truth-in-Lending Act.
    B. Florida Uniform Land Sales Practices Act.
    C. Florida "Little FTC Act."
    D. Real Estate Settlement Procedures Act.

19. Mr. Tenant's lease expired November 30. He continued to occupy the premises and to mail his monthly rent payment to the landlord on the same schedule he had observed prior to the expiration of the formal lease. Mr. Tenant is a
    A. lessor.
    B. life tenant.
    C. tenant at will.
    D. tenant at sufferance.

20. A broker receives conflicting demands from the buyer and seller. The broker properly notifies the FREC and requests an escrow disbursement order (EDO). However, before the order is issued, the buyer and seller sue one another. What must the broker do in this situation?
    A. The broker must notify the FREC of the situation within ten business days.
    B. The broker need not do anything because the lawsuits are a separate action.
    C. The broker must follow the instructions of the EDO when received because it was timely filed.
    D. The broker must notify the FREC of the lawsuit within 15 business days.

21. The purpose of the Save Our Home amendment is to
    A. provide a procedure for retaining ownership of one's home after foreclosure proceedings are initiated.
    B. limit the increase in the amount of property taxes on homestead property.
    C. provide low cost mortgage financing for first time homebuyers.
    D. reduce the amount of income taxes owed by homeowners.

22. Mr. Freno lived next door to a real estate broker. Mr. Freno referred his sister to the broker next door, and she purchased a home costing $120,000. To show his appreciation, the broker may
    A. take Mr. Freno and his wife out to dinner.
    B. give Mr. Freno a bottle of his favorite wine.
    C. send Mrs. Freno a small gift.
    D. express his thanks to Mr. Freno.

23. Which entity is a HUD agency?
    A. DIF
    B. OTS
    C. Ginnie Mae
    D. Fannie Mae

24. Broker Nocount listed a commercial lot belonging to Mr. Favor for $48,000. Later, Nocount learned that a firm that owned the building adjoining Favor's lot was going to need the lot for expansion and would be willing to pay up to $62,000 for the lot. Broker Nocount told Mr. Favor that he wanted to terminate his brokerage relationship and buy the lot himself for $46,000 cash. Mr. Favor agreed to the offer and sold the lot to Broker Nocount, who then sold the lot to the neighboring firm. This is an example of
    A. a legitimate business transaction.
    B. conversion.
    C. culpable negligence.
    D. concealment.

25. Mrs. Allday, a widow and a veteran with 25 percent disability due to service-connected injuries, has resided in Florida since 1971. Mrs. Allday is entitled to a maximum property tax exemption on her homesteaded property of
    A. $5,500.
    B. $25,500.
    C. $26,000.
    D. $30,500.

26. Tom has been a licensed real estate sales associate for 26 years. His license expires every even year on the 31st of March. On March 15, 20XX, Tom completed his renewal card and wrote a check for his renewal fee. Tom purchased a continuing education correspondence course and planned to complete the course on the last weekend of the month. On March 24 Tom received a call that his father had suffered a heart attack. Tom flew immediately to Indiana to be with his father. Tom put his license renewal in the mail before leaving for the airport because he did not want to be charged a late fee. Tom's father passed away so Tom remained in Indiana until late April to settle his father's affairs. Tom intended to complete his education course when he returned to Florida. On April 28 Tom received a letter informing him that he is being audited for compliance with Rule 61J2-3.009. What action will the Commission likely take when the audit reveals that Tom has not completed his continuing education?
    A. The Commission will likely grant Tom a six-month extension under the hardship rule.
    B. The usual action of the Commission under such circumstances is to impose an administrative fine and require Tom to complete his education requirement.
    C. Tom will have to take 21 hours of continuing education and pay a late fee.
    D. The usual action of the Commission in situations such as this is suspension or revocation of the real estate license.

27. DBPR auditors conducted a routine check of Broker Smith's escrow accounts. Office records revealed that Broker Smith had made 22 sales during the time period checked and that only two of the sales had closed with appropriate disbursements totaling $9,000. Binder deposit receipts showed Broker Smith had collected an overall total of $88,000 in binder deposits. Total commissions earned by all 22 sales amounted to $58,500. Smith's escrow balance at the time of the audit was $20,400. Which statement is most correct?
    A. Broker Smith's license can be suspended or revoked due to the condition of his escrow account.
    B. Broker Smith has not violated Chapter 475, F.S., because he can account for every penny of binder deposits.
    C. The DBPR has violated Broker Smith's rights without valid justification or authority.
    D. Broker Smith has shown that his escrow account records are maintained adequately.

28. The clause in a mortgage that ensures that the mortgage cannot be foreclosed so long as all payments are current and other conditions are fulfilled is the
    A. redemption clause.
    B. defeasance clause.
    C. escalation clause.
    D. release clause.

29. When the Commission decides that a real estate licensee's activities may have been grounds for suspension or revocation, the licensee is informed by the use of a
    A. notice and a copy of the complaint.
    B. writ of certiorari.
    C. notice of noncompliance.
    D. writ of injunction.

30. Jim is unlicensed and lives in Chicago. Jim referred a prospective buyer to Broker Donna in Tallahassee, Florida. Broker Donna reimbursed Jim for his out-of-pocket expenses associated with making the referral. Which statement applies to this situation?
    A. This is legal because the expenses were actually incurred.
    B. Jim can accept the expense money as long as he does not come to Florida.
    C. The expense money can be considered a referral fee and therefore must be disclosed to the prospective buyer before Jim can accept the money.
    D. Both Jim and Broker Donna have violated Chapter 475 because it is illegal to pay an unlicensed person for performing real estate services.

31. Sales associate Dirk is employed by Broker Jones. Dirk sold a house owned by Broker Jones's customer, and the transaction was closed on May 20. On October 10 of the same year, Dirk sued the customer for his commission, which amounted to $4,100. Which statement is FALSE?
    A. Dirk may be penalized by suspension.
    B. Dirk may be penalized by fine.
    C. Dirk may be penalized by probation.
    D. Dirk did nothing wrong because he earned the commission.

32. Aveda Realty is the exclusive representative of the developer of Blues Creek subdivision. Aveda sales staff will temporarily work out of a mobile home that the developer has placed in the subdivision until the model home is completed. Transactions will be closed at the main office. Does Aveda Realty need to register the mobile home as a branch office?
    A. License law prohibits the use of mobile homes as temporary shelters.
    B. The broker must make the mobile home stationary before registering it as a branch office.
    C. The broker must register the branch office and pay a fee before assigning any sales staff there.
    D. The mobile home is a temporary shelter and therefore is not considered to be a branch office.

33. Broker Tate lists a tract that has three mortgages amounting to approximately 90 percent of total market value. In order to convey title properly to a buyer, which statement is most correct?
    A. All subordinate mortgages must be either paid off or merged with the first mortgage.
    B. The property must be refinanced.
    C. A deed must be voluntarily delivered.
    D. All mortgages must be paid off.

34. Sales associate Dean is employed by Developer Bob to sell new homes in Capri subdivision. The developer is also building in Winder and Mile Trail subdivisions, which are organized as affiliated companies. Bob wants to have Dean sell homes in the other subdivisions because Capri recently was sold out. Which statement applies?
    A. Dean must work out of Winder or Mile Trail but not both because sales associates must be registered with a single office.
    B. Dean may request and be issued a group license so that he can work in any of the developer's subdivisions.
    C. Developer Bob must contact the FREC and request a multiple license.
    D. The sales offices of the subdivisions are considered temporary shelters. Therefore, Dean doesn't need to do anything in order to work for the various affiliated entities.

35. Broker Dudley Doright received an offer and an earnest money deposit on Thursday, July 10, at 9:30 AM. The owner of the property will not be in town until Wednesday, July 16, to consider the offer. Doright's next normal banking day will be Monday, July 14; however, he has a large safe built into the wall of his office. FREC rules require Broker Doright to
    A. hold the earnest money deposit in his safe until his principal can accept or reject the offer.
    B. hold the earnest money deposit in his safe until his banking day on Monday, July 14.
    C. deposit the earnest money in his escrow account by the close of business on Tuesday, July 15.
    D. deposit the earnest money in his escrow account by the close of business on Friday, July 11.

36. Buyer Brown entered into a purchase and sale agreement with Seller Sam to buy Sam's condominium. Two days later, Brown canceled the contract and requested that the broker return his earnest money deposit. Which statement applies to this situation?
    A. The broker may return the earnest money deposit because it is within the buyer's three-day rescission period.
    B. The broker must get a release of the earnest money deposit from both the buyer and the seller before releasing the funds. Otherwise, the broker must notify the FREC of conflicting demands.
    C. This is a breach of contract, and the seller may be entitled to the earnest money deposit as liquidated damages.
    D. The broker must request the FREC to issue an escrow disbursement order.

37. A Georgia broker has a prospective buyer who wants to buy some land in Florida for the purpose of building between 100 and 150 luxury condominiums. The Georgia broker contacts a Florida broker to help locate some suitable tracts for the prospect to consider. Together, they work with the buyer and show him five separate tracts. Their cooperation pays off when the buyer purchases a 60-acre tract for $558,000 and they evenly divide a 10 percent commission. Which is most correct?
    A. If the Georgia broker's license is current, this is a legal arrangement.
    B. Only the Florida broker is legally entitled to a commission.
    C. Both brokers are legally entitled to a commission.
    D. Both brokers have violated Chapter 475, F.S.

38. For a limited partnership to register as a real estate broker with the FREC, the limited partnership must
    A. file a copy of the partnership agreement with the FREC.
    B. have all general partners who will deal with the public licensed as active brokers.
    C. register all unlicensed limited partners.
    D. register all sales associates who are general partners.

39. A broker deposited a $5,000 earnest money deposit in his escrow account in a timely manner. A sale contract was signed by the buyer and seller. Later, the two parties disagree about which equipment and furnishings are to be conveyed with the property. Each accuses the other of breaching the contract, and each demands that the broker turn over the deposit to him. The broker worked almost two months to sell the property, and he feels that he has earned his commission of $4,000 and therefore wants to be paid. The broker should notify the FREC and
    A. request the FREC to issue an escrow disbursement order.
    B. seek arbitration of the dispute or instruct his attorney to file a request for a writ of certiorari.
    C. seek arbitration of the dispute, or file a bill of interpleader, or recommend that the two disagreeing parties litigate the matter.
    D. request the FREC to issue an escrow disbursement order, seek arbitration of the dispute, seek adjudication by a court of law, or seek mediation of the dispute.

40. Which type of deed will provide the grantor the best assurance of no future liability?
    A. Warranty deed
    B. Special warranty deed
    C. Quitclaim deed
    D. Fiduciary's deed

41. In an effort to obtain more listings and subsequent commissions, a licensee urges people in an older neighborhood to sell because "a group belonging to a religious cult has recently moved in and property values will fall." This is an example of the illegal and unethical practice called
    A. redlining.
    B. blockbusting.
    C. reverse discrimination.
    D. steering.

42. The mandatory distance between lot lines and building improvements is known as
    A. zoning.
    B. variance.
    C. frontage.
    D. setback.

43. If the interest paid for borrowed funds is greater than the overall rate of return to an investor, this is an example of
    A. positive leverage.
    B. negative leverage.
    C. increased yield.
    D. increased cash reversion.

44. Mr. Sims and Mr. Frey are primarily owner-developers, although both are active real estate broker licensees. Together they hire Mr. Mica, an accountant and CPA who is not a licensee, to supervise the overall development of a large tract of land they are jointly developing into a high-quality, recreation-oriented subdivision. Mr. Mica is not experienced in selling real estate; however, he is an astute businessman and manages to exceed the first 18 months' sales projections in just nine months. As a reward for his achievement, Sims and Frey agree to pay Mr. Mica a bonus of 15 percent of the amount in excess of the first 12 months' sales projections. Which is most correct?
    A. This is a perfectly legal arrangement.
    B. All three men have violated Chapter 475, F.S.
    C. Mr. Sims and Mr. Frey have violated Chapter 475, F.S.
    D. Mr. Mica has violated Chapter 475, F.S.

45. The Florida Real Estate Time-Share Act applies to time-share plans consisting of
    A. more than seven time-share periods over at least a three-year period.
    B. more than three time-share periods over at least a seven-year period.
    C. more than seven time-share periods with no minimum span of time.
    D. two or more time-share periods with no minimum span of time.

46. Management Services Inc. represents a residential landlord who has obtained a writ of possession to evict a tenant. The writ has been executed by the sheriff. The tenant's belongings are inside the apartment. Which statement is true regarding this situation?
    A. The landlord, or Management Services Inc. as agent, may remove the personal belongings and place them on the property line.
    B. Only the sheriff may remove the tenant's personal belongings.
    C. The property manager must notify the tenant by certified mail of the intent to remove the personal property.
    D. The landlord or property manager must get an executed judgment lien on the personal property before taking possession of it.

47. Widow Jane is always looking for good, safe investments for her money. Jane decides to bid on a cute bungalow home at a foreclosure sale. Jane feels that the fair market value of the home is approximately $84,000. There is a first mortgage lien of $68,000 held by the lender who has initiated the foreclosure action. The property is homesteaded by the current owner. Property taxes are two years in arrears. Which statement applies?
    A. Widow Jane's opening bid should be high enough to cover the existing first mortgage so that the mortgage lien can be satisfied from the sale proceeds.
    B. Widow Jane will be responsible for the prior property tax liens.
    C. The mortgage lien and back taxes will not survive a foreclosure sale.
    D. Because this is homesteaded property, the home is protected from foreclosure.

48. Which statement(s) describes a purchase-money mortgage?
    A. It is alternative financing between buyer and seller that usually excludes a third party.
    B. It enables a buyer to purchase with less equity funds than required by a financial institution.
    C. It is given by the buyer to the seller for all or part of the purchase price of the property.
    D. All of the statements describe purchase-money mortgages.

49. If licensees are not state-certified appraisers, they may still evaluate real property for the purpose of obtaining a listing. They must, however, refer to the value determined as a(n)
    A. estimate of value.
    B. listing analysis.
    C. appraised value.
    D. comparative market analysis (CMA).

50. A buyer and seller executed a sale and purchase agreement. Buyer and seller have a dispute over the earnest money deposit. The buyer has agreed to arbitrate the matter. However, the seller will not agree. Can the broker proceed to have the dispute resolved by arbitration?
    A. Yes, the broker can choose any one of several methods to resolve an escrow dispute, provided the Commission is notified in a timely manner.
    B. No, the broker is required to first request an escrow disbursement order.
    C. Yes, the earnest money deposit was pledged by the buyer; therefore, the buyer may choose arbitration to resolve the dispute.
    D. No, the seller would also have to agree to arbitration.

51. To be enforceable in court, a contract for the sale of real property must
    A. be signed by two subscribing witnesses.
    B. be in writing and signed by both parties.
    C. be acknowledged by an official of the court or a notary public.
    D. specify the type of deed that will convey the title.

52. When a buyer stipulates that he will agree to make each monthly mortgage payment on the house he is buying but takes no responsibility for the note, he is
    A. buying with an assumption of the mortgage.
    B. releasing the seller from his obligation regarding the mortgage.
    C. purchasing the house subject to the mortgage.
    D. assigning the mortgage.

53. A real estate instructor was citing examples of freehold estates and nonfreehold estates. Which did she correctly use as an example of an estate that is nonfreehold?
    A. Estate for years
    B. Life estate
    C. Fee estate
    D. Estate by the entireties

54. In a community property state, the real property owned by a wife prior to her marriage is known after her marriage as
    A. common property.
    B. joint property.
    C. community property.
    D. separate property.

55. Young Dan was not licensed with the DBPR but helped his father (Harry) by finding buyers for his father's lots. Dan did not receive any money, but his father agreed to give Dan a choice lot, free and clear, after Dan found buyers for five lots. Dan was offered a well-paying job some distance from home after he had found buyers for only three lots. Dan took the job and did not earn his lot. Which statement is correct?
    A. Dan need not have been licensed because his father owned the lots.
    B. Dan violated Chapter 475, F.S., and is subject to fine or imprisonment.
    C. Dan did not violate Chapter 475, F.S., because he received no compensation.
    D. Dan and his father both violated Chapter 475, F.S., due to intent.

56. Sam Elder, a widower, was 83 years old and the owner of a popular restaurant business. His business assets consisted of goodwill, regular customers, all the restaurant equipment, and the building housing the restaurant. The land was leased and had 54 years remaining on a 99-year lease. Sam told his headwaiter that he would like his help in selling the business for $200,000. Sam agreed to give the headwaiter $7,000 if he, the headwaiter, found a buyer for the business. The headwaiter approached one of the regular customers who agreed to buy the business if the headwaiter would contract to manage the business. An agreement was reached, and Sam sold the business. When Sam learned that the headwaiter was going to take over as manager, Sam refused to pay the promised $7,000. Which is most correct?
    A. The headwaiter can force Sam to pay on the strength of a verbal contract.
    B. Sam's age would cause doubt to be cast on the compensation agreement.
    C. The headwaiter violated Chapter 475, F.S., and can be fined or jailed.
    D. Because the headwaiter received no compensation, he did not violate Chapter 475, F.S.

57. Curable functional obsolescence results in a change in value that is
    A. less than the cost to cure the defect.
    B. equal to the cost to cure the defect.
    C. greater than the cost to cure the defect.
    D. unrelated to the actual cost to cure the defect.

58. When a broker is unable to convince a property owner that the current market value is the price at which the property should be listed, the broker should
    A. take the listing at the owner's price and hope to sell the property.
    B. take the listing at the owner's price and later return to negotiate a reduction.
    C. diplomatically decline to accept the listing.
    D. take the listing and forget about it.

59. The individual whom a single agent represents in his or her dealings with the public is the
    A. buyer.
    B. mortgagor.
    C. customer.
    D. principal.

60. Which offense is a misdemeanor of the first degree?
    A. False advertising
    B. Unlicensed practice of real estate
    C. Culpable negligence
    D. Collecting a fee for inaccurate and out-of-date rental information

61. Streets, parks, and school sites are transferred from developers to counties or communities by an act or process called
    A. subdivision.
    B. subrogation.
    C. descent.
    D. dedication.

62. A mortgage note or bond provides legal evidence of a personal debt and also
    A. permits legal action to collect the debt wherever the mortgagee may be located.
    B. pledges all the assets of the mortgagor.
    C. neutralizes the defeasance clause in the mortgage.
    D. creates a lien on the property.

63. A broker has a farm listed for $164,000 with a negotiated sale commission of 8 percent. An immigrating retiree sees the For Sale sign and voluntarily offers $185,000 for the farm. The broker buys the farm from his seller for $160,000, and then he sells it to the retiree for $185,000. Later, the seller learns of the sequence of transactions. Which statement is most correct?
    A. The broker must reimburse the seller $25,000 plus any commission received.
    B. No legal or ethical violation has occurred.
    C. The broker's purchase price may be regarded as a legal option.
    D. The law does not apply to this transaction.

64. In determining market value, the principle of substitution is the basis for which approach to value?
    A. Comparable sales approach
    B. Cost-depreciation approach
    C. Income capitalization approach
    D. The principle of substitution is the basis for all three approaches

65. Which statement is FALSE regarding a new condominium complex?
    A. A declaration must be filed before any units may be sold.
    B. Each unit owner has a fractional, undivided interest in the common areas and facilities.
    C. Each unit owner is responsible for his or her own mortgage payments.
    D. Unit ownership requires the purchase of shares of stock in the association.

66. When a new lending agreement releases the seller and substitutes the buyer as the party liable for the mortgage debt, this act is called
    A. subrogation.
    B. subject to the mortgage.
    C. novation.
    D. negative amortization.

67. Which statement is TRUE with respect to a composite closing statement?
    A. The balance due from the buyer is paid directly to the seller.
    B. The balance due from the seller is paid directly to the buyer.
    C. The balance due the seller is paid directly by the buyer.
    D. The balance due the seller is paid by the closing agent.

68. The risk associated with an investment's ability to provide sufficient funds to pay operating costs is referred to as
    A. purchasing power risk.
    B. interest rate risk.
    C. business risk.
    D. financial risk.

69. A consideration that is legally sufficient to result in an enforceable real estate sale contract could be
    A. a specified sacrifice by one contracting party.
    B. receipt of some benefit in lieu of cash.
    C. a promise to accomplish some particular act.
    D. any of the considerations described above.

70. Bill offered $150,000 for Terri's home. Terri countered at $160,000. Bill did not accept Terri's counteroffer. Terri told her broker that she was revoking the counteroffer and accepting Bill's original offer. Which statement is TRUE regarding this situation?
    A. Bill and Terri have entered into a sale and purchase agreement for $150,000.
    B. Terri can revoke her counteroffer and accept Bill's original offer up until the time Bill rejects the counteroffer.
    C. Terri cannot accept the original offer because it was extinguished by the counteroffer.
    D. None of the statements are true.

71. The intent of the Legislature with respect to Florida's laws regulating professions and occupations is to
    A. control licensed professions and occupations in every way possible for the protection of the public.
    B. exercise strict control over a selected group of professions to screen and limit persons desiring to enter those professions.
    C. permit any qualified person to engage in any profession regulated by the State of Florida.
    D. permit anyone who wants to enter a profession to do so.

72. The purpose of recording documents relating to real property is to
    A. make the documents legal.
    B. give notice to future purchasers and creditors.
    C. prevent loss by adverse possession.
    D. eliminate squatters' rights.

73. A quitclaim deed differs from a bargain-and-sale deed because
    A. the bargain-and-sale deed has a covenant of seisin.
    B. the quitclaim deed gives a full warranty of title.
    C. only the bargain-and-sale deed has a granting clause.
    D. the quitclaim deed is enforceable longer.

74. The real taxable value of a Florida resident's home will NOT be known until the
    A. age of the homeowner is known.
    B. total tax millage is applied to the assessed value.
    C. total existing exemptions are subtracted from the current market value.
    D. total existing exemptions are subtracted from the current assessed value.

75. Broker Don purchased some raw acreage and developed it into several hundred building lots. He wrote Mr. Milling, a licensed real estate broker in Alabama, and offered Mr. Milling $150 for every prospect he sent to Florida who bought a lot from him (Broker Don). Which statement is correct?
    A. Broker Don has violated Chapter 475, F.S.
    B. Mr. Milling cannot legally accept compensation from Broker Don unless he is licensed as a broker in Florida.
    C. Broker Don can be fined and imprisoned.
    D. This is a perfectly legal arrangement.

76. Mr. Brown is a sales associate with Honest Realty, Inc. After two months of negotiation and effort, he succeeded in obtaining a tentative offer from Mr. Marshall to buy an undeveloped apartment site. Mr. Marshall refused to sign any sale agreement until he returned from a vacation in Alaska. While Mr. Marshall was on vacation, Mr. Brown took a two-week vacation but still returned several days ahead of Mr. Marshall. Within a few days after returning, Mr. Marshall contacted Mr. Brown and purchased the apartment site. Neither Mr. Brown nor Mr. Marshall was aware that, during their vacations, the zoning for the property had been changed from multifamily to single-family zoning, thereby prohibiting the use of the property Mr. Marshall had intended. Mr. Marshall brought suit against Mr. Brown and his employer, which resulted in collection of damages. What legal basis did Mr. Marshall have for his suit?
    A. Conversion
    B. Concealment
    C. Culpable negligence
    D. Commingling of interests

77. To determine the correct amount of property tax for property, multiply the tax rate by the
    A. assessed value of the property.
    B. last recorded sale price.
    C. taxable value of the property.
    D. appraised value of the property.

78. Mr. Cohen is a broker who overlooked the expiration date of September 30 on his license for the first time in 15 years as a real estate broker. Five days later, on October 5, an old friend brings a relative to Mr. Cohen's real estate office to discuss purchase of an office building listed by Ms. Dennis, another broker. Mr. Cohen contacts Ms. Dennis, who agrees to cobroker the transaction on a 50/50 basis. Mr. Cohen obtains a binding offer and a substantial earnest money deposit from the prospective buyer and presents them both to Ms. Dennis for her to obtain approval from the owner. Two months of offer and counteroffer follow. Finally, a mutually acceptable arrangement is negotiated by Mr. Cohen and Ms. Dennis. The closing is held and the sale commission is paid to Ms. Dennis, who then refuses to share the commission with Mr. Cohen because she learned the month before that Mr. Cohen's license had expired. Which is correct?
    A. Both brokers have violated Chapter 475, F.S.
    B. Ms. Dennis has violated Chapter 475, F.S., due to conversion.
    C. Mr. Cohen has violated Chapter 475, F.S.
    D. Neither broker actually has violated Chapter 475, F.S.

79. Mr. Park decided he would pay the requested purchase price of a house to the owner, Mr. Dino, if the owner agreed to accept $6,000 cash as the total down payment. Mr. Dino agreed to accept the offer on the condition that Mr. Park arrange his own financing and pay the balance of the purchase price at closing. Mr. Park accepted this condition with the stipulation that his $6,000 be returned to him in the event he was unsuccessful in obtaining adequate financing. Mr. Dino agreed to the financing contingency and instructed his broker, Mr. Chase, to prepare a contract for sale incorporating the agreed conditions and contingencies.

    Four weeks after Mr. Park and Mr. Dino signed the sale contract, Mr. Park met with Mr. Dino to announce that he was unable to obtain financing and therefore had to revoke the sale contract under the provisions of the financing contingency. He then requested the return of his $6,000. Mr. Dino agreed with Mr. Park's request and notified Mr. Chase to return Mr. Park's deposit. To the surprise of both Park and Dino, the broker (Mr. Chase) pointed out a clause in the small print of the sale contract giving the broker the deposit in the event the transaction did not go through. Mr. Park and Mr. Dino consulted their respective attorneys. What will their lawyers tell them is the proper action or result under the laws regulating contracts?
    A. The $6,000 must be turned over to Broker Chase.
    B. The $6,000 must be returned to Mr. Park (the buyer).
    C. The $6,000 must be split between Mr. Dino (the seller) and Mr. Chase (the broker).
    D. The $6,000 must be split between Mr. Park (the buyer) and Mr. Dino (the seller).

80. A broker, representing a newly formed syndicate of investors, arranged the purchase of 1,800 acres of ranch land for $1,650,000 from a citizen of Venezuela. The seller demanded all cash, with the buyers to arrange their own financing. The broker helped her investors arrange the financing. Further, the broker recommended that the buyers only pay the seller what percent of the selling price in order to comply with an IRS regulation?
    A. 10%
    B. 40%
    C. 60%
    D. 90%

81. A real estate broker followed the instructions of an escrow disbursement order. The seller sued the broker and obtained a judgment against the broker for $15,000 in damages plus $10,000 in attorney's fees and court costs. The broker incurred $3,000 in attorney's fees. The Commission is authorized to pay
    A. $15,000.
    B. $18,000.
    C. $25,000.
    D. $28,000.

82. John manages a residential rental property. The owner has decided she wants another real estate office to manage the property and asks John to transfer the security deposits to the new rental agent. Which statement applies to this situation?
    A. John must first secure the tenants' permission to transfer the deposits.
    B. John must close the bank accounts and return the funds directly to the owner.
    C. John must transfer the funds to the new agent along with an accounting.
    D. The deposits must be reimbursed to the tenants.

83. In the cost-depreciation approach to estimating value, land value is commonly estimated by
    A. comparable sales analysis.
    B. development cost analysis.
    C. residual value subtraction analysis.
    D. subtracting building value from total property value.

84. The VA total monthly obligations ratio is determined by dividing the total monthly
    A. housing expenses (PITI) by the net monthly income.
    B. obligations by the gross monthly income.
    C. housing expenses (PITI) by the gross monthly income.
    D. obligations by the net monthly income.

85. Where the government survey system is used to describe real property, the primary north-south line and the primary east-west line that form the basic reference point for the system are correctly called the
    A. principal meridian and base line.
    B. primary meridian and primary base line.
    C. principal meridian and primary base line.
    D. primary meridian and principal base line.

86. An up-front fee paid to the lender in exchange for a reduced interest rate, generally for the first one to three years, is referred to as
    A. commitment fees.
    B. points.
    C. the discount rate.
    D. a buydown.

87. For income tax purposes, the term *adjusted sale price* means the sale price of a home
    A. less the original cost.
    B. less allowable fix-up and selling expenses.
    C. less the down payment when seller financing is involved.
    D. adjusted to reflect the negotiation and acceptance of a counteroffer.

88. The real estate term *situs* refers to
    A. commercial properties designated on a site plan.
    B. properties listed in the historic properties register.
    C. scenic rural or farm areas.
    D. value derived from preferred property locations.

89. The master plan developed by planning commissions to manage local growth and preserve living conditions is called the
    A. growth management plan.
    B. comprehensive plan.
    C. development plan.
    D. environmental impact plan.

90. Broker Betty purchased two adjoining lots, each of which measured 150' across the front and 180' in depth. She paid $7,500 for each lot. She then divided the property into three equal lots and sold each one for $125 per front foot. What percent of profit did she make on her original investment?
    A. 25%
    B. 60%
    C. 67%
    D. 150%

91. A homebuyer has arranged a conventional mortgage of $30,000 at 13 percent interest for 30 years. By agreement, the first three monthly payments are to consist of interest only with payment on principal to begin with payment number four. How much total interest will the homebuyer pay during the first three months?
    A. $975
    B. $325
    C. $3,900
    D. $11,700

92. The closing date is September 10. Day of closing belongs to the seller. Property taxes for the year are $1,700. Calculate the proration using the 365-day method.
    A. $1,178.36 debit seller, credit buyer
    B. $1,173.70 debit seller, credit buyer
    C. $521.64 credit seller, debit buyer
    D. $516.99 debit seller, credit buyer

93. The sale price of a home is $66,000. A savings association has agreed to lend 80 percent of the sale price. The prospective buyer has made a binder deposit of $2,200. How much more cash must the buyer produce at closing?
    A. $10,760
    B. $11,000
    C. $13,200
    D. $14,960

94. A developer purchased a tract measuring 1,452 feet by 1,200 feet for $3,000 per acre. The sale contract provided for the developer to pay the seller 29 percent of the purchase price in cash, the developer to assume a $50,000 existing first mortgage, and the seller to take back a new second mortgage for the remainder of the purchase price. How much must the seller pay for the tax stamps he must place on the deed before it can be recorded?
    A. $596.40
    B. $660
    C. $720
    D. $840

95. Buyer Bettie bought a new home for $230,000. The lender agreed to loan Bettie $200,000 at 9 percent interest with six points discount. What approximate yield will this provide the lender?
    A. 9.5%
    B. 9.67%
    C. 9.75%
    D. 10.25%

96. Which parcel contains 2½ acres of land?
    A. W½ of the NE ¼ of the NW¼
    B. S½ of the NW¼ of the N½ of the NE¼
    C. SE¼ of the SW¼ of the SW¼
    D. SW¼ of the NE¼ of the NW¼ of the NE¼

97. Your county government has estimated its budget for the coming year to be $24,000,000. Income from nonproperty tax revenues is estimated to be $8,000,000. The county property assessor reports a total of $1,050,000,000 in taxable property. Homestead exemptions are found to total $100,000,000. Compute the tax rate for your county.
    A. 25.3 mills
    B. 22.9 mills
    C. 16.8 mills
    D. 15.2 mills

98. Mr. Gillian engages you to estimate the value of his office building prior to his putting it up for sale. The building is seven years old, and it would now cost $90,000 to reproduce the structure new. Originally, the economic life of the structure was estimated at 40 years. The land is valued at $20,000. Mr. Gillian paid $70,000 for the building and the land five years ago. What is the estimated value of Mr. Gillian's property?
    A. $98,750
    B. $94,250
    C. $90,750
    D. $81,250

99. Sales associate Sam listed a parcel of undeveloped commercial property for $215,000. The agreed sale commission is 10 percent on the first $50,000, 5 percent on the next $100,000, and 3 percent on any balance. Sales associate Sarah sold the property for $210,000, and the owner paid the sale commission per the listing agreement. The broker paid the listing sales associate 10 percent of the total commission and split the remaining commission 65 percent to Sarah and 35 percent to himself. What was Sarah's commission?
    A. $7,670
    B. $6,903
    C. $4,130
    D. $3,717

100. On March 1, an investor bought a ten-unit apartment building for $360,000. He paid $72,000 in cash and obtained a 30-year mortgage in the amount of $288,000. A review of the accounts over the preceding two years revealed that vacancy and collection losses were stable at 4 percent. Potential gross income for the property is $70,400 and the operating expenses are $12,770, including reserve for replacements of $2,812. Mortgage payments are $2,742.71. Calculate the net operating income.
    A. $49,259
    B. $52,002
    C. $54,814
    D. $67,584

100 Multiple-Choice Question
Exam 2

Instructions. This second practice examination is designed to give you additional help in preparing for your state license examination. Mark your answer choices on the Answer Sheet provided on page 199. Explanations of the correct answers are provided in the Practice 2 Answer Key at the end of the book.

1. Martha decided she wanted to leave her summer cottage to her granddaughter, so she executed a general warranty deed to the property and gave it to her granddaughter. Martha died a few weeks later, prior to the recording of the deed. Which statement applies to this situation?
    A. The cottage is part of Martha's estate and must be probated.
    B. Title to the property was conveyed to the granddaughter when Martha executed and delivered the deed to her granddaughter.
    C. The deed must be recorded in order to convey title to the granddaughter.
    D. The granddaughter will have to pay inheritance taxes on the taxable value of the home prior to recording the deed.

2. Neal has a broker license and wants to become associated with Carol Homes Realty, Inc. What is Neal required to do in order for him to maintain an active broker license with the company?
    A. Neal must have an ownership interest in the company.
    B. Neal must be registered as an officer or director of the corporation.
    C. Neal's name must appear on the brokerage entrance sign.
    D. Neal must register with the Florida Department of State.

3. Sales associate Joshua Comelately has not completed his continuing education prior to the expiration of his license. In a previous renewal cycle, Joshua completed his post-licensing requirement. What should Joshua do?
    A. Mail in his renewal card and fee prior to the expiration of his license and then do his continuing education requirement at the earliest opportunity.
    B. Complete his education requirement and send in the renewal fee, renewal application, late fee, and the appropriate DRE form to reactivate his license.
    C. Complete 21 hours of in-class instruction.
    D. Retake the 45-hour post-licensing course.

4. Beth Thomas is considering making an offer to purchase a 50-unit beachfront time-share development from Dan Waterbury. The buyer and seller have requested that Mr. Chime, a licensed real estate sales associate, act as a single agent representative for each of them. Which statement applies to this situation?
   A. Beth Thomas and Dan Waterbury must each have assets in excess of $1 million for this to be permissible.
   B. The sales associate must give the buyer and seller the single agent disclosure.
   C. This arrangement is a violation of Chapter 475, F.S.
   D. Because this is residential property, it does not qualify for designated sales associate representation.

5. Broker Mike has appointed sales associates Rebecca and Joshua to be designated sales associates in a real estate transaction. Chapter 475, F.S., requires
   A. the buyer and seller to each sign an asset disclosure indicating that each has assets of at least $1 million.
   B. that the designated sales associates give the buyer and seller the single agent disclosure explaining the duties of a single agent.
   C. that the designated sales associates give the buyer and seller a disclosure explaining how confidential information will be handled.
   D. all of the actions described above.

6. Motivated Molly regularly does cold calling for potential listings. One day, Molly called a party who informed her that he was on the national do-not-call list and did not want to be disturbed. Which statement applies to this situation?
   A. Molly can be fined for calling a person who is listed on the do-not-call list.
   B. Molly made an honest mistake and should jot down the phone number so that she won't disturb the man again.
   C. Real estate licensees are not bound by the national do-not-call restrictions.
   D. As long as Molly initially identified herself and the name of the brokerage company she works for, she has acted properly.

7. Sales associate Sara decides to mail personalized notepads to the residents of a neighborhood. The notepads include Sara's picture plus her name, phone number, and e-mail address. Sara paid the cost of printing and mailing the notepads. Which statement applies to this situation?
   A. The notepads are a form of real estate advertisement and therefore must include the name of the brokerage firm.
   B. The name of the brokerage firm is required in newspaper advertisements and For Sale signs only.
   C. Because Sara paid for the printing and mailing of the notepads, she can choose the wording and content.
   D. Sara needs to add her license status to the information printed on the notepads.

8. Buyer Bonnie made an offer on Jim's home which Jim accepted. The contract was contingent on several inspections. Several weeks prior to the closing, the sale fell through due to one of the inspections. Which statement is true regarding the retention of documents?
   A. The broker is not obligated to retain copies of the agency disclosure forms because the transaction did not close.
   B. The broker is required to keep copies of the brokerage relationship disclosure forms for five years.
   C. The broker may dispose of the "dead files" after two years.
   D. The broker is only obligated to retain documentation regarding disbursement of the earnest money deposit.

9. Sales associate John has become frustrated with buyers who use his time and expertise and then make an offer to purchase through another real estate company. To help "tie" prospective buyers to John, he now requires prospective buyers to deposit $500 with the real estate company to show intent to deal through John's broker. If the buyer makes a purchase, the $500 is applied to the earnest money deposit. However, if the prospective buyer does not make a purchase, the deposit is forfeited. Which statement is true regarding this arrangement?
   A. This is a constructive way to prevent buyers from jumping from one sales associate to another.
   B. The $500 is an illegal kickback.
   C. The $500 is a trust fund and must be paid to John's broker.
   D. The $500 is a referral fee.

10. A licensed real estate sales associate conducted an appraisal for a fee. The FREC found the licensee to be in violation of the Uniform Standards of Professional Practice.
    A. Real estate licensees are not required to abide by the USPAP.
    B. The licensee is subject to suspension or revocation of his or her real estate license.
    C. Only the Appraisal Board can impose a penalty in this case—the FREC does not have authority over appraisal matters.
    D. Real estate sales associates may not conduct appraisals for a fee unless they are also certified or licensed real estate appraisers.

11. Sales associate John has a dispute with his former broker over a commission. What recourse does John have to resolve the commission dispute?
    A. John can request the FREC to issue an escrow disbursement order.
    B. John can sue the principal named in the listing contract that is in dispute.
    C. John can sue his former broker and request the civil courts to resolve the matter.
    D. John can seek relief from the Real Estate Recovery Fund.

12. Broker Bertha purchased a list of FHA foreclosure properties from Neal who is an employee of the FHA. Broker Bertha has promised to pay Neal a percentage of all commissions earned by her company resulting from FHA foreclosure sales on the list.
    A. Bertha has violated Chapter 475, F.S., by compensating an unlicensed person for performing services that require a real estate license.
    B. Bertha may compensate Neal because he is a salaried employee of a government agency.
    C. FHA foreclosure properties are exempt from the Florida Real Estate License Law.
    D. Bertha is allowed to compensate Neal as long as he does not provide real estate services to the buyer and seller.

13. To be in compliance with federal laws regarding lead-based paint, which is (are) required regarding dwellings built prior to 1978?
    A. Sellers and lessors must disclose the presence of known lead-based paint in residential dwellings.
    B. Sale contracts and leases must include specific lead-based paint warning and disclosure language.
    C. Buyers and tenants must acknowledge that they have received the warning and disclosure.
    D. All of the above are required.

14. Broker Carol has a multiple license. She is an active broker for ABC Realty Company as well as XYZ Company. Rebecca, a sales associate for ABC Realty, has procured a listing to sell Mike's condo. Joshua, a sales associate for XYZ Realty, is a single agent of a buyer who has entered into a contract to purchase Mike's condo. Which applies here?
    A. Because Carol is the broker of ABC Realty and XYZ Realty, this is an illegal dual agency relationship.
    B. This is a legal arrangement because two separate real estate firms are involved.
    C. The buyer and seller must agree to allow Carol to transition to a transaction broker to complete this sale.
    D. Broker Carol has violated Chapter 475, F.S.

15. Broker Ellen Sammis of Newcomer Realty, Inc., is opening a real estate office. The following information must be included on her exterior entrance sign EXCEPT
    A. Ellen Sammis.
    B. Licensed Real Estate Broker.
    C. REALTOR®.
    D. Newcomer Realty, Inc.

16. Buyer and seller have entered into a real estate contract. The broker neglected to include a closing date on the contract.
    A. This is a valid and enforceable contract.
    B. This is an unenforceable contract.
    C. The contract is void.
    D. The broker can be disciplined for fraud and misrepresentation.

17. A licensed real estate sales associate recently purchased a condo and moved out of his former apartment. Is the sales associate required to notify the DBPR?
    A. As long as the sales associate continues to work under the same broker, there is no need to notify the DBPR.
    B. The sales associate must notify the DBPR of the change in his current mailing address within ten days after the change.
    C. The sales associate must notify the Commission within 60 days of a change in residency.
    D. If the sales associate's license is inactive, he or she is not required to notify the DBPR.

18. Jack and Jill are close friends who own Hilltop Nursery as joint tenants with right of survivorship. Jill died unexpectedly in a terrible fall. Does Jack now solely own the nursery?
    A. If Jill was married at the time of her death, her interest in the nursery will descend to her heirs.
    B. Jack will have to wait until Jill's estate is probated before taking sole ownership of the property.
    C. If Jill has minor children, the children will receive a remainder estate for Jill's interest in the nursery and Jack will take a life estate.
    D. Jack becomes sole owner of the nursery by operation of law.

19. Broker Mike wants to change one of his branch office locations. What must Mike do?
    A. Mike must send a letter to the DBPR notifying it that he is transferring his branch office registration from one location to another.
    B. Mike must fill out a change of address form only.
    C. Mike must register the new location and pay the appropriate fee.
    D. Mike must register the new location without paying an additional fee.

20. Briley is a student working on her master's degree at the university. Briley owns a duplex that she rents to college students. Briley has an inactive real estate license and collects the rent on her own behalf. Which statement is TRUE regarding this situation?
    A. Briley is required to maintain deposit money and advance rents in compliance with the Florida Residential Landlord and Tenant Act.
    B. Because there are only two dwelling units, Briley does not have to set aside rental deposits and advance rent.
    C. Because Briley has a real estate license, she must set aside the rental deposits.
    D. Owners are exempt from rental deposit requirements stipulated in the Florida Residential Landlord and Tenant Act.

21. A broker may NOT establish an escrow account in a Florida
    A. credit union.
    B. commercial bank.
    C. savings association.
    D. stock brokerage account.

22. A broker chooses not to maintain an escrow account. Which statement is TRUE regarding this situation?
    A. Brokers are required to maintain an escrow account.
    B. If the title company is handling the closing, the title company may hold the earnest money deposit in escrow.
    C. If an attorney is conducting the closing, the attorney may hold the deposit in escrow provided the broker is a signatory on the account.
    D. The broker is subject to disciplinary action by the FREC.

23. Discount points are
    A. a charge to financial lenders for borrowing from the Federal Reserve Bank.
    B. an up-front charge, usually paid by the developer to lower the buyer's mortgage interest rate for the first one to three years.
    C. up-front charges to the FHA for mortgage insurance.
    D. a charge by a lender to increase the interest yield on a mortgage.

24. A prospective tenant wants to install a ramp to the front door and handrails in the bathroom of a bungalow cottage. Which applies here?
    A. If the landlord is the property owner (no management company is involved), the owner does not have to allow the tenant to make modifications to the property.
    B. The owner is responsible for the cost of modifying the dwelling, provided the tenant agrees to sign a one-year (or longer) lease agreement.
    C. The tenant may make the modification at her own expense.
    D. Owners of less than four units do not have to allow a tenant to make modifications to a residential dwelling.

25. The township located due East of T1N, R1E is
    A. T1N, R2E.
    B. T1N, R1W.
    C. T2N, R1E.
    D. T1S, R2E.

26. Mary responded "No" to the question on her real estate application regarding whether she had ever been found guilty of a crime. Four years ago Mary was divorced and lost her job. She found another job a short time later but went ahead and cashed two unemployment checks totaling $700. Mary went to court for illegally cashing the unemployment checks. She repaid the $700 and adjudication of her guilt was withheld. What action, if any, will the FREC likely take?
    A. Because the incident took place four years ago, the FREC will probably take no action.
    B. Because adjudication of guilt was withheld, the Commission will not have any information concerning the case.
    C. The Commission will likely consider this to be a case of obtaining a license by fraud, misrepresentation, or concealment and revoke or suspend the license, or deny a license if not yet issued.
    D. The FREC will likely issue a notice of noncompliance.

27. The subject property is a three-bedroom, two-bath home. A comparable property is a three-bedroom, two and one-half-bath home. An appraiser has determined that the extra half bath is worth about $2,200. What adjustment should the appraiser make?
    A. Subtract $2,200 from the estimated value of the subject property.
    B. Subtract $2,200 from the comparable's transaction price.
    C. Add $2,200 to the comparable's transaction price.
    D. Add $2,200 to the estimated value of the subject property.

28. In 1990, at age 19, Barbara was charged with one count of petty theft. She paid a fine during a ten-minute court proceeding and was not sentenced to probation or any other penalty. Nine years later, Barbara is completing her sales associate application. How should Barbara respond to the question on her application concerning whether she has ever been convicted of a crime, found guilty, or entered a plea of guilty or no contest even if adjudication was withheld?
    A. Barbara was a minor when the incident occurred, so it was expunged at age 21.
    B. Because Barbara was not sentenced, there is no record of the petty theft, and therefore, she does not need to disclose the incident on her application.
    C. Barbara must disclose the petty theft incident on her application.
    D. The crime will most likely not be discovered in the fingerprint check, so she can simply answer "No" to the question on her application.

29. Loreen is a 65-year-old widow who is legally blind. Her condo is homesteaded. Her total tax exemption is
    A. $25,000.
    B. $25,500.
    C. $26,000.
    D. $26,500.

30. Briley has become frustrated that one of her tenants has not paid his rent, so while the tenant is away, she has a locksmith change the locks on the apartment.
    A. Briley is within her rights as a property owner-landlord to regain possession of her property.
    B. Briley's actions are a violation of Florida's Landlord and Tenant Act.
    C. As long as Briley posted a three-day notice and the three days have passed, she may legally change the locks.
    D. Only the sheriff may legally change the locks.

31. If a real estate sales associate fails to complete the 45-hour post-licensing course prior to the expiration of his or her initial license, what happens to the license?
    A. The license automatically reverts to an involuntary inactive license.
    B. The license remains inactive until the licensee completes the education requirement and pays a late fee.
    C. The license reverts to inactive status and the licensee is issued a notice of noncompliance.
    D. The license becomes null and void.

32. Under the Truth-in-Lending Act, certain words trigger disclosures of the amount or percentage of down payment, the terms of repayment, and the annual percentage rate. Which of the following is (are) "triggering terms"?
    A. The amount of down payment in a credit sale transaction
    B. The amount of any payment
    C. The number of payments
    D. All of the above are triggering terms

33. A commercial tenant pays a pro-rata share of the property taxes, hazard insurance, and utilities. The tenant has what type of lease?
    A. Net lease
    B. Expense lease
    C. Prorated lease
    D. Percentage lease

34. Muffy is a prospective tenant. Muffy was evicted from her previous apartment for failure to pay rent. Muffy has inspected an apartment and wishes to enter into a lease agreement with Action Property Management Company. May the landlord refuse to rent to Muffy?
    A. No, this would be a violation of the Fair Housing Act.
    B. Yes, provided Muffy is not disabled.
    C. Yes, based on Muffy's poor credit history.
    D. No, this would be a violation of the Fair Credit Act.

35. Which statement is TRUE regarding townships?
    A. A township is a parcel containing 36 square miles.
    B. A township contains 640 acres.
    C. Townships are a part of the metes-and-bounds method of legal description.
    D. Checks are smaller units that make up a township.

36. Fred obtained a judgment against a real estate licensee for negligent conduct involving a real estate brokerage transaction. The licensee had an inactive license at the time that the negligence occurred. If Fred is unable to collect on the judgment, can he be reimbursed from the Real Estate Recovery Fund?
    A. Yes, it is irrelevant that the real estate license was inactive.
    B. Yes, provided the amount of the claim does not exceed $25,000.
    C. No, the license must have been active when the incident occurred.
    D. No, because of negligence on the part of the licensee.

37. The Commission's authority to adopt administrative rules is an exercise of which power?
    A. Executive
    B. Administrative
    C. Quasi-judicial
    D. Quasi-legislative

38. Broker Sue obtained a judgment from a Florida court against the seller for a commission due her. May Sue record the judgment?
    A. Real estate licensees are prohibited from doing anything that would create a lien on an owner's property.
    B. Sue is prohibited from recording a judgment against a principal.
    C. Sue's only recourse is to seek relief from the Real Estate Recovery Fund.
    D. Sue may record the judgment in the county where the debtor owns property.

39. The market value of a site is determined by its
    A. current use.
    B. zoning.
    C. highest and best use.
    D. physical characteristics.

40. The income capitalization approach to value requires collection of data pertaining to
    A. reproduction costs of improvements.
    B. expected future expenses.
    C. market evidence of depreciation.
    D. recent land sales.

41. Which survey method is used when developed subdivisions have been recorded?
    A. Survey method
    B. Lot and block method
    C. Subdivision method
    D. Metes-and-bounds method

42. If probable cause is found to exist, the probable cause panel will direct the DBPR to file a formal complaint against the subject of the investigation. Which statement is TRUE?
    A. At this point the licensee will be scheduled to attend an informal hearing before the FREC.
    B. At this point the findings of the probable cause panel are reduced to a stipulation and mailed to the licensee.
    C. The licensee is entitled to either a formal or informal hearing, or the licensee may agree to a stipulation.
    D. The FREC makes a determination regarding whether to dismiss the case.

43. Tom makes an offer to purchase John's property. Sales associate Mike presents Tom's offer, which John accepts. Before Mike is able to contact Tom to tell him that his offer has been accepted, Tom is killed in a car accident. The sale contract is
    A. valid because the seller accepted Tom's offer.
    B. valid and binding on Tom's heirs.
    C. void because of Tom's death unless the contract provided otherwise.
    D. none of the above.

44. A court awarded a judgment to Mr. and Mrs. Smith against Broker Jones for $30,000 actual damages and $45,000 punitive damages regarding a real estate brokerage transaction. What is the maximum amount of reimbursement available to the Smiths from the Real Estate Recovery Fund?
    A. $30,000
    B. $50,000
    C. $75,000
    D. $150,000

45. Sales associate Mike finds a buyer for another brokerage firm's listing. The buyer gives Mike an earnest money deposit check made payable to Mike personally. What should Mike do?
    A. Deposit the check in his own account and then immediately write a check payable to the listing company
    B. Put a limited endorsement on the back of the check to the listing broker's escrow account
    C. Return the check to the buyer and request that the buyer make out a new check payable to the escrow account of Mike's broker
    D. Cash the check and then turn the money over to Mike's employing broker

46. Which parties constitute an arm's length transaction?
    A. Medallion Financial Services, Inc., to Medallion Taxi Enterprises, Inc.
    B. Mrs. Sammis, mother, to Dean Sammis, son
    C. Mr. Perez to Miss Root (not related)
    D. Microfirm, Inc., to Net, Inc. (Microfirm is a shareholder of Net, Inc.)

47. Mike purchased a weather vane. He bolted the weather vane to his roof ridge. The weather vane is
    A. personal property.
    B. a fixture.
    C. constructive property.
    D. considered air rights.

48. Sales associate Tom works for ABC Realty Company in Naples, Florida. While Tom is visiting a friend in St. Petersburg, he sees a waterfront lot listed by XYZ Realty. Tom sells the lot to his friend, and XYZ Realty pays Tom a 10 percent commission.
    A. As long as Tom's real estate license is active, it is legal for XYZ Realty to pay Tom a commission.
    B. Tom may be compensated by XYZ Realty because it is the listing company.
    C. For this transaction to be legal, the 10 percent commission must be classified as a finder's fee.
    D. Both Tom and the broker of XYZ have violated Florida's Real Estate License Law.

49. The process by which private property is acquired through judicial process to build a police station is called
    A. condemnation.
    B. escheat.
    C. foreclosure.
    D. hypothecation.

50. Neal loves to spend money but he sometimes is a little slow in paying his debts. Neal owns homesteaded property. The homesteaded property is protected from which debt?
    A. The tax collector's office for delinquent property taxes on the principal residence
    B. Blue Lagoon Pool Company for an in-ground swimming pool at Neal's principal residence, which he charged on his credit card
    C. Delinquent mortgage payments on his principal residence
    D. None of the above

51. Awax Candle Company pays the property owner rent in the amount of $500 per month plus 3 percent of gross sales revenue. Awax Candle Company has entered into what type of lease agreement?
    A. Gross lease
    B. Percentage lease
    C. Indexed lease
    D. Step-up lease

52. Buyer Mike makes a written offer on Seller Joshua's property. Joshua makes a counteroffer, which Mike accepts. The listing broker conveys Mike's written acceptance to Joshua. At this point, the offer becomes a(n)
    A. express contract.
    B. parol contract.
    C. ratified offer.
    D. contingent contract.

53. Which expense associated with a principal residence is deductible for income tax purposes?
    A. Depreciation
    B. Operating expenses
    C. Maintenance costs
    D. Property taxes

54. Broker Mario had an exclusive listing to sell a small apartment complex. The owner canceled the listing agreement before an offer was presented and then entered into a lease-management agreement with a third party. Is Mario entitled to a commission?
    A. Yes, because the seller has entered into an agreement with another broker
    B. Yes, if Mario can find a buyer for the property prior to the expiration date specified in the original listing agreement
    C. No, because Mario did not meet the conditions for payment of commission prior to the cancellation of the agreement
    D. None of the above

55. Which business structure is designed to protect personal assets?
    A. General partnership
    B. Sole proprietorship
    C. Corporation
    D. None of the above

56. Broker Muffy was served a citation for not having a proper entrance sign. Muffy contends that she does have a proper sign and wants to dispute the citation. Which statement applies to this situation?
    A. Muffy may dispute the citation within 30 days of its being served.
    B. Muffy must pay the fine and then petition for a reconsideration.
    C. Muffy must pay the citation without challenge or risk further disciplinary action.
    D. Muffy may dispute the citation by attending the next scheduled Commission meeting.

57. Sales associate Sara's first license renewal period expires at the end of March. What education is required for Sara to renew her license?
    A. 14-hour continuing education course
    B. 45-hour post-licensing course
    C. Broker prelicense course
    D. 7-hour core law course

58. A buyer made an offer to purchase and paid a $500 earnest money deposit. The seller accepted the offer. A few weeks later the transaction fell through. Neither the buyer nor the seller has made a claim on the escrowed deposit. Attempts to contact the buyer and seller have been unsuccessful. What should the broker do with the earnest money deposit?
    A. The broker should give the buyer and seller at least one month to make a claim for the deposit.
    B. The broker should notify the FREC that the broker is holding abandoned funds.
    C. The broker should refund the deposit to the buyer because that is who paid the earnest money deposit.
    D. The broker must notify the FREC within 15 business days that the broker has a good-faith doubt.

59. A Florida-licensed broker wants to register an office located in New York City as his principal real estate office. May he do so?
    A. No, the brokerage office must be located within the State of Florida.
    B. Yes, a broker's principal office may be located outside the State of Florida as long as the broker's escrow account is maintained in a Florida institution.
    C. No, only a branch office may be located outside the State of Florida.
    D. Yes, a broker's registered principal office may be located outside the State of Florida. However, the broker must have all escrow funds held in trust by a Florida-based title company.

60. Broker Badder sold a home for $150,000. The broker then, at the request of the buyer and seller, prepared a second contract at $180,000 to present to a mortgage company. Which statement is true regarding this situation?
    A. As long as the property will appraise for $180,000, this is legal.
    B. As long as the seller agrees to the dual contract arrangement, this is legal.
    C. It is illegal to enter into a dual contract for the purpose of securing a larger loan.
    D. Broker Badder has violated his fiduciary duty to the seller.

61. The purpose of the Real Estate Settlement Procedures Act is to ensure
    A. uniform credit costs.
    B. that elderly applicants have an opportunity to secure long-term financing.
    C. that buyers are informed regarding the amount and type of charges they can expect at closing.
    D. that the annual percentage of interest is disclosed.

62. Can a real estate licensee working in a nonrepresentative role with a seller provide the seller a CMA?
    A. No, providing a CMA for a seller can only be done in a transaction broker or single agent capacity.
    B. No, providing a CMA would constitute a fiduciary relationship with the seller.
    C. Yes, provided the seller signs a notice that states that the seller will not construe the CMA to create an agency relationship.
    D. Yes, there is no restriction in Chapter 475, F.S., to prevent a licensee from preparing a CMA for a buyer or seller.

63. William and his wife Hildigard have homesteaded property. William owns investment real estate in severalty. William dies testate and bequeaths his investment real property to Mona.
    A. Mona is the remainder of William's entire estate.
    B. Hildigard owns the principal residence in severalty and 50 percent of the investment property.
    C. Hildigard may file for an elective share of the investment property in addition to having 100 percent interest in the principal residence.
    D. Hildigard is entitled to all of the homesteaded property only.

64. A railroad track easement is which type of easement?
    A. Appurtenant
    B. Necessity
    C. Prescription
    D. In gross

65. An acknowledgment is a
    A. notary seal.
    B. recorded document.
    C. declaration by the signer that the signing is of his or her own free will.
    D. constructive notice.

66. Dorothy and Carl have been married for 40 years. They have owned and sold several homes during their marriage and have rolled over the gain from the sale of previous homes. Carl is planning on retiring at age 60, and so the couple has decided to sell their spacious family home and buy a smaller condo. How does the current tax law affect their capital gains on the sale of their family home?
    A. Carl and Dorothy can take their one-time tax exclusion on the gain from the sale of their home.
    B. As long as the couple meets the two-year principal-residence test, they may exclude up to $500,000 of gain when they sell the home, if filing jointly.
    C. Carl and Dorothy must pay all of the deferred gain on the previous homes. However, any gain on their current residence is excluded up to $500,000, if filing jointly.
    D. Carl and Dorothy must pay a reduced long-term capital gain on the rollover only.

67. A mortgage must include
    A. a due-on-sale clause.
    B. a legal description.
    C. a granting clause.
    D. the mortgagee's signature.

68. Broker Steve receives a $100 referral fee from Full Title Services for every transaction that closes through the title company. Because of this, Broker Steve has inserted a sentence into his standard contract for sale and purchase requiring the buyer to use Full Title Services. Which of the following applies to this situation?
    A. This is a legal referral fee because the title company is disclosed to the buyer and seller in the sale and purchase agreement.
    B. The broker may be disciplined for requiring the buyer to use a particular title company.
    C. Florida law prohibits a title company from paying a referral fee for recommending the use of its services.
    D. Both B and C are true.

69. The statement that there must be at least a two-hour fire wall rating between attached common walls would most likely appear in the
    A. zoning code.
    B. building code.
    C. condominium documents.
    D. deed restrictions.

70. Sales associate Lucy changes her residence from 100 Gator Lane to 305 Seminole Terrace in Tallahassee, Florida. She remains employed by Bobby's Realty Company. Which statement is TRUE?
    A. Lucy must notify the DBPR of her change in mailing address within ten days after the change.
    B. Because Lucy did not change employers, she does not need to notify the DBPR.
    C. Lucy must notify the DBPR of the change in residence within 60 days of the change.
    D. Lucy's broker must notify the DBPR of the change in mailing address.

71. Variables that influence demand do NOT include
    A. availability of mortgage credit.
    B. population size and household composition.
    C. availability of skilled labor.
    D. consumer tastes or preferences.

72. Sales associate Lucy decided to move from Tallahassee to Macon, Georgia. Which statement(s) is (are) true?
    A. Lucy must notify the DBPR of her change in mailing address within ten days after the change.
    B. Lucy must notify the DBPR of the change in residency within 60 days of becoming a nonresident and execute an irrevocable consent to service.
    C. Lucy must place her real estate license in an inactive status.
    D. Both A and B are true.

73. Which individual is required to have a real estate license?
    A. A mortgage broker working for a lender in the loan processing department
    B. A property manager who is paid an annual salary plus is provided with an apartment
    C. A broker who exclusively markets business opportunities
    D. A person who sells cemetery lots

74. Which brokerage relationship disclosure notice must be signed by the buyer or seller before the licensee can proceed?
    A. Consent to transition to transaction broker notice
    B. Single agent disclosure notice
    C. No brokerage relationship notice
    D. Transaction broker notice

75. A transaction broker does NOT have which duty?
    A. Accounting for all funds
    B. Disclosing all known facts that materially affect the value of residential real property and are not readily observable to the buyer
    C. Using skill, care, and diligence in the transaction
    D. Loyalty

76. If a broker receives conflicting demands on escrowed property, the broker must notify the FREC, in writing, within 15 business days of the last demand and institute one of four settlement procedures *unless* the transaction
    A. concerns a time-share unit.
    B. concerns a residential sale contract on HUD-owned property.
    C. involves commercial real estate.
    D. concerns the sale of a business opportunity on leased land.

77. Murl is the broker of record for Little Mo Realty. He is working with a buyer as a buyer's single agent. The buyer has become interested in a property listed by Little Mo Realty as a transaction broker. Which statement applies to this situation?
    A. Little Mo Realty may serve as a transaction broker with the seller and as a single agent for the buyer to complete this transaction.
    B. Murl must appoint a designated sales associate to represent the buyer before completing the transaction.
    C. Little Mo Realty cannot be a transaction broker for one party and a single agent for the other party.
    D. Broker Murl may complete the transaction but he can only collect a commission from the buyer.

78. Mary's listing is a beautiful home in the historic district of Tampa. The home was built in the early 1900s. Mary gives the buyer a lead-based paint disclosure at the closing. Which statement applies to this situation?
    A. The law requires Mary to give the buyer the disclosure prior to contract.
    B. Homes located in a historic district are exempted from the lead-based paint disclosure requirements.
    C. Mary's actions are in compliance with the law.
    D. The disclosure is only required if the buyer intending to occupy the property has children under age five.

79. A Presbyterian church owns a nursing home for its members. The church admits only church members to the nursing facility. Is this legal?
    A. No, this is a violation of the Fair Housing Act.
    B. Yes, the church is exempt under the Fair Housing Act and may restrict the use of the facility to its members.
    C. The church has violated the Civil Rights Act of 1866.
    D. The church may only exclude others if they paid cash for the facility and did not finance the purchase of the nursing home facility.

80. An individual is eligible to seek recovery from the Real Estate Recovery Fund if
    A. the seller was an active licensed sales associate selling the home for-sale-by-owner.
    B. at the time the real estate contract was executed, the sales associate's license was in inactive status.
    C. the claim is based on a final judgment against the active licensee involved in a real estate brokerage transaction.
    D. he or she wishes to avoid a court process.

81. Sue rents a college apartment and pays her rent on the tenth of every month. Sue has a written agreement with the property owner; however, there is no specified termination date. Which statement is TRUE?
    A. Sue is a tenant at sufferance.
    B. Sue must be given at least 15 days' notice to vacate prior to the end of the monthly period.
    C. Sue is a holdover tenant.
    D. Sue must be given 30 days' notice to vacate if the owner wants to end the lease.

82. A previous owner has stipulated that future owners of a tract of land may not operate any type of business on the property that produces a toxic substance of any kind and might potentially harm a natural spring on the property. Where would a real estate licensee interested in listing this property find this information?
    A. EPA property report
    B. Local zoning code
    C. Deed restrictions
    D. Survey of the property

83. What is the distance between the south boundary of Section 1 and the north boundary of Section 36?
    A. 3 miles
    B. 4 miles
    C. 5 miles
    D. 6 miles

84. The following are paired relationships EXCEPT
    A. 36 sections—1 township.
    B. 24 miles square—check.
    C. range—north-south.
    D. meridian—east-west.

85. Bob and Mark discuss the purchase and sale of a tract of land over a beer one Friday night. They jot down the sale price and other terms and conditions on a bar napkin and each signs his name on the napkin. This is a(n)
    A. unenforceable contract.
    B. valid contract.
    C. parol contract.
    D. offer.

86. Kathleen makes an offer to purchase a home built in the early 1970s that is listed by XYZ Realty. Prior to signing the contract for purchase and sale, what must occur?
    A. Kathleen must give an earnest money deposit to the broker.
    B. The seller must disclose any known presence of lead-based paint in the home.
    C. The buyer must sign a release waiving the right to a paint inspection.
    D. All of the above must occur.

87. If a prospective buyer suspects that there is an encroachment on a property she is considering purchasing, to which document should she refer?
    A. A recent survey
    B. Seller's deed
    C. Title insurance policy
    D. Blueprints

88. Which entity may NOT register as a real estate broker?
    A. Nonprofit corporation
    B. Sole proprietorship
    C. Corporation sole
    D. Limited liability partnership

89. If the Fed wants to stimulate a sluggish economy, it may choose to
    A. raise the reserve requirement.
    B. sell securities in the open market.
    C. decrease the prime rate.
    D. lower the discount rate.

90. Three individuals purchase a property without the right of survivorship. Their estate is referred to as a
    A. joint tenancy.
    B. leasehold estate.
    C. tenancy in common.
    D. tenancy by the entireties.

91. Annual property taxes are $1,460. Closing is June 1. Using the 365-day method of proration, how is this entered on the composite closing statement? Charge day of closing to the buyer.
    A. Debit seller $608, credit buyer $608
    B. Debit buyer $856, credit seller $604
    C. Debit buyer $856, credit seller $856
    D. Debit seller $604, credit buyer $604

92. A property sold two years ago for $120,000. An appraiser estimates that properties in the market area where the parcel is located have appreciated 5 percent annually. How much is the property worth today, assuming no other factors?
    A. $126,000
    B. $132,000
    C. $132,300
    D. $144,000

93. The adjusted sale prices of three comparables are $87,900, $88,500, and $82,750. The appraiser applies weights of 30 percent, 50 percent, and 20 percent, respectively. Calculate the indicated value of the subject property.
    A. $86,383
    B. $87,170
    C. $87,950
    D. $88,100

94. Robert owns a 30-unit apartment complex that produces a net monthly rental income of $9,200. This monthly income represents a 9.5 percent annual return for the owner during the first year of ownership. What did Robert pay for the building? (Round to the nearest dollar.)
    A. $96,842
    B. $116,211
    C. $1,042,100
    D. $1,162,105

95. The N½ of the NE¼ of the SW¼ and the S½ of the SE¼ of a section contains
    A. 2.5 acres.
    B. 20 acres.
    C. 80 acres.
    D. 100 acres.

96. A 130-unit apartment complex contains 80 one-bedroom apartments which rent for $750 per month and 50 two-bedroom apartments which rent for $950 per month. The one-bedroom units are 10 percent vacant, and the two-bedroom units are 5 percent vacant. Calculate the projected annual effective gross income for this investment property.
    A. $107,500
    B. $1,189,500
    C. $1,290,000
    D. $1,344,000

97. Sales associate Ted sells a property for $98,500. Ted receives 55 percent of the total sale commission of 8 percent. How much commission did Ted earn?
    A. $3,546
    B. $3,940
    C. $4,334
    D. $7,880

98. The city is proposing to pave the streets in your neighborhood at a cost of $47 per foot. The city will absorb 30 percent of the cost. Your lot has a front footage of 110 feet. Assuming there are homes on both sides of the street, calculate the amount of your paving assessment.
    A. $1,551.50
    B. $1,809.50
    C. $3,619
    D. $5,170

99. The loan-to-value ratio offered by a local financial institution is 75 percent. If a buyer wishes to acquire a property selling for $129,500, the buyer will need to make a down payment of
    A. $1,727.
    B. $5,180.
    C. $32,375.
    D. $97,125.

100. The monthly payment for principal and interest on a $92,000 loan at 7½ percent for 30 years is $643.28. What amount of the second month's payment will be applied to principal?
    A. $68.28
    B. $68.71
    C. $574.57
    D. $575

ANSWER SHEET

PRACTICE EXAM

Score: _____

Wrong Ways to mark answers:

✔ ⊗ ⊙ Ⓚ

RIGHT WAY to mark answers:

●

1 Ⓐ Ⓑ Ⓒ Ⓓ	21 Ⓐ Ⓑ Ⓒ Ⓓ	41 Ⓐ Ⓑ Ⓒ Ⓓ	61 Ⓐ Ⓑ Ⓒ Ⓓ	81 Ⓐ Ⓑ Ⓒ Ⓓ
2 Ⓐ Ⓑ Ⓒ Ⓓ	22 Ⓐ Ⓑ Ⓒ Ⓓ	42 Ⓐ Ⓑ Ⓒ Ⓓ	62 Ⓐ Ⓑ Ⓒ Ⓓ	82 Ⓐ Ⓑ Ⓒ Ⓓ
3 Ⓐ Ⓑ Ⓒ Ⓓ	23 Ⓐ Ⓑ Ⓒ Ⓓ	43 Ⓐ Ⓑ Ⓒ Ⓓ	63 Ⓐ Ⓑ Ⓒ Ⓓ	83 Ⓐ Ⓑ Ⓒ Ⓓ
4 Ⓐ Ⓑ Ⓒ Ⓓ	24 Ⓐ Ⓑ Ⓒ Ⓓ	44 Ⓐ Ⓑ Ⓒ Ⓓ	64 Ⓐ Ⓑ Ⓒ Ⓓ	84 Ⓐ Ⓑ Ⓒ Ⓓ
5 Ⓐ Ⓑ Ⓒ Ⓓ	25 Ⓐ Ⓑ Ⓒ Ⓓ	45 Ⓐ Ⓑ Ⓒ Ⓓ	65 Ⓐ Ⓑ Ⓒ Ⓓ	85 Ⓐ Ⓑ Ⓒ Ⓓ
6 Ⓐ Ⓑ Ⓒ Ⓓ	26 Ⓐ Ⓑ Ⓒ Ⓓ	46 Ⓐ Ⓑ Ⓒ Ⓓ	66 Ⓐ Ⓑ Ⓒ Ⓓ	86 Ⓐ Ⓑ Ⓒ Ⓓ
7 Ⓐ Ⓑ Ⓒ Ⓓ	27 Ⓐ Ⓑ Ⓒ Ⓓ	47 Ⓐ Ⓑ Ⓒ Ⓓ	67 Ⓐ Ⓑ Ⓒ Ⓓ	87 Ⓐ Ⓑ Ⓒ Ⓓ
8 Ⓐ Ⓑ Ⓒ Ⓓ	28 Ⓐ Ⓑ Ⓒ Ⓓ	48 Ⓐ Ⓑ Ⓒ Ⓓ	68 Ⓐ Ⓑ Ⓒ Ⓓ	88 Ⓐ Ⓑ Ⓒ Ⓓ
9 Ⓐ Ⓑ Ⓒ Ⓓ	29 Ⓐ Ⓑ Ⓒ Ⓓ	49 Ⓐ Ⓑ Ⓒ Ⓓ	69 Ⓐ Ⓑ Ⓒ Ⓓ	89 Ⓐ Ⓑ Ⓒ Ⓓ
10 Ⓐ Ⓑ Ⓒ Ⓓ	30 Ⓐ Ⓑ Ⓒ Ⓓ	50 Ⓐ Ⓑ Ⓒ Ⓓ	70 Ⓐ Ⓑ Ⓒ Ⓓ	90 Ⓐ Ⓑ Ⓒ Ⓓ
11 Ⓐ Ⓑ Ⓒ Ⓓ	31 Ⓐ Ⓑ Ⓒ Ⓓ	51 Ⓐ Ⓑ Ⓒ Ⓓ	71 Ⓐ Ⓑ Ⓒ Ⓓ	91 Ⓐ Ⓑ Ⓒ Ⓓ
12 Ⓐ Ⓑ Ⓒ Ⓓ	32 Ⓐ Ⓑ Ⓒ Ⓓ	52 Ⓐ Ⓑ Ⓒ Ⓓ	72 Ⓐ Ⓑ Ⓒ Ⓓ	92 Ⓐ Ⓑ Ⓒ Ⓓ
13 Ⓐ Ⓑ Ⓒ Ⓓ	33 Ⓐ Ⓑ Ⓒ Ⓓ	53 Ⓐ Ⓑ Ⓒ Ⓓ	73 Ⓐ Ⓑ Ⓒ Ⓓ	93 Ⓐ Ⓑ Ⓒ Ⓓ
14 Ⓐ Ⓑ Ⓒ Ⓓ	34 Ⓐ Ⓑ Ⓒ Ⓓ	54 Ⓐ Ⓑ Ⓒ Ⓓ	74 Ⓐ Ⓑ Ⓒ Ⓓ	94 Ⓐ Ⓑ Ⓒ Ⓓ
15 Ⓐ Ⓑ Ⓒ Ⓓ	35 Ⓐ Ⓑ Ⓒ Ⓓ	55 Ⓐ Ⓑ Ⓒ Ⓓ	75 Ⓐ Ⓑ Ⓒ Ⓓ	95 Ⓐ Ⓑ Ⓒ Ⓓ
16 Ⓐ Ⓑ Ⓒ Ⓓ	36 Ⓐ Ⓑ Ⓒ Ⓓ	56 Ⓐ Ⓑ Ⓒ Ⓓ	76 Ⓐ Ⓑ Ⓒ Ⓓ	96 Ⓐ Ⓑ Ⓒ Ⓓ
17 Ⓐ Ⓑ Ⓒ Ⓓ	37 Ⓐ Ⓑ Ⓒ Ⓓ	57 Ⓐ Ⓑ Ⓒ Ⓓ	77 Ⓐ Ⓑ Ⓒ Ⓓ	97 Ⓐ Ⓑ Ⓒ Ⓓ
18 Ⓐ Ⓑ Ⓒ Ⓓ	38 Ⓐ Ⓑ Ⓒ Ⓓ	58 Ⓐ Ⓑ Ⓒ Ⓓ	78 Ⓐ Ⓑ Ⓒ Ⓓ	98 Ⓐ Ⓑ Ⓒ Ⓓ
19 Ⓐ Ⓑ Ⓒ Ⓓ	39 Ⓐ Ⓑ Ⓒ Ⓓ	59 Ⓐ Ⓑ Ⓒ Ⓓ	79 Ⓐ Ⓑ Ⓒ Ⓓ	99 Ⓐ Ⓑ Ⓒ Ⓓ
20 Ⓐ Ⓑ Ⓒ Ⓓ	40 Ⓐ Ⓑ Ⓒ Ⓓ	60 Ⓐ Ⓑ Ⓒ Ⓓ	80 Ⓐ Ⓑ Ⓒ Ⓓ	100 Ⓐ Ⓑ Ⓒ Ⓓ

A N S W E R S H E E T

PRACTICE EXAM

Score: _____

Wrong Ways to mark answers:

☑ ☒ ⊙ Ⓞ

RIGHT WAY to mark answers:

●

1 Ⓐ Ⓑ Ⓒ Ⓓ	21 Ⓐ Ⓑ Ⓒ Ⓓ	41 Ⓐ Ⓑ Ⓒ Ⓓ	61 Ⓐ Ⓑ Ⓒ Ⓓ	81 Ⓐ Ⓑ Ⓒ Ⓓ
2 Ⓐ Ⓑ Ⓒ Ⓓ	22 Ⓐ Ⓑ Ⓒ Ⓓ	42 Ⓐ Ⓑ Ⓒ Ⓓ	62 Ⓐ Ⓑ Ⓒ Ⓓ	82 Ⓐ Ⓑ Ⓒ Ⓓ
3 Ⓐ Ⓑ Ⓒ Ⓓ	23 Ⓐ Ⓑ Ⓒ Ⓓ	43 Ⓐ Ⓑ Ⓒ Ⓓ	63 Ⓐ Ⓑ Ⓒ Ⓓ	83 Ⓐ Ⓑ Ⓒ Ⓓ
4 Ⓐ Ⓑ Ⓒ Ⓓ	24 Ⓐ Ⓑ Ⓒ Ⓓ	44 Ⓐ Ⓑ Ⓒ Ⓓ	64 Ⓐ Ⓑ Ⓒ Ⓓ	84 Ⓐ Ⓑ Ⓒ Ⓓ
5 Ⓐ Ⓑ Ⓒ Ⓓ	25 Ⓐ Ⓑ Ⓒ Ⓓ	45 Ⓐ Ⓑ Ⓒ Ⓓ	65 Ⓐ Ⓑ Ⓒ Ⓓ	85 Ⓐ Ⓑ Ⓒ Ⓓ
6 Ⓐ Ⓑ Ⓒ Ⓓ	26 Ⓐ Ⓑ Ⓒ Ⓓ	46 Ⓐ Ⓑ Ⓒ Ⓓ	66 Ⓐ Ⓑ Ⓒ Ⓓ	86 Ⓐ Ⓑ Ⓒ Ⓓ
7 Ⓐ Ⓑ Ⓒ Ⓓ	27 Ⓐ Ⓑ Ⓒ Ⓓ	47 Ⓐ Ⓑ Ⓒ Ⓓ	67 Ⓐ Ⓑ Ⓒ Ⓓ	87 Ⓐ Ⓑ Ⓒ Ⓓ
8 Ⓐ Ⓑ Ⓒ Ⓓ	28 Ⓐ Ⓑ Ⓒ Ⓓ	48 Ⓐ Ⓑ Ⓒ Ⓓ	68 Ⓐ Ⓑ Ⓒ Ⓓ	88 Ⓐ Ⓑ Ⓒ Ⓓ
9 Ⓐ Ⓑ Ⓒ Ⓓ	29 Ⓐ Ⓑ Ⓒ Ⓓ	49 Ⓐ Ⓑ Ⓒ Ⓓ	69 Ⓐ Ⓑ Ⓒ Ⓓ	89 Ⓐ Ⓑ Ⓒ Ⓓ
10 Ⓐ Ⓑ Ⓒ Ⓓ	30 Ⓐ Ⓑ Ⓒ Ⓓ	50 Ⓐ Ⓑ Ⓒ Ⓓ	70 Ⓐ Ⓑ Ⓒ Ⓓ	90 Ⓐ Ⓑ Ⓒ Ⓓ
11 Ⓐ Ⓑ Ⓒ Ⓓ	31 Ⓐ Ⓑ Ⓒ Ⓓ	51 Ⓐ Ⓑ Ⓒ Ⓓ	71 Ⓐ Ⓑ Ⓒ Ⓓ	91 Ⓐ Ⓑ Ⓒ Ⓓ
12 Ⓐ Ⓑ Ⓒ Ⓓ	32 Ⓐ Ⓑ Ⓒ Ⓓ	52 Ⓐ Ⓑ Ⓒ Ⓓ	72 Ⓐ Ⓑ Ⓒ Ⓓ	92 Ⓐ Ⓑ Ⓒ Ⓓ
13 Ⓐ Ⓑ Ⓒ Ⓓ	33 Ⓐ Ⓑ Ⓒ Ⓓ	53 Ⓐ Ⓑ Ⓒ Ⓓ	73 Ⓐ Ⓑ Ⓒ Ⓓ	93 Ⓐ Ⓑ Ⓒ Ⓓ
14 Ⓐ Ⓑ Ⓒ Ⓓ	34 Ⓐ Ⓑ Ⓒ Ⓓ	54 Ⓐ Ⓑ Ⓒ Ⓓ	74 Ⓐ Ⓑ Ⓒ Ⓓ	94 Ⓐ Ⓑ Ⓒ Ⓓ
15 Ⓐ Ⓑ Ⓒ Ⓓ	35 Ⓐ Ⓑ Ⓒ Ⓓ	55 Ⓐ Ⓑ Ⓒ Ⓓ	75 Ⓐ Ⓑ Ⓒ Ⓓ	95 Ⓐ Ⓑ Ⓒ Ⓓ
16 Ⓐ Ⓑ Ⓒ Ⓓ	36 Ⓐ Ⓑ Ⓒ Ⓓ	56 Ⓐ Ⓑ Ⓒ Ⓓ	76 Ⓐ Ⓑ Ⓒ Ⓓ	96 Ⓐ Ⓑ Ⓒ Ⓓ
17 Ⓐ Ⓑ Ⓒ Ⓓ	37 Ⓐ Ⓑ Ⓒ Ⓓ	57 Ⓐ Ⓑ Ⓒ Ⓓ	77 Ⓐ Ⓑ Ⓒ Ⓓ	97 Ⓐ Ⓑ Ⓒ Ⓓ
18 Ⓐ Ⓑ Ⓒ Ⓓ	38 Ⓐ Ⓑ Ⓒ Ⓓ	58 Ⓐ Ⓑ Ⓒ Ⓓ	78 Ⓐ Ⓑ Ⓒ Ⓓ	98 Ⓐ Ⓑ Ⓒ Ⓓ
19 Ⓐ Ⓑ Ⓒ Ⓓ	39 Ⓐ Ⓑ Ⓒ Ⓓ	59 Ⓐ Ⓑ Ⓒ Ⓓ	79 Ⓐ Ⓑ Ⓒ Ⓓ	99 Ⓐ Ⓑ Ⓒ Ⓓ
20 Ⓐ Ⓑ Ⓒ Ⓓ	40 Ⓐ Ⓑ Ⓒ Ⓓ	60 Ⓐ Ⓑ Ⓒ Ⓓ	80 Ⓐ Ⓑ Ⓒ Ⓓ	100 Ⓐ Ⓑ Ⓒ Ⓓ

Sample Exam Questions

Answers to 470 multiple-choice sample exam questions are grouped in
the sequence license law, general law, principles and practices, and math.
The chapter number (in parentheses) indicates where the question topics can be found in
the textbooks *Florida Real Estate Principles, Practices & Law* and *Florida Real Estate Broker's Guide*.
The correct letter answer is followed by a brief explanation of the correct answer.

Florida Real Estate License Law Chapters

■ LICENSE LAW AND QUALIFICATIONS (CHAPTER 2) FLORIDA REAL ESTATE BROKER'S GUIDE (CHAPTER 1)

1. (C) An individual who does not intend to engage actively in the real estate business, such as an officer of a real estate corporation, simply registers this information with the DRE so that the information can be entered into the FREC's records.

2. (D) Section 475.01, F.S., defines a broker associate as, "a person who is qualified to be issued a license as a broker but who operates as a sales associate in the employ of another."

3. (C) *Caveat emptor* is a Latin term meaning "let the buyer beware."

4. (B) If a nonresident applicant or licensee wishes to become licensed in Florida, he or she must sign the irrevocable consent of service section on the application form. This agreement provides that lawsuits and other legal actions may be initiated against the applicant in any county of Florida in which the person bringing suit resides.

5. (C) Any resident licensee who becomes a nonresident must notify the Commission within 60 days of the change in residency and comply with all nonresident requirements.

6. (A) There are eight real estate services (A BAR SALE): advertise, buy, appraise, rent or provide rental lists (information), sell, auction, lease, and exchange.

7. (C) Pursuant to 61J2-26.001, F.A.C., mutual recognition agreements apply exclusively to nonresidents licensed in other jurisdictions.

8. (B) A sales associate or broker associate may have only one registered employer at any time.

9. (A) U.S. citizenship is not required to hold a Florida real estate license.

10. (C) Pursuant to Section 475.011, F.S., persons acting within the limitations of their duties as designated by a will, proper court, or statutory authority to serve as a personal representative or trustee are specifically exempted from licensure.

11. (C) It is not a violation of rules to serve as a broker for one company and concurrently serve on the board of directors of another real estate company. Pursuant to 61J2-5.015, F.A.C., all officers and directors of a real estate brokerage corporation must be registered. Because he is also an active broker for Richard Realty, he must hold an active broker license.

12. (B) Section 475.181, F.S., states that if an applicant does not pass the licensing examination within two years after the successful course completion date, the applicant's successful course completion is invalid for licensure.

13. (A) Prima facie evidence is a legal term used to refer to evidence that is good and sufficient on its face to establish a given fact or prove a case.

■ LICENSE LAW AND ADMINISTRATION (CHAPTER 3)

14. (C) Florida statutes prohibit Commission members from serving more than two consecutive terms.

15. (D) The FREC's quasi-legislative responsibilities include the power to enact administrative rules and regulations.

16. (C) The FREC must inform the Division of Florida Land Sales, Condominiums and Mobile Homes when any disciplinary action is taken by the FREC against any of its licensees.

17. (A) The Commission is obligated to report any criminal violation of Chapter 475, when knowledgeable of such violations, to the state's attorney having jurisdiction.

18. (D) The powers of the FREC are limited to administrative matters and do not extend to criminal actions. The FREC cannot impose imprisonment as a penalty.

19. (C) Individuals who previously qualified for current license status but who do not renew their licenses before they expire are placed on involuntary inactive status.

20. (D) A member of the U.S. Armed Forces who at the time of entry to active duty was a Florida licensee in good standing is exempt from all renewal requirements while on active duty and for six months thereafter. When the military duty is out of state, the exemption also applies to a licensed spouse.

21. (B) A license that has been in involuntary inactive status for more than two years expires automatically and becomes null and void. At that point an individual would have to meet the requirements for a new real estate license.

22. (C) A sales associate's license is placed in involuntary inactive status when an employer's license is suspended or revoked. The sales associate is, however, entitled to receive a new registration as soon as new employment is secured.

23. (D) A Florida broker may be issued, on request, additional Florida broker licenses whenever it is shown that the additional licenses are necessary to the conduct of business. A broker who holds more than one Florida broker license is said to hold multiple licenses.

24. (B) When a broker changes his or her business address, the broker must notify the Commission of the change within ten days after the change occurs. The licenses of sales associates working for a broker who changes his or her business address remain effective and in force.

25. (B) When a broker changes business address the brokerage firm permit holder must file with the Commission a notice of the change of address, along with the names of any sales associates who are no longer employed by the brokerage. Sales associates who are no longer employed with the broker of record are placed in involuntary inactive status.

■ BROKERAGE RELATIONSHIPS AND ETHICS (CHAPTER 4) FLORIDA REAL ESTATE BROKER'S GUIDE (CHAPTER 10)

26. (B) Brokers must retain brokerage relationship disclosure documents for five years for all residential transactions that result in a written contract to purchase and sell real property. This requirement includes files of properties that may have failed to close.

27. (B) A special agent is authorized by the buyer or seller to handle only a specific business transaction or to perform only a specific act. A real estate broker typically is authorized by the buyer or seller to act as a special agent.

28. (C) The disclosure is not required from a builder because the builder is not regulated by the FREC. However, the builder's licensed sales associates would have to give a disclosure only if it was not clear through name tags, signage, and so on, that the sales associates worked for the builder.

29. (B) The broker and the broker's sales associates are obligated to follow the lawful instructions of the owner.

30. (C) An agency relationship exists between a broker and a sales associate (agent) who is either an employee of or an independent contractor of the broker (principal). The sales associate is obligated to act in conformity with the broker's instructions as long as they are legal and relevant to the contractual relationship. Otherwise, the sales associate should withdraw from the relationship.

31. (D) The broker must provide the single agent notice to the seller before, or at the time of, entering into a listing agreement.

32. (B) A sales associate or broker associate owes the same fiduciary obligations to the principal as does his or her broker, regardless of whether the associate, for tax purposes, is an employee or an independent contractor.

33. (C) The licensee must secure the written consent and approval of the seller (or buyer, if the licensee is a buyer's agent) before transitioning to another relationship.

34. (B) The disclosures do not apply to the rental or leasing of real property, unless an option to purchase all or a portion of the property improved with four or fewer residential units is involved.

35. (D) Effective October 1, 1997, dual agency was revoked in the State of Florida.

36. (C) Transaction brokers have a duty of limited confidentiality, unless waived in writing. This limited confidentiality will prevent disclosure that the seller will accept a price less than the asking or listing price, the motivation of any party for buying or selling property, or any other information requested by a party to remain confidential.

37. (C) A transaction broker has a duty of limited confidentiality (not full disclosure). Undivided loyalty is a single agent duty. Transaction brokers have a duty to disclose all known facts that materially affect the value of real property and are not readily observable to the buyer.

38. (A) In nonresidential transactions involving a buyer and seller who each have assets of $1 million or more, the broker at the request of the buyer and seller may designate sales associates to act as single agents for different customers in the same transaction. Such designated sales associates have the duties of a single agent, including disclosure requirements.

39. (B) A transaction broker has a duty to account for all funds entrusted to him or her with regard to a real estate transaction. Loyalty and confidentiality are single agent duties.

■ REAL ESTATE BROKERAGE OPERATIONS (CHAPTER 5) FLORIDA REAL ESTATE BROKER'S GUIDE (CHAPTERS 2 AND 4)

40. (D) Yard signs and classified ads must include the registered name of the brokerage firm.

41. (A) Florida law requires that the broker be a signatory on the escrow account.

42. (C) A "broker associate" is a person who is qualified to be licensed as a broker, but who operates as a sales associate. Therefore, the licensee must use the full title, "broker associate" on her business card.

43. (D) Because a licensee has superior knowledge and expertise in real estate, to reduce liability the "by owner" licensee-seller should disclose at the first point of meaningful negotiation that the seller is a real estate licensee.

44. (A) Commingling of funds is the illegal practice of mixing a buyer's or seller's funds with the broker's own money or of mixing escrow money with the broker's personal funds or business funds.

45. (C) In the case of a corporation, brokerage entrance signs must contain the name of the corporation, the name of at least one of the active brokers, and the words "Licensed Real Estate Broker" or "Lic. Real Estate Broker."

46. (B) "Immediately" for brokers is defined as not later than the end of the third business day following receipt of a deposit by a sales associate or employee of the brokerage firm.

47. (B) If a broker receives conflicting demands on escrowed property, the broker must notify the FREC, in writing, within 15 business days of the party's last demand.

48. (D) Acceptable depositories for escrow accounts are Florida-based title companies having trust powers, a commercial bank, a credit union, a savings association, or, if designated in the sale contract, a Florida attorney.

49. (B) Real estate licensees are prohibited from sharing commission with an unlicensed person. However, Florida law does allow the sharing of part of the commission with the buyer or seller in a real estate transaction.

50. (C) The Telephone Consumer Protection Act restricts solicitation calls to the hours of 8:00 AM to 9:00 PM.

51. (A) The FREC may choose not to issue an escrow disbursement order (EDO). If the broker is informed in writing by the Commission that an EDO will not be issued, the broker must utilize another settlement procedure, such as mediation, arbitration, or litigation.

52. (D) According to Rule 61J2-14.0110(1), Florida Administrative Code (FAC), at least one broker of a brokerage firm must be a signatory on the escrow account.

53. (D) It is illegal for a licensee to pay an unlicensed person any sum of money for the referral of real estate business.

54. (B) There are three exceptions to the notice requirements (1) escrow deposits concerning a residential sale contract utilized by HUD in the sale of HUD-owned property; (2) buyers of residential condominium units who timely deliver written notice of their intent to cancel the contract as authorized by the Condominium Act; and (3) buyers who in good faith fail to satisfy the terms specified in the financing clause of a contract for sale and purchase.

55. (B) If a prospective tenant does not obtain a rental, he or she is entitled to a refund of 75 percent of the fee paid if requested within 30 days of the contract/receipt date.

56. (A) When a buyer or seller refuses to pay a broker's commission after the commission has been earned, the broker may take action to collect by filing a suit against the party for the amount due. Florida law prohibits a licensee from placing a lien on residential property for the purpose of collecting a commission, unless expressly permitted by contractual agreement.

57. (C) Pursuant to Rule 61J2-10.028, F.A.C., a licensee, prior to the acceptance of a kickback or rebate, must fully advise the principal and all affected parties in the transaction of all the facts pertaining to the arrangement.

58. (D) A broker may be disciplined by the FREC for failure to secure the written permission of all interested parties prior to placing trust (escrow) funds in an interest-bearing escrow account.

59. (C) All monies earned by a sales associate as a result of any real estate service must be paid to the sales associate by his or her employer and not directly by the buyer or seller.

60. (B) Chapter 673, F.S., provides for checks and other negotiable instruments to be postdated; however, extreme caution should be taken in handling such deposits. In all cases, the seller's approval must be obtained before accepting the postdated check.

61. (A) If a sales associate takes the original listings from an employer's office, the sales associate is guilty of larceny (theft) and is subject to administrative penalties by the FREC, civil action in court, and criminal penalties.

62. (A) A foreign corporation is a corporation organized under the laws of a state other than Florida but that conducts business in Florida.

63. (A) Brokers are allowed to place in a sales escrow account an amount up to $1,000 in order to open and maintain the account and to cover monthly service charges. Additionally, brokers may keep up to $5,000 of their own monies in a property management escrow account.

64. (A) In a general partnership, each of the partners is responsible for all the debts incurred in conducting the business.

65. (A) A quasi-partnership exists where there is not a real partnership but the parties act, or do business, in such a manner that the public, having no knowledge of the private relations of the parties, would reasonably be deceived into believing that a partnership exists.

66. (D) A sales associate or broker associate may not be a general partner in a partnership registered as a real estate broker.

67. (C) Licensed real estate brokers are exempt from complying with the provisions of the Florida Fictitious Name Act because they must register their trade name (if one is used) directly with the Commission.

68. (B) A joint venture is a temporary form of business arrangement. The joint venture structure is normally used when two or more parties combine their efforts to complete a single business transaction or a fixed number of business transactions.

69. (D) The broker must institute one of the settlement procedures within 30 business days from the time the broker received the conflicting demands. Because 12 business days have already passed, the broker has 18 business days remaining to implement one of the settlement procedures.

■ COMPLAINTS, VIOLATIONS, AND PENALTIES (CHAPTER 6) FLORIDA REAL ESTATE BROKER'S GUIDE (CHAPTER 5)

70. (A) Pursuant to Section 475.25(2), F.S., a license may be revoked or canceled if it was issued through a mistake or inadvertence of the Commission. Such revocation or cancellation will not prejudice any future application for licensure filed by the person against whom action was taken.

71. (D) The DBPR is empowered to administer oaths, take depositions, and examine respondents, witnesses, and plaintiffs. It can also issue subpoenas to anyone thought to possess information relevant to the case.

72. (C) Once a case has been investigated and found valid, the Probable Cause Panel determines whether probable cause exists.

73. (D) A person may not disseminate or cause to be disseminated by any means any false or misleading information for the purpose of offering for sale, or for the purpose of causing or inducing any other person to purchase; lease; or rent, real estate located in the state or for the purpose of causing or inducing any other person to acquire an interest in the title to real estate located in the state. To do so is a misdemeanor of the second degree.

74. (C) The Commission is empowered to enact (and modify) administrative rules. The administrative rule concerning real estate practice is Rule 61J2, F.A.C. Only the legislature can modify a statute.

75. (A) A licensee has 30 days from receipt of a citation to accept or reject the alleged violation(s), as specified in the citation. Failure to pay the fine in a timely manner will give rise to the filing of an administrative complaint.

76. (B) Any final order issued as a result of a hearing for a summary suspension must be issued by the DBPR Secretary or a legally appointed designee. A summary suspension must be followed promptly by a formal suspension or revocation hearing.

77. (D) Possible administrative penalties that may be imposed by the FREC include denial of an application for licensure; refusal to recertify a license for renewal; revocation of a license; suspension of a license for not more than ten years; a fine not to exceed $5,000 for each F.S. 455 or F.S. 475 violation or separate offense; and probation, reprimand, citation, notice of noncompliance, or other penalty.

78. (B) Pursuant to Rule 61J2-24.003, the Commission sets forth a list of minor violations for which the DBPR must issue a notice of noncompliance as a first response to a minor violation by a licensee.

79. (D) The FREC is empowered to revoke a license for a violation of Chapter 475, F.S.

80. (A) The FREC is authorized to order reimbursement to any licensee who is required by a court of law to pay money damages as a result of the licensee's compliance with an escrow disbursement order. If the licensee had previously requested an EDO and complied with it, no action will be taken against the licensee.

81. (B) Section 475.41, F.S., provides that such contracts are invalid. An inactive license does not allow a broker to do licensed real estate activity for compensation.

82. (C) Licensees are not required to report misdemeanor convictions to the FREC. However, pursuant to Chapter 475.25(2)(p), a licensee who pleads guilty or nolo contendere to, or is convicted of, or found guilty of, any felony must notify the FREC, in writing, within 30 days.

83. (B) One of the probable-cause panel members may be a former Commissioner. However, if a former professional board member serves on the panel, the former Commissioner must currently hold an active real estate license.

84. (A) The licensee-respondent must be given at least 14 days notice of a hearing. The notice of hearing informs the licensee-respondent of the time, place, nature of the hearing, and includes a statement regarding the legal authority and jurisdiction under which the hearing is being held.

General Real Estate Law Chapters

■ FEDERAL AND STATE HOUSING LAWS (CHAPTER 7) FLORIDA REAL ESTATE BROKER'S GUIDE (CHAPTERS 2, 12, AND 18)

85. (A) In 1968 the U.S. Supreme Court, in the case of *Jones v. Mayer*, upheld the Civil Rights Act of 1866, which prohibits discrimination on the basis of race.

86. (A) The Civil Rights Act of 1968 made discrimination illegal in sales, leasing, advertising sales or rentals, financing, or brokerage services if such discrimination is based on race, color, religion, sex, national origin, handicap, or familial status.

87. (D) The Fair Housing Act is part of the Civil Rights Act of 1968.

88. (A) Blockbusting refers to using the entry, or rumor of the entry, of a protected class into a neighborhood to persuade owners to sell.

89. (B) Denying loans or insurance coverage or other restrictive practices by a lending institution or insurer that represents different terms or conditions for homes in certain neighborhoods is known as redlining.

90. (C) Channeling protected-class homeseekers away from areas that are not mixed with that class into areas that are is known as steering.

91. (A) The Equal Credit Opportunity Act ensures that financial institutions and firms engaged in extending credit will make credit available with fairness and without discrimination on the basis of race, color, religion, national origin, sex, marital status, age, or receipt of income from public assistance programs.

92. (D) The Interstate Land Sales Full Disclosure Act is designed to protect consumers from misrepresentation by land developers. Purchasers must be furnished a Property Report before signing a purchase contract or lease.

93. (A) The Truth-in-Lending Act is implemented by Federal Reserve Regulation Z and requires that lenders disclose the annual percentage rate of interest and finance charges imposed by consumers.

94. (C) The Truth-in-Lending Act requires that lenders disclose the annual percentage rate of interest and finance charges imposed on consumers.

95. (B) RESPA requires the use of a uniform settlement statement by the closing agent for all loan closings that are not exempt. Included in transactions exempt from RESPA are construction loans, except those intended for conversion into permanent loans.

96. (B) Brokers must obey the lawful instructions of the owner. It is not a violation of the Fair Housing Act to inform the member of the protected class that the property cannot be shown while the owner is out of town *provided* the statement is the truth and the refusal to show the property in the owner's absence applies to *all* prospective buyers.

97. (B) Transactions exempt from RESPA include loans to finance the purchase of 25 acres or more.

98. (B) The landlord is obligated to account for security deposits and advance rents in one of three ways. One of the three methods is to post a surety bond with the clerk of the circuit court in the total amount of the security deposits and advance rents or $50,000, whichever is less, and pay the tenant 5 percent per year simple interest.

99. (A) The Florida Residential Landlord and Tenant Act requires that the landlord inform tenants in writing, within 30 days from the receipt of advance rent or security deposit, of the manner in which the tenant's funds are being held.

100. (D) If a tenant vacates rented premises at the end of a lease, the landlord is required to notify the tenant within 30 days if the landlord intends to claim a part or all of the tenant's security deposit.

101. (D) At the time the sheriff executes the writ of possession or any time thereafter, the landlord or the landlord's agent may remove any personal property found on the premises to or near the property line. Subsequent to executing the writ of possession, the landlord may request the sheriff to stand by to keep the peace while the landlord changes the locks and removes the personal property from the premises.

102. (A) Any right or duty stated in Chapter 83, Part II, F.S., is enforceable by civil action, which means that all legal remedies sought by either tenant or landlord are pursued through the civil courts.

103. (D) After entry of judgment in favor of the landlord, the clerk of the court issues a writ to the sheriff to put the landlord in possession after a 24-hour notice has been posted on the premises.

■ PROPERTY RIGHTS: ESTATES, TENANCIES, AND MULTIPLE OWNER- SHIP INTERESTS (CHAPTER 8)

104. (D) Pursuant to Section 475.01, F.S., real property is any interest or estate in land and any interest in business enterprises or business opportunities, including any assignment, leasehold, subleasehold, or mineral right.

105. (C) Riparian rights are associated with land abutting the banks of a river, stream, or other watercourse.

106. (A) Real property includes the land and anything permanently attached to it.

107. (A) Real property can become personal property by the act of severance. For example, timber is real property but when cut becomes personal property by the act of severance.

108. (B) A trade fixture is an item of personal property attached to real property that is owned by a tenant and is used in a business. It is legally removable by the tenant.

109. (C) Pursuant to Chapter 83, F.S., a notice of fifteen days is required to terminate a month-to-month tenancy at will.

110. (C) A freehold estate is a tenancy in real property with no set termination date; it can be measured by the lifetime of an individual or can be inherited.

111. (C) A joint tenancy is an estate owned by two or more persons, each having equal rights of possession and ownership, and right of survivorship.

112. (C) A freehold estate is an ownership interest for an indefinite period that can be inherited. A proprietary lease is associated with cooperatives. A tenancy by the entireties is a joint tenancy between a husband and wife.

113. (A) A true joint tenancy cannot be created unless specific wording in the deed conveying the property provides for survivorship.

114. (C) A tenancy in common is a form of ownership by two or more persons each having an equal or unequal interest and passing the interest to heirs, not to surviving tenants.

115. (B) A tenancy in common provides the best protection for each owner's families because each tenant in common's legal interest will descend to the legal heirs.

116. (B) The right of disposition allows the owner to sell, mortgage, dedicate, give away, or otherwise dispose of all or any portion of the property.

117. (B) A tenancy in common is the most frequently used form of co-ownership, except for husband and wife ownership.

118. (D) A joint tenant who wants to sell his or her share of a property may do so. However, the person who buys that share cannot be a joint tenant with the other original owners, but instead will be a tenant in common.

119. (C) Any property that a husband or wife owned before the marriage is separate property and is owned independently of the other spouse.

120. (B) As joint tenants die, their shares are divided among the surviving tenants until only one owner is left. The sole survivor then has a fee simple estate in severalty.

121. (A) The fact that the purchase took place at different times tells us this is a tenancy in common rather than a joint tenancy because at least one of the four "unities" of time, title, interest, and possession is not present.

122. (B) An estate for years is a tenancy with a definite termination date. An estate for years is a leasehold estate that must be created by a properly executed lease agreement.

123. (C) An estate for years exists for a designated period, which may be any length of time from less than a year to a period of many years.

124. (D) When a life estate ends, the property reverts (returns) to the original grantor or goes to a third party, called a remainderman. If the life estate reverts to the original grantor, an estate in reversion is created.

125. (B) If an individual is a salaried employee of an owner-developer whose primary business is the development and sale of time-share units, the sales person is not required to hold a real estate license, provided he or she is not paid a commission or otherwise compensated on a transactional basis, such as with bonuses based on sales quotas. Jenny receives bonuses based on sales production so she must be licensed.

126. (A) The bylaws of a condominium association govern the administration of the association and include the rules and regulations.

127. (A) It is an estate for years because there is a definite beginning and ending date.

128. (B) A tenant at sufferance has no estate or title but only "naked" possession.

129. (C) The current homestead tax exemption is $25,000 for all qualifying homesteads and is deducted from the assessed value when calculating taxable value.

130. (C) The bundle of rights under the allodial system includes (DUPE): disposition; use (or control); possession; and exclusion (or quite enjoyment).

131. (C) Common elements include all portions of the condominium property not included in the individual units.

132. (C) A tenancy at will is a leasehold in which the tenant holds possession of the premises with the owner's permission but without a fixed term.

133. (A) A condominium is created by recording a declaration in the public records of the county where the land is located, executed, and acknowledged with the requirements of a deed.

134. (B) Purchase of stock in the corporation entitles the purchaser to a proprietary lease and the right to occupy a particular unit in the cooperative.

135. (C) Condominium documents that define the rights and obligations of condominium owners include the declaration, bylaws, and articles of incorporation.

136. (A) Accretion is the process of land buildup from water-borne rock, sand, and soil.

137. (D) Developers of 20 or more new residential units must prepare a prospectus in addition to the other condominium documents. A copy of the prospectus must be given to prospective purchasers.

■ TITLES, DEEDS, AND OWNERSHIP RESTRICTIONS (CHAPTER 9)

138. (C) A lis pendens is a notice of pending legal action.

139. (B) Transfer by devise involves a will; transfer by descent involves heirs; and escheat is the reversion of property to the state when an owner dies without leaving a will or any known heirs.

140. (D) Adverse possession requires hostile possession of the property (without the owner's permission).

141. (B) A gift of real property in a will is known as a devise, and the recipient of the gift is the devisee.

142. (D) Adverse possession must continue for seven or more consecutive years without the consent of the owner.

143. (B) Constructive notice refers to information that has been made public by recording the information in the public records.

144. (D) A deed or other conveyance instrument will not be effective in transferring title to property until it is delivered to and accepted by the grantee.

145. (C) Acknowledgment is the formal declaration before a notary public by the grantor that his or her signing is a free act.

146. (D) Legal title can be conveyed by descent (inheritance), quitclaim deed, or eminent domain. *Novation* is the term used for the substitution of a new party and/or new terms to an existing obligation.

147. (D) The grantee is the person who received the deed (buyer). The grantor is the person conveying title (seller).

148. (D) Option D describes the lender's title insurance policy.

149. (A) When the Lakes took physical possession of the property, they gave actual notice of legal title.

150. (B) Essential elements of a deed include consideration, execution (signed) by a competent grantor and two witnesses, and voluntary delivery and acceptance. Seal refers to a mark, emblem, or impression on a document used to authenticate a signature. A seal is not required to make a deed valid.

151. (A) The granting clause contains the necessary words used to convey property, such as "grants, bargains, and sells" or similar words.

152. (C) The habendum clause is a provision in a deed to real property that stipulates the estate or interest the grantee is to receive and the type of title conveyed.

153. (C) Only attorneys may draft leases on someone else's behalf. Property owners may draft leases for their own property, but owners may not delegate that authority to nonattorneys.

154. (A) The seisin clause is a covenant in a deed that warrants that the grantor (seller) holds the property by virtue of a fee simple title and has a complete right to dispose of the property.

155. (B) Instead of the usual wording "grants, bargains, and sells," the quitclaim deed uses the words "remise, release, and quitclaim." This allows the grantor to sign a deed transferring any and all interests he or she may have, without claiming ownership of any right of title whatsoever.

156. (B) Police powers, eminent domain, and escheat are all governmental restrictions on ownership. Deed restrictions are among the broadest restrictions in the private category.

157. (A) The covenant of further assurance is a provision in a deed containing a covenant of warranty to perform any further acts the buyer might require to perfect title to the property.

158. (C) Condemnation is the taking of private real property for a public purpose under the right of eminent domain for a fair price.

159. (B) Escheat is the reversion of property to the state when an owner dies without leaving a will (intestate) or any known heirs.

160. (B) Under police power, the use of real property may be regulated. Eminent domain is the taking for just compensation.

161. (B) The constitutions of the federal government and state governments grant eminent domain power to take private property for a public use.

162. (B) An easement is a right given or belonging to another for some specific use of an owner's property.

163. (A) Escheat is the reversion of property to the state when an owner dies without leaving a will or any known heirs.

164. (C) An easement by necessity is created by court order to allow property owners to enter and exit their landlocked property.

165. (C) The requirements of a valid lease include names of the lessor and lessee, legal capacity, consideration, the term of the lease, and the property identification.

166. (B) A lease is for a specified time period and conveys upon sale of the leased property. A buyer who wanted a tenant to vacate during the remaining lease period would have to "buy out" the tenant's remaining interest.

167. (D) A sublease is effected when the lessee assigns less than the entire property or assigns all of the property for less than the full remaining period. Subleasing is also called subrogation or subordination of space.

168. (A) A quitclaim deed is a conveyance by which the grantor transfers whatever interest he or she has in the real estate, without making any warranties or obligations. Quitclaim deeds are often used to clear clouds on title.

169. (C) An encroachment is the unauthorized use of another's property. It is an infringement or intrusion on property without the owner's consent.

170. (B) When the use of property such as a roadway has continued openly without interruption for more than 20 years, an easement by prescription is created.

171. (D) A lease is an interest in, but not title to, real property.

172. (C) Any oral contract or agreement between the lessor and lessee is legally a tenancy at will.

173. (B) A leasehold is an estate in real property held under a lease arrangement for a definite number of years.

174. (D) The terms eviction, assignment, and subrogation apply to leasing real property.

175. (B) Police power is the government's right to impose laws, statutes, and ordinances to protect the public health, safety, and welfare. Police power represents the broadest power of the government to limit the rights of property owners.

176. (A) A lien is an encumbrance on the title to real property; however, not all encumbrances on property are liens. Specific liens affect only a certain property (not all property of a debtor). A property tax lien is an example of a specific (not a general) lien.

177. (D) A lease is an agreement (contract) between the lessor and lessee. A lease constitutes an interest in real property, but it does not convey ownership.

178. (B) Deed restrictions are private restrictions that restrict the use of real property but do not create a lien on the property.

179. (D) An assignment of a lease occurs when a lessee assigns to another party all of the leased property for the full remaining period.

180. (B) A sublease is affected when the lessee assigns less than the entire property or assigns all of the property for less than the full remaining period.

181. (D) An income tax lien is a general lien meaning that it is not restricted to one property but may affect all properties of a debtor.

182. (C) Eminent domain is the right of a government or a municipal quasi-public body to acquire property for a public use through a court action known as condemnation.

183. (D) A mortgage is a lien voluntarily placed on real property by a borrower who pledges his or her property as security to the lender.

184. (A) The date the mortgage is filed and recorded with the clerk of the circuit court establishes the priority of the lien against other claims on the property.

185. (B) The date of recordation establishes the priority.

186. (B) A specific lien is a claim that affects only the property designated in the lien instrument. Property taxes are involuntary because they become liens as soon as the assessment is complete.

187. (A) When litigation is initiated involving a specific parcel of real property, a lis pendens (notice of pending legal action) usually is filed with the clerk of the county in which the property is located.

188. (C) An attachment is a legal writ obtained to prevent removal of property that is expected to be used to satisfy a judgment.

189. (B) A vendor's lien is a claim against property giving the seller the right to hold the property as security for any unpaid purchase money.

190. (B) Equitable title is a beneficial interest in real estate that implies that an individual will receive legal title at a future date.

◼ REAL ESTATE CONTRACTS (CHAPTER 11) FLORIDA REAL ESTATE BROKER'S GUIDE (CHAPTER 11)

191. (B) Pursuant to the statute of frauds, certain contracts, including those pertaining to the transfer of interests in real property, must be in writing to be enforceable.

192. (D) A real estate contract typically is not recorded.

193. (B) An essential element of a valid real estate contract is an offer and acceptance (or a meeting of the minds).

194. (D) To be enforceable, a contract must have a lawful purpose; one that is not prohibited by law or contrary to public policy.

195. (D) A minor's contract is voidable because the minor can choose to void the contract.

196. (D) The signatures of the buyer and seller indicate that they agree to the terms of the contract.

197. (A) A unilateral contract is one that obligates only one party to an agreement without any obligation on the part of the other party involved. The broker is obligated to pay the bonus if the sales associate sells 20 homes; however, the sales associate is not obligated to sell 20 homes.

198. (B) The statute of frauds mandates that real estate contracts must be in writing and signed to be enforceable, *except* in two specific instances: (1) when the buyer has paid part of the purchase price and then has either taken possession of the property or made some improvements to the property, or (2) if both parties have fully performed all of the terms of the oral agreement.

199. (A) An option contract is an agreement in which a property owner grants a prospective buyer the right to buy the property within a specified period for a specified price and terms.

200. (C) When a counteroffer is made, it actually kills the original offer and substitutes a new offer in its place.

201. (C) When a prospective buyer submits a real estate contract accompanied by an earnest money deposit, an offer is considered to have been made. It does not become a contract for sale and purchase until the seller acknowledges acceptance of the price and terms by signing the sale and purchase agreement.

202. (A) A counteroffer indicates a willingness to contract, but on terms or conditions different from those contained in the offer. The original offer is dead forever and cannot be accepted later.

203. (C) When the seller made a counteroffer, it extinguished the buyer's original offer. At that point, the buyer was released from the original offer and is under no further obligation.

204. (C) An offeror may revoke an offer at any time until notice of the offeree's acceptance is received by the offeror or his or her designated agent.

205. (C) The desired outcome of any contract is performance.

206. (C) "Time is of the essence" is a phrase in a contract making failure to perform by a specified date a breach or violation of the agreement.

207. (A) A wronged party may sue for specific performance to have the courts force the other party to perform as the contract specifically states.

208. (D) A contract is breached when one of the parties to a contract fails to perform and the law does not recognize the reason for failure to perform as valid.

209. (B) The statute of limitations designates the period of time during which the terms of a contract may be enforced and protects people from being compelled to perform or otherwise be sued after a specific period of time has expired.

210. (D) Power of attorney is the designation of another person to act for a principal.

211. (A) An attorney-in-fact can bargain and sign for the person who granted power of attorney, provided that power is specifically granted.

212. (C) Real estate licensees may not draw lease agreements. However, licensees may fill in the blanks on Florida Supreme Court preapproved lease instruments for lease periods that do not exceed one year. Real estate licensees are allowed to assist buyers and sellers with the drawing of four types of contracts listing, buyer-brokerage, sale, and option contracts.

213. (D) A net listing is created when a seller agrees to sell a property for a stated minimum amount.

214. (A) In an open listing the owner gives a listing to a number of brokers and also reserves the right to sell the property himself. The seller is not obligated to pay a commission to any broker except the broker who first finds a buyer to purchase the property. In an open listing, the broker who is the procuring cause is the only broker entitled to compensation.

215. (C) If the prospective buyer (optionee) pays a consideration to the seller (optionor), the seller is obligated not to sell to anyone other than the optionee during the option period; however, the optionee is not obligated to buy.

216. (C) An option contract is an agreement in which the seller grants the optionee the right (but not the obligation) to buy the property within a specified period for a certain price and terms.

217. (C) Any contract that obligates both parties to perform in accordance with the terms of the contract is a bilateral contract.

218. (B) Letters and telegraphic communications can be part of a valid sale contract.

219. (D) A minor's contract is voidable because the minor can choose to void the contract.

220. (B) An express contract is an agreement wherein the terms are specifically stated by the parties, either orally, in writing, or a combination of the two.

221. (C) The broker must give a copy of the written listing agreement to the seller within 24 hours after the seller signs the agreement. Failure to do so is a violation of Section 475.25(1)(r), F.S., which is punishable by a $200 fine.

222. (A) A contract may be terminated by performance, mutual rescission, or impossibility of performance. Offers may be terminated by rejection but not contracts.

223. (B) Frequently, a contract includes an amount of money (usually the earnest money deposit) to be paid to the seller in the event of default by the buyer.

224. (B) One remedy for breach of contract is a suit for damages. Usually the party bringing suit seeks an amount of money equal to the extent of loss suffered, called compensatory damages.

225. (D) A contract can contain all of the essentials of a valid contract (competent parties, mutual assent, legal purpose, and consideration) and yet it is an unenforceable contract. A contract may be unenforceable because it is not in writing, as required by the statute of frauds, or because the statute of limitations has passed, or because the property is destroyed.

■ PLANNING AND ZONING (CHAPTER 20) FLORIDA REAL ESTATE BROKER'S GUIDE (CHAPTER 16)

226. (C) The concurrency provision in Florida's Growth Management Act of 1985 mandates that the infrastructure, such as roads and water and waste treatment facilities needed to support additional population, be in place before new development is allowed.

227. (B) A buffer zone is a strip of land separating one land use from another.

228. (B) Economic base studies analyze the effect of base-industry employment in the area.

229. (C) Zoning ordinances authorize segmentation of a community into districts or zones in keeping with the character of the land and structures. Each zone is assigned a specific land-use classification. "R" is usually reserved for residential classification.

230. (B) Building codes establish minimum standards for a building's design, construction, use and occupancy, and quality.

231. (D) A variance allows a property owner to vary from strict compliance with all or part of a zoning code (such as the minimum number of parking spaces) because to comply would force an undue hardship on the property owner.

232. (A) One example of a variance is to vary from strict compliance with a setback requirement because of the shape of the lot.

233. (A) Nonconforming use properties usually are not allowed to be increased in size or to undergo structural changes. Most zoning authorities restrict repairs and maintenance to those needed for sanitation and safety purposes.

234. (D) Local government enforces building codes. The process begins by issuing a building permit. Municipal inspectors visit each job site to conduct periodic building inspections. A final certificate of occupancy is issued once construction is completed. A condemnation proceeding is associated with eminent domain *not* building code enforcement.

235. (B) An environmental impact statement (EIS) is a required description of the probable cost-benefit impact that a proposed large development project will have on the environment during all phases of development.

236. (A) Both a legal and a development design concept, a planned unit development permits a mix of land uses along with a high density of residential units.

Real Estate Principles and Practices Chapters
■ THE REAL ESTATE BUSINESS (CHAPTER 1)

237. (A) Business brokers are real estate licensees who engage in the sale, purchase, or lease of businesses. To do so, they must hold active real estate licenses.

238. (B) Dedication is the gift of land by an owner, typically a developer, to a government body for public use.

239. (B) Tract building involves building model homes in a new subdivision so that buyers can choose a floor plan and then have a home built on a lot in the new subdivision.

240. (C) Property management is devoted to the leasing, managing, marketing, and overall maintenance of property for others. The scope of a property manager's functions goes far beyond rent collection, maintenance, and repair. Absentee ownership has increased (not decreased) demand for property managers.

241. (C) Follow-up is what a sales associate does after the sale to maintain customer contact and goodwill.

242. (D) Federal law (FIRREA) mandates that appraisal reports involving a federally related transaction must be prepared by a state-certified or licensed appraiser.

243. (B) A subdivision plat map indicates the size and location of individual lots, streets, and public utilities, including water lines and arrangements for sewage disposal.

244. (B) An absentee owner is a property owner who does not reside on the property and who often relies on a professional property manager to manage the owner's investment.

■ LEGAL DESCRIPTIONS (CHAPTER 10)

245. (A) A metes-and-bounds description begins with a starting reference point, called a point of beginning (POB). Metes refers to "distance" and bounds refers to "direction."

246. (D) Sections are numbered beginning in the northeast corner of a township with section number 1. The section numbers progress consecutively from east to west—from the upper right corner of the township across the top row of sections to number 6. Immediately to the west of section 6 a new township begins, numbered beginning in the northeast corner of the township with section number 1.

247. (C) North is 0 degrees on a compass. Therefore, the direction closest to 0 degrees is most northerly. Because 30 minutes is closer to 0 than 45 minutes, option C is the most northerly of the answer choices.

248. (B) Opposite of south is north. Opposite of east is west; therefore, N 45° W is a straight line opposite to S 45° E.

249. (D) Principal meridians and base lines intersect to form basic reference points in the government survey system. There are 36 sets of principal meridians and base lines. In Florida, the principal meridian and base line cross at a point in the city of Tallahassee.

250. (C) There are 640 acres in a section. There are 23,040 acres in a township (640 acres × 36 sections).

251. (C) $640 \div 4 \div 4 = 10$ acres

252. (A) Range lines are numbered consecutively from 1 both east and west of the principal meridian. Because the principal meridian runs north-south through the city of Tallahassee, a small numbered range (2) will be closest to Tallahassee.

253. (B) Section 36 is directly due south of section 1 of the same township. There are four sections between sections 1 and 36, which equals a distance of 4 miles.

254. (B) Range lines are numbered consecutively, from 1 both east and west of the principal meridian.

255. (A) Sections are numbered beginning in the northeast corner of the township with section 1 and progress consecutively from east to west through section 6. The second horizontal row begins directly under section 6 and progresses west to east from section 7 to section 12. Section 13 is directly under number 12. The row is numbered consecutively from east to west to section 18. Section 19 is directly under 18 and then the sections are numbered consecutively from west to east through section 24. Section 13 therefore is directly above (north) of section 24.

256. (C) The most common type of legal description used for single-family dwellings located in developed subdivisions is the lot and block method, which can be used only where plat maps of developed subdivisions have been recorded in the public records.

257. (D) 640 ÷ 4 ÷ 2 = 80 acres;
640 ÷ 4 ÷ 4 = 40 acres;
80 + 40 = 120 acres

■ REAL ESTATE FINANCE (CHAPTER 12)
FLORIDA REAL ESTATE BROKER'S GUIDE (CHAPTER 12)

258. (B) A deed in lieu of foreclosure is a way for the mortgagor (borrower) to avoid foreclosure. The borrower who is in default under the terms of the mortgage gives a deed to the lender.

259. (B) The promissory note is the legal instrument that represents the primary evidence of a debt.

260. (A) A defeasance clause included in mortgages in title theory states provides that the conveyance of title by the borrower to the lender is "defeated" when all of the terms and conditions of the mortgage have been met. It is the vehicle by which title is returned to the borrower when the debt has been repaid.

261. (D) The promissory note states the total amount of indebtedness, interest rate, repayment method, and term or time period to repay.

262. (C) The mortgagor is the borrower who signs the note.

263. (A) When the mortgage debt is paid in full, the lender executes a satisfaction of mortgage.

264. (D) Florida is a lien theory state, meaning the borrower retains title to the property.

265. (A) The acceleration clause authorizes the lender to accelerate (advance) the due date of the entire unpaid balance should the mortgagor fail to fulfill any of the covenants contained in the mortgage.

266. (D) A prepayment penalty clause provides for the lender to charge a penalty for early payment. Both FHA and VA mortgages allow early payment of the debt without penalty.

267. (B) An applicant's credit history is the best indicator of his or her willingness to repay debt. Lenders use credit scores to determine applicants' willingness to repay debt. A credit score is a financial snapshot of a borrower's credit history and current credit usage at a given point in time.

268. (D) The receivership clause allows the mortgagee to appeal to the courts to appoint a receiver to take over management of a property and collection of rents or other income.

269. (A) Equitable redemption allows the borrower to prevent foreclosure from occurring by paying the mortgagee the principal and interest due plus any expenses the mortgagee has incurred in attempting to collect the debt and initiating foreclosure proceedings.

270. (B) A subordination clause is a provision in a mortgage in which the lender voluntarily permits a subsequent mortgage to take priority over the lender's otherwise superior mortgage; the act of yielding priority.

271. (A) The exculpatory clause requires that the lender waive the right to a deficiency judgment against the borrower, relieving the borrower of personal liability to repay the loan.

272. (D) A due-on-sale clause is a provision in the mortgage that states that the entire balance of the note is immediately due and payable if the mortgagor transfers (sells) the property. The due-on-sale clause prevents a third party from assuming the mortgage.

273. (C) Once a mortgagor has paid off a mortgage loan in full, Florida statute requires the mortgagee to cancel the mortgage and send the recorded satisfaction to the mortgagor within 60 days.

274. (C) An estoppel certificate is a legal instrument setting forth the exact unpaid balance of a mortgage, the current rate of interest and the date to which interest has been paid.

275. (C) The Department of Veterans Affairs (VA) has the authority to partially guarantee mortgage loans made to veterans by private lenders.

276. (A) The VA establishes loan guarantee limits referred to as the "VA loan guarantee" or the "maximum entitlement."

277. (D) The maximum mortgage amount for an FHA residential loan is based on a percentage of the property's sale price (or appraised value, if less) exclusive of closing costs. This assures FHA that the borrower makes a minimum cash investment of at least 3 percent.

278. (C) FHA functions as an insurance company, insuring mortgage loans made by lending institutions.

279. (B) FHA requires borrowers to escrow property taxes and hazard insurance.

280. (A) The loan-to-value ratio is the relationship between the amount borrowed and the appraised value (or sale price) of a property.

281. (C) Loans are based on the amount borrowed (loan amount), loan duration (term), interest rate charged, and monthly mortgage payment.

282. (C) A loan amortization schedule indicates payments of principal and interest required to pay off the loan based on loan amount, term, and interest rate.

283. (B) FHA loans feature a monthly mortgage insurance premium payment (MIP). Lenders require private mortgage insurance (PMI) on the amount of loan over 80 percent LTV ratio. VA charges borrowers a funding fee or user's fee. VA loans do *not* require a down payment.

284. (D) On a fully amortized fixed-rate loan, the same amount is paid each month. However, the portion used to pay interest decreases each month, while the portion used to repay principal increases each month.

285. (C) Term mortgages require payment of interest only, until the full term of the mortgage has expired.

286. (C) The most popular loan payment plan is the fully amortized, fixed-rate mortgage with a term of 25 years or 30 years.

287. (D) When a buyer secures new financing, the seller pays off the old debt and a release of mortgage is recorded.

288. (B) In an assumption, the buyer signs a new promissory note.

289. (D) A contract for deed is also called a land contract, agreement for deed, or installment sale contract.

290. (C) A wraparound mortgage is a financing technique in which the payment of the existing mortgage is continued (by the seller) and a new, higher interest rate mortgage, which is larger than the existing mortgage, is paid by the buyer-borrower.

291. (D) In a contract for deed, the title to the real property remains with the seller until the loan is repaid. The contractual agreement grants equitable title to the buyer.

292. (B) Lending institutions legally are permitted to link the interest rate of an ARM with any recognized index (for example, the three-year treasury security).

293. (A) Buydowns are a financing technique in which points are paid to the lender by the seller or builder that lowers (buys down) the effective interest rate paid.

294. (B) Qualifying a buyer involves determining the potential buyer's real property needs (housing objectives) and determining the buyer's economic capability to satisfy those needs (financial abilities).

■ THE MORTGAGE MARKET (CHAPTER 13)

295. (D) The major federal agencies active in secondary market activities are Fannie Mae, Ginnie Mae, and Freddie Mac.

296. (C) Fannie Mae deals in conventional as well as FHA and VA mortgage loans.

297. (B) When the Fed decides to sell securities through open-market bulk trading, all funds received are held by the Fed. This reduces the supply of money in circulation.

298. (D) Fannie Mae recycles capital by purchasing loans previously made by primary lenders. Fannie Mae does not originate new loans.

299. (B) Mortgage bankers can originate and service loans, often with the expectation of reselling the loans to an institutional lender.

300. (D) The Rural Housing Service offers direct loans and other services to farmers, rural residents, and rural communities.

301. (C) Freddie Mac provides a secondary market for loans originated by savings associations.

302. (B) The discount rate is the interest rate charged member banks for borrowing money from the Fed.

303. (D) The Savings Association Insurance Fund (SAIF) insures the deposits of federally chartered savings associations.

304. (C) National banks are members of the Federal Reserve System.

305. (A) Mortgage companies package loans and sell them to institutional investors and secondary market participants.

306. (D) Interest is the price paid for the use of borrowed funds.

307. (A) When calculating the actual cost in dollars added by discount points, each point is equal to 1 percent of the loan amount (1 point = 1%).

308. (C) Discount points are based on the loan amount, not on the selling price.

309. (B) An origination fee is a charge by a lender for taking a mortgage in exchange for a loan.

■ ESTIMATING REAL PROPERTY VALUE (CHAPTER 15) FLORIDA REAL ESTATE BROKER'S GUIDE (CHAPTERS 6–9)

310. (D) Plottage is the added value as a result of combining two or more properties into one large parcel.

311. (B) Market value is defined as the most probable price that a property should bring in a competitive and open market under all conditions requisite to a fair sale, the buyer and seller each acting prudently and knowledgeably, and assuming the price is not affected by undue stimulus.

312. (A) Section 475.25, F.S., empowers the Commission to discipline brokers and sales associates who violate any of the standards of the USPAP; however, CMAs are exempted from compliance with the USPAP.

313. (D) If the capitalization rate is held constant and the NOI is increased, the result is an increase in value. For example, $6,000 NOI ÷ .08 cap rate = $75,000 value. However, $8,000 NOI ÷ .08 cap rate = $100,000.

314. (B) Cost is the total expenditure required to bring a new improvement into existence plus the cost of the land.

315. (B) The four characteristics of value are demand, utility, scarcity, and transferability.

316. (A) A vacant lot in a residential subdivision is not suitable to the income or cost approaches. A comparative market analysis is not a formal appraisal. The most suitable approach for appraising a vacant lot is to consider the selling prices of comparable lots.

317. (D) Apartment buildings are best suited to the income approach. Hospitals are best suited to the cost approach. Single-family dwellings are best suited to the sales comparison approach. Raw land is best suited to the sales comparison (or market) approach.

318. (C) The cost approach is the most applicable approach for special purpose buildings.

319. (B) The objective of the income capitalization approach is to measure a flow of income projected into the future.

320. (B) If a comparable is superior on a given feature, a downward adjustment is made to the comparable property (subtract the value of the difference).

321. (B) The basis of the cost approach is to estimate the cost to acquire an equivalent site (land value) and to reproduce a structure as if new, and then subtract accrued depreciation.

322. (D) The gross income multiplier (GIM) is the ratio to convert annual income into market value.

323. (C) A gross rent multiplier (GRM) is the ratio between a property's gross monthly income and its selling price.

324. (B) The unit comparison method is the predominant costing method used for appraisal purposes. However, its use is limited to relatively small, uncomplicated structures such as single-family homes and small office buildings.

325. (B) Exterior dimensions are used to calculate gross living area.

326. (D) Land is not depreciated in the cost-depreciation approach; only the buildings or other improvements to land are subject to depreciation.

327. (D) A property owner has least control over loss in value caused from factors in the surrounding area that are external to the subject property.

328. (B) Anything that is inferior due to operational inadequacies, poor design, or changing tastes and preferences is classified as functional obsolescence.

329. (C) Layout of the traffic pattern concerns poor design and is an example of functional obsolescence.

330. (A) Poor design is an example of functional obsolescence. An incurable defect is one in which the cost of curing the defect is greater than the value added by the cure.

331. (B) External obsolescence results from a loss in value due to influences originating outside the boundaries of the property.

332. (C) Anything that is inferior due to operational inadequacies (one-car garage) is classified as functional obsolescence.

333. (A) An incurable defect is one in which the cost of curing the defect is greater than the value added by the cure; or in other words, the value added by the cure is less than the cost of the cure.

334. (D) Economic life is the period of time a property may be expected to be profitable or productive; its useful life.

335. (D) Owner-occupied property is not income producing.

336. (C) The first step in the income capitalization approach is to estimate potential gross income (PGI). Vacancy and collection losses are subtracted from PGI to arrive at effective gross income (EGI). Operating expenses are subtracted from EGI to arrive at net operating income.

■ PRODUCT KNOWLEDGE (CHAPTER 16)

337. (C) Balloon construction is used for some two-story construction, especially if the structure has a masonry exterior.

338. (D) A built-up roof is a flat roof that allows for the placement of air conditioning and other mechanical equipment on its surface.

339. (A) A three-wire system provides two lines each carrying 120 volts of current and a third grounded neutral wire. Both hot wires and the neutral provide 240 volts of electricity for large appliances.

340. (B) U-shaped pipes called "traps" stay full of water. The water forms a seal in the pipe and prevents odors from entering the home.

■ REAL ESTATE INVESTMENT ANALYSIS (CHAPTER 17) FLORIDA REAL ESTATE BROKER'S GUIDE (CHAPTER 15)

341. (C) Liquidity refers to the ability to sell an investment quickly without loss of one's capital.

342. (B) Leverage is the use of borrowed funds to finance the purchase of an asset; the use of another's money to make more money.

343. (D) Advertising and marketing are business expenses and may not be deducted.

344. (A) The installment sale method relieves the seller of paying tax on gain not yet collected. Generally, it calls for the gain to be reported only as payments are actually received, with each payment treated as part profit and part recovery of investment.

345. (D) The loan-to-value ratio is a measure of the financial risk associated with lending and borrowing money.

346. (C) The balance sheet shows the company's financial position at a stated moment in time, the close of business on the date of the balance sheet.

347. (D) Goodwill is the intangible asset attributed to a business's reputation and the expectation of continued customer loyalty.

348. (C) Going concern value is the value of an established business property, compared with the value of just the physical assets of a business that is not yet established.

349. (A) The use of leverage may increase or decrease equity return. If the equity leverage is positive, it means that the borrower's return on equity was positive; there is a positive return on the cash investment after taking into account the financing cost.

350. (C) The methods used to arrive at an estimate of a business's value are comparable sales analysis, reproduction or replacement cost less depreciation analysis, income capitalization analysis, and liquidation analysis.

■ TAXES AFFECTING REAL ESTATE (CHAPTER 18) FLORIDA REAL ESTATE BROKER'S GUIDE (CHAPTER 14)

351. (A) Florida statutes require that all property be assessed at just value based on objective valuation methods. County property appraisers apply the three approaches to value to arrive at a fair and reasonable value.

352. (A) The Value Adjustment Board is made up of five members three county commissioners and two county school board members.

353. (B) Florida has a three-step protest procedure. The first step is to seek an adjustment by contacting the county property appraiser's office.

354. (B) $25,000 homestead + $500 surviving spouse + $500 disability = $26,000 cumulative tax exemption.

355. (B) Property owned by a church that is used for nonprofit purposes is exempt from property taxes. Property that once was part of the tax base, if changed to exempt property, will require higher taxes on taxable property.

356. (D) County hospitals and consolidated high schools are immune properties. Churches are exempt properties. Undeveloped farmland is subject to property taxation.

357. (A) Florida law authorizes county property appraisers to assess agricultural land by a more favorable method than that used for other properties. Florida's Green Belt law was designed to protect farmers from having taxes increased just because the land might be suited for development.

358. (C) To calculate the dollar amount of property taxes owed, the taxable value is multiplied by the appropriate millage rate. A mill is one one-thousandth of a dollar (or one-tenth of a cent).

359. (B) The tax rate is calculated based on the following formula:

Approved budget – Nonproperty tax revenue
Total assessed value – Exemptions

360. (A) The city or county government is responsible for the cost of its day-to-day operation and must collect delinquent taxes. To accomplish this, property tax certificates in the amount of taxes owed are issued for each delinquent property.

361. (A) The Save Our Home amendment limits the allowable increase in assessed value of homesteaded property to the lesser of 3 percent or the CPI for the previous year.

362. (B) Homeowners who itemize their deductions may deduct the interest portion of their mortgage payment and their property taxes.

363. (A) Special assessments are a one-time tax levied on properties to help pay for some public improvement that benefits the property.

364. (B) Exclusion of gain from the sale of a principal residence is allowed only once every two years. However, homeowners who do not meet the two-year requirement due to change in health or place of employment may be eligible for a prorated exclusion of gain.

365. (C) The Taxpayer Relief Act of 1997 allows homeowners to exclude up to $250,000 ($500,000 for married couples filing a joint return) realized on the sale or exchange of a principal residence. The taxpayer is not required to reinvest the sale proceeds in a new residence to claim the exclusion.

366. (B) Depreciation allowance deductions are allowed on investment property only.

367. (C) The IRS has established the useful asset life of 39 years for nonresidential income-producing property.

■ THE REAL ESTATE MARKET (CHAPTER 19)

368. (B) The price of real estate is based on what buyers in the marketplace are willing to pay.

369. (C) No two tracts of land are identical. There is no standard product. The uniqueness of land is referred to as heterogeneity.

370. (B) The household is the basis for most population analysis.

371. (C) Variables that influence supply include the availability of skilled labor, construction loans and financing, land, and materials.

372. (C) Whenever the supply and demand equilibrium is upset by excess demand, a seller's market develops. This allows sellers to demand higher prices from buyers, who are forced to compete for available space.

■ COMPUTATIONS AND TITLE CLOSING (CHAPTER 14) FLORIDA REAL ESTATE BROKER'S GUIDE (CHAPTER 13)

373. (D) The customary method of accounting and delivery of all monies is to have the closing agent prepare and deliver closing statements to the buyer and the seller, plus a summary that reconciles all the debits and credits involved.

374. (B) In some areas or by negotiation, the day of closing will be charged to the seller. In that situation, the seller is charged with an additional day.

375. (A) Mortgage interest is paid at the end of the period (in arrears). It is therefore charged to the seller up to the date of closing, and that amount is credited to the buyer in the offsetting double entries.

376. (B) Closing statement items credited to the buyer include the earnest money deposit, new and assumed mortgages, prorated taxes, interest, and prepaid rent.

377. (D) The seller is usually required to remove any encumbrances on the title.

378. (A) Any rental income collected in advance belongs to the new owner as of the date of closing. The buyer is credited for the rent from day of closing through the remainder of the month. The seller is debited the same amount.

Math Problems

379. (B) (9, 14)
$546 doc stamps ÷ $.70 rate × 100 increments = $78,000 sale price

380. (A) (18)
$117,500 assessed value –
$25,000 exemption =
$92,500 taxable value;
$92,500 × .026 millage rate =
$2,405 taxes due

381. (D) (18)
$25,000 homestead × .030 millage rate =
$750 savings

382. (C) (18)
100 ft. + 125 ft. = 225 total ft. ×
$24 per foot = $5,400 total paving cost;
$5,400 × .50 city share =
$2,700 total private share;
$2,700 ÷ 2 = $1,350 owner's side of street

383. (C) (18)
180 ft. × $24 per foot =
$4,320 total paving cost;
180 ft. × .70 = $3,024 total private share;
$3,024 ÷ 2 = $1,512 owner's side of street

384. (B) (14)
$18,000 second mortgage × .002 rate =
$36 intangible tax;
$18,000 note ÷ $100 increments =
180 taxable increments;
180 × $.35 = $63 doc stamps on note;
$72,000 ÷ $100 increments =
720 taxable increments;
720 × $.35 = $252; $252 + $63 =
$315 doc stamps on note

385. (B) (14)
$116,000 × .70 = $81,200 mortgage;
$81,200 × .002 rate =
$162.40 intangible tax

386. (C) (14)
$825.30 doc stamps ÷ $.70 = $1,179;
$1,179 × $100 increments =
$117,900 purchase price

387. (A) (18)
$5,600,000 × .10 withholding =
$560,000 due IRS

388. (C) (10)
640 acres per section ÷ 2 = 320 acres

389. (B) (18)
$235,000 × .80 =
$188,000 depreciable basis;
$188,000 ÷ 27.5 years = $6,836.36, or
$6,836 rounded annual depreciation deduction

390. (C) (10)
Rectangle measures 891 ft. by 440 ft;
891 × 440 = 392,040 sq. ft.;
392,040 ÷ 43,560 sq. feet per acre = 9 acres

391. (C) (10)
640 acres per section ÷ 4 ÷ 2 = 80 acres;
80 acres × $4,000 per acre =
$320,000 sale price

392. (B) (10)
4,000 ft. × 2,000 ft. = 8,000,000 sq. ft.;
8,000,000 sq. ft. ÷ 43,560 = 183.65 acres;
$1,306,800 sale price ÷ 183.65 acres =
$7,115.71 per acre, or approx. $7,116

393. (D) (10)
73 × 120 = 8,760 sq. ft.;
8,760 ÷ 43,560 = .20 or $\frac{1}{5}$

394. (A) (14)
$60 ÷ .002 rate = $30,000 mortgage;
$30,000 note ÷ $100 increments =
300 taxable increments;
300 × $.35 = $105 doc stamps on note

395. (B) (12)
$140,000 loan ÷ $180,000 sale price =
.7778, or 78% LTV

396. (D) (12)
$129,500 sale price × .25 =
$32,375 down payment

397. (A) (18)
($12,000,000 approved budget – $750,000
nonproperty revenue) ÷ ($1,500,000,000
total assessed value – $50,000,000
exemptions) =
$11,250,000 ÷ $1,450,000,000 =
.0077586 millage rate, or .008 rounded

398. (B) (14)
$734 P&I year 1 × 1.15 =
$844.10 P&I year 2;
$844.10 × 1.15 = $970.715 × 12 months =
$11,648.58 annual mortgage expense year 3

399. (A) (12)
$696 monthly housing expenses ÷
$2,400 monthly gross income =
.29 FHA housing expense ratio

400. (C) (13)
$2,500 discount ÷ $50,000 loan =
.05 or 5 points

401. (D) (13)
$105,000 mortgage × .03 points =
$3,150 cost of points;
$105,000 mortgage × .01 =
$1,050 loan origination fee;
$3,150 + $1,050 =
$4,200 total loan charges

402. (B) (13)
$90,000 × .10 = $9,000 down payment;
$90,000 – $9,000 down payment =
$81,000 loan;
$81,000 loan × .01 =
$810 loan origination fee;
$9,000 + $810 = $9,810 total cash

403. (D) (14)
$\frac{1}{4}$ = $\frac{2}{8}$ + $\frac{1}{8}$ = $\frac{3}{8}$ for pond and road;
$\frac{8}{8}$ – $\frac{3}{8}$ = $\frac{5}{8}$ usable area;
5 ÷ 8 = .625;
43,560 sq. ft. × .625 =
27,225 usable sq. ft.

404. (D) (14)
$100,000 net to seller + closing costs =
$105,000;
100% – commission rate = .94;
$105,000 ÷ .94 = $111,702.13
(round to $111,702) sale price

405. (B) (14)
$320,000 sale price × .07 rate =
$22,400 total commission;
100% – .45 sales associate split =
.55 broker's split;
$22,400 × .55 =
$12,320 broker's commission

406. (D) (14)
110 front feet × $325 per front foot =
$35,750 per lot;
$35,750 × 5 lots = $178,750 total cost;
8 lots × $28,000 sale price =
$224,000 total received;
$224,000 – $178,750 cost =
$45,250 made on sale;
$45,250 made ÷ $178,750 cost =
25.3 or approximately 25% profit.

407. (A) (14)
$98,400 × .07 = $6,888 total commission;
$6,888 ÷ 2 = $3,444 each broker's share

408. (C) (14)
2¾ = 2⁹⁄₁₂; 3⁵⁄₁₂; 4⅚ = 4¹⁰⁄₁₂;
2⁹⁄₁₂ + 3⁵⁄₁₂ + 4¹⁰⁄₁₂ = 9²⁴⁄₁₂ = 11 acres

409. (C) (14)
15 years × 12 payments a year =
180 payments to date:
$450 × 180 = $81,000 total paid to date;
$45,000 mortgage × .50 paid =
$22,500 principal paid;
$81,000 − $22,500 =
$58,500 interest paid to date

410. (A) (15)
$200,000 lease income + $12,000 other
income = $212,000 total income;
$1,395,000 ÷ $212,000 = 6.58 or 6.6 GIM

411. (B) (14)
$70,000 home × 2 = $140,000 home;
$30,000 lot × 300% = $90,000 amount of
increase + $30,000 orig. cost = $120,000;
$70,000 + $90,000 = $160,000 profit;
$160,000 profit ÷ $100,000 cost = 1.6 or 160%

412. (D) (15)
$320 × 12 months = $3,840;
$340 × 12 months = $4,080;
$300 × 12 months × 3 apartments = $10,800;
$3,840 + $4,080 + $10,800 =
$18,720 gross income;
$18,720 × .55 = $10,296 expenses;
$18,720 − $10,296 = $8,424 net income

413. (B) (15)
$8,424 net income ÷ .105 rate =
$80,228.57 value

414. (C) (14)
$8,050 income − $700 salary =
$7,350 commission;
$7,350 ÷ .028 rate =
$262,500 value properties sold

415. (A) (14)
$80,000 sale price × .20 down =
$16,000 down payment;
$80,000 − $16,000 = $64,000 loan;
$64,000 × .03 points = $1,920 points;
$16,000 down payment + $1,920 =
$17,920 − ($2,000 earnest money already
paid + $325 credit for taxes);
$17,920 − $2,325 = $15,595 cash at closing

416. (D) (14)
$85,000 − $80,000 = excess sale price;
$5,000 × .07 rate =
$350 excess commission

417. (C) (14)
100% cost − 10% loss = selling price;
90% = $36,000;
$36,000 sale price ÷ .90 = $40,000 cost

418. (C) (14)
100% + 20% more sales =
180 home sales;
120% = 180;
180 ÷ 1.20 =
150 home sales last year

419. (D) (14)
$5,600 × .20 =
$1,120 overage to Broker Bob's office;
$1,120 ÷ 2 = $560 Broker Bob's overage
after split to sales associate

420. (A) (14)
$94,500 × .15 = $14,175 down payment;
$14,175 + $1,575 closing costs = $15,750;
$15,750 total buyer costs −
$10,150 earnest money =
$5,600 cash at closing

421. (C) (18)
$190,000 assessed value −
$25,000 exemption =
$165,000 taxable value;
$165,000 × .0286 mills = $4,719 taxes due

422. (D) (14)
½ of a ¼ section = 640 ÷ 4 ÷ 2 = 80 acres;
80 acres × 43,560 sq. ft. per acre =
3,484,800 sq. ft.;
3,484,800 − 484,800 =
3,000,000 buildable sq. ft.; 3,000,000 ÷
12,000 sq. foot lots = 250 lots;
$160,000 cost × 5 =
$800,000 development cost;
$160,000 + $800,000 = $960,000 total cost;
$960,000 × 1.10 = $1,056,000 ÷ 250 lots =
$4,224 average per lot

423. (B) (14)
$20,000 × 9% interest =
$1,800 annual int. ÷ 12 months =
$150 interest month 1;
$161 − $150 =
$11.00 principal paid month 1;
$20,000 − $11 = $19,989 unpaid balance;
$19,989 × 9% interest =
$1,799.01 ÷ 12 months =
$149.92 interest month 2;
$161 − $149.92 =
$11.08 principal paid month 2;
$19,989 − $11.08 = $19,977.92;
$19,977.92 × 9% interest =
$1,798.01 ÷ 12 months =
$149.83 interest month 3;
$161 − $149.83 =
$11.17 principal paid month 3;
$19,977.92 − $11.17 =
$19,966.75 mortgage balance Sept. 1

424. (B) (14)
$96,800 × .75 = $72,600 mortgage amount;
$72,600 × 10% interest =
$7,260 ÷ 12 months =
$605 interest month 1;
$849.50 − $605 =
$244.50 principal month 1;
$72,600 − $244.50 =
$72,355.50 unpaid balance;
$72,355.50 × 10% =
$7,235.55 ÷ 12 months = $602.96;
$849.50 − $602.96 =
$246.54 principal month 2

425. (A) (14)
$2,400 ÷ 8 apartments ÷ 12 months =
$25 rent increase

426. (A) (14)
31 + 28 + 31 + 30 = 120 seller unpaid days;
$1,095 ÷ 365 days per year × 120 days =
$360 debit

427. (C) (14)
June 15 belongs to buyer, therefore
16 days due buyer;
$465 × 10 units =
$4,650 total rent collected;
$4,650 ÷ 30-day month × 16 days =
$2,480 credit to buyers

428. (B) (15)
$140,000 sale price − $12,500 location +
$8,000 size + $5,000 age =
$140,500 adjusted sale price

429. (B) (15)
$89,500 cost ÷ 50-year useful life =
$1,790 annual depreciation;
$1,790 × 4 years =
$7,160 accumulated depreciation

430. (C) (14)
$600 × 2 units = $1,200 monthly rent;
$1,200 ÷ 30 days = $40 per day;
$40 × 16 days belong to buyer = $640;
Entered on closing statement;
$640 debit seller; $640 credit buyer

431. (C) (15)
Sale 1: $36,720 ÷ (100′ × 120′ =
12,000 sq. ft.) = $3.06 per sq. ft.;
Sale 2: $29,800 ÷ (100′ × 100′ =
10,000 sq. ft.) = $2.98 per sq. ft.;
Sale 3: $36,800 ÷ (110′ × 110′ =
12,100 sq. ft.) = $3.04 per sq. ft.;
Sale 4: $29,700 ÷ (90′ × 110′ =
9,900 sq. ft.) = $3 per sq. ft.;
$3.06 + $2.98 + $3.04 + $3 =
$12.08 ÷ 4 = $3.02 average;
100′ × 110′ = 11,000 sq. ft. × $3.02 =
$33,220 market value

432. (B) (15)
Sale 1: $5,600 ÷ (100' × 130' =
13,000 sq. ft.) = $.431 per sq. ft.;
Sale 2: $5,800 ÷ (104' × 132' =
13,728 sq. ft.) = $.422 per sq. ft.;
Sale 3: $5,600 ÷ (102' × 130' =
13,260 sq. ft.) = $.422 per sq. ft.;
Sale 4: $5,600 ÷ (102' × 130' =
13,260 sq. ft.) = $.422 per sq. ft.;
Sale 5: $5,400 ÷ (100' × 132' =
13,200 sq. ft.) = $.409 per sq. ft.;
$.431 + $.422 + $.422 + $.422
+ $.409 = $2.106 ÷ 5 = $.4212;
110' × 130' = 14,300 sq. ft. × $0.4212 =
$6,023 (rounded to the nearest dollar)

433. (C) (15)
$72,000 ÷ 1,800 sq. ft. = $40 per sq. foot

434. (C) (15)
$48,750 ÷ $375 monthly rent = 130 GRM

435. (D) (15)
1,800 sq. ft. × $0.24 = $432 monthly rent;
$432 rent × 120 GRM =
$51,840 market value

436. (B) (15)
$480,000 reproduction cost ÷ 40 years =
$12,000 annual depreciation;
$12,000 annual depreciation × 6 years =
$72,000 accrued;
$480,000 − $72,000 depreciation +
$100,000 site value =
$508,000 market value

437. (C) (15)
40' × 60' = 2,400 sq. ft.;
$57,000 sale price ÷ 2,400 sq. ft. =
$23.75 per sq. foot

438. (C) (15)
100% ÷ 20 years = 5% loss per year

439. (D) (15)
20' × 40' = 800 sq. ft.;
$840 monthly rent × 12 months =
$10,080 annual rent;
$10,080 ÷ 800 sq. ft. = $12.60 per sq. foot

440. (B) (15)
$4,800 monthly net × 12 months =
$57,600 annual NOI;
$57,600 NOI ÷ .12 rate =
$480,000 original cost

441. (A) (15)
$475 rent × 8 units × 12 months =
$45,600 PGI;
$45,600 × .10 = $4,560 vacancy loss;
$45,600 − $4,560 = $41,040 EGI;
$41,040 EGI − ($1,875 × 12 months =
$22,500 operating expense) =
$18,540 NOI;
$18,540 NOI ÷ .12 cap rate =
$154,500 market value

442. (C) (15)
$96,400 EGI − $36,600 operating expense =
$59,800 NOI

443. (D) (18)
120' × 150' × 2 stories = 36,000 total sq. ft.;
36,000 × .90 = 32,400 sq. ft. available for
bin storage;
10' × 12'= 120 sq. ft. per bin;
32,400 sq. ft. ÷ 120 sq. ft. = 270 bins

444. (D) (15)
$185,000 × .08 cap rate = $14,800 NOI;
$14,800 NOI ÷ .40 = $37,000 EGI

445. (B) (15)
Project 1: $39,400 NOI ÷
$345,000 sale price = .114;
Project 2: $45,680 NOI ÷
$464,000 sale price = .098;
Project 3: $36,800 NOI ÷
$386,000 sale price = .095;
Project 4: $43,790 NOI ÷
$424,000 sale price = .103;
.114 + .098 + .095 + .103 = .41 ÷ 4 =
.1025 = 10.25%

446. (B) (12)
$80,000 loan ÷ $100,000 price =
.80 or 80% LTV

447. (C) (12)
$145,000 loan + $55,000 down payment =
$200,000 sale price;
$145,000 ÷ $200,000 = .725 or 72.5% LTV

448. (A) (15)
$26,750 EGI – $8,350 operating expense =
$18,400 NOI

449. (B) (15)
$26,750 PGI – ($8,350 fixed expense +
$450 reserves);
$26,750 PGI – $8,800 operating expense =
$17,950 NOI

450. (B) (18)
(A) $49,500 value × 100% = $49,500
(B) $66,900 value × 75% = $50,175
(C) $81,400 value × 60% = $48,840
(D) $119,600 value × 40% = $47,840

451. (B) (14)
Seller owes 31 days in May + 15 days in
June = 46 days;
$105,500 mortgage balance × .08 =
$8,440 ÷ 365 = $23.12 interest per day;
$23.12 × 46 days = $1,063.52 debit

452. (D) (12)
FHA allows up to 29% for housing
expense ratio (HER); FHA allows up to
41% for total obligations ratio (TOR);
HER = $658 monthly housing expense ÷
$2,350 monthly gross income = 28%;
$658 monthly housing expense +
$282 other credit obligation = $940;
TOR = $940 total monthly obligation ÷
$2,350 monthly gross income = 40%

453. (C) (15)
8 years effective age ÷
55 years economic life = .145;
.145 × $300,000 =
$43,500 accrued depreciation

454. (C) (17)
$1,500,000 value – $1,250,000 mortgage =
$250,000 equity

455. Determine proper description *and* acreage for the *numbered areas*

Description	Acreage
1 = NW ¼	160 acres
2 = W ½ of NE ¼	80 acres
3 = NE ¼ of NE ¼	40 acres
4 = E ¼ of NW ¼ of SE ¼	20 acres
5 = SW ¼ of SW ¼ of SE ¼	10 acres
6 = E ½ of NE ¼ of SE ¼ of SE ¼	5 acres
7 = SE ¼ of SE ¼ of SE ¼ of SE ¼	2.5 acres

Provide an *alternative* way of describing
3 = N ½ of E ½ of NE ¼
5 = W ½ of S ½ of SW ¼ of SE ¼

Description	Acreage
A = SE ¼ of NE ¼	40 acres
B = NW ¼ of SW ¼	40 acres
C = N ½ of S ½ of SE ¼ of SW ¼ and N ½ of SE ¼ of SW ¼	30 acres
D = S ½ of S ½ of SE ¼ of SW ¼	10 acres
E = W ½ of NW ¼ of SE ¼	20 acres
F = N ½ of NE ¼ of SE ¼	20 acres
G = NE ¼ of SW ¼ of SE ¼	10 acres
H = S ½ of SW ¼ of SE ¼ of SE ¼	5 acres
I = W ½ of NE ¼ of SE ¼ of SE ¼	5 acres
J = NE ¼ of SE ¼ of SE ¼ of SE ¼	2.5 acres

The acreage for SE ¼ of NE ¼ and N ½ of NE ¼ of SE ¼ is *60* acres.

Broker Investment Problems

456. (C) $650 rent × 12 units × 12 months = $93,600 PGI

457. (B) $93,600 PGI × .05 V&C rate = $4,680 V&C loss;
$93,600 - $4,680 = $88,920 effective gross income

458. (C) $88,920 EGI × .30 = $26,676 operating expenses

459. (D) $88,920 EGI - $26,676 operating expenses = $62,244 NOI

460. (A) $1,995.91 × 12 months = $23,950.92 rounded to $23,951 annual debt service

461. (D) $62,244 NOI ÷ $23,951 = 2.599 or 2.60 rounded

462. (D) $62,244 NOI - $23,951 annual debt service = $38,293 before-tax cash flow

463. (C) $26,676 operating expenses ÷ $88,920 EGI = .30

464. (D) $38,293 before-tax cash flow ÷ $50,000 down payment = .7658 or 76.6%

465. (B) $350,000 purchase price - $50,000 land = $300,000 depreciable basis;
$300,000 ÷ 27.5 years = $10,909 annual depreciation

466. (A) $26,676 operating expenses - $10,000 reserves + $23,951 annual debt service = $40,627;
$40,627 ÷ $93,600 PGI = .434 or 43.4%

467. (A) $345,000 appraised value × .80 maximum loan/value ratio = $276,000 maximum loans allowed;
$276,000 total loans allowed - $181, 435 current 1st mortgage = $94,565 available for 2nd mortgage

468. (D) $995,000 total purchase price + $4,000 appraisal + $700 survey + $2,400 title insurance = $1,003,800 total acquisition cost; $1,003,800 × .80 allocated to the building = $803,040 depreciable basis

469. (C) $1,675,000 purchase price × .80 building allocation = $1,340,000 depreciable basis;
$1,340,000 ÷ 39 years = $34,358.97 rounded to $34,359 typical depreciation

470. (D) $3,250 base rent × 12 months = $39,000 annual base rent;
$39,000 ÷ .05 percentage rate = $780,000 annual sales before additional rent is due

Math Cross-Reference Key

You will find each type of real estate math problem explained and worked out in the companion textbook, *Florida Real Estate Principles, Practices & Law.*

Textbook Chapter	Math Subject
3	license fees
6	administrative fines
6	Real Estate Recovery Fund payments
9, 14	state documentary stamp tax on deeds
10	legal descriptions; measurements
10, 14, 20	lots per acre and lot prices
10, 14	building square footages and prices
12, 14	state intangible tax on mortgages
12, 14	state documentary stamp tax on notes
12	FHA mortgage insurance program (MIP)
12	FHA down payments and loan amounts
12	VA down payments and loan amounts
12	loan-to-value ratios (LTV)
12	private mortgage insurance (PMI)
12	adjustable-rate mortgage (ARM)
12	housing expense ratio; total obligations ratio
13	discount points
13	loan origination and service fees
14	fractions, decimals, and percentages
14	sale commissions
14	selling price, cost, and profit
14	mortgage amortization
14	mortgage interest
14	prorated expenses—two methods
14	prepaid rent
14, 18	property taxes
14	hazard insurance
14	state taxes—three

Textbook Chapter	Math Subject
14	other charges at closings
15	estimating value comparable sales
15	comparable market analysis (CMA)
15	net adjustments
15	gross rent (income) multipliers (GRM, GIM)
15	estimating value cost-depreciation
15	depreciation (straight-line)
15	economic (useful) life
15	estimating value income capitalization
15	potential gross income (PGI)
15	effective gross income (EGI)
15	net operating income (NOI)
15	overall capitalization rate (OAR)
15	return on investment
18	federal income taxes
18	homestead tax exemptions
18	property tax rates
18	special assessments
18	capital gains
18	sale of residence
20	density for zoning, land-use requirements

Practice Exam 1 Answer Key

Note: Correct letter answer is followed (in parenthesis) by *Florida Real Estate Principles, Practices & Law* chapter number(s) and a brief explanation of the correct answer.

1. **(C) (5)** It is illegal for real estate brokers to conspire to fix commissions or fees for the services they perform. The amount of commission to be paid is negotiable, and it is arrived at by agreement between the broker and buyer or seller.

2. **(C) (5)** Rule 61J2-10.028(2) provides that a licensee may share a commission with a party to a real estate transaction, which includes real estate sale and purchase agreements and lease agreements, provided the arrangement is disclosed to all interested parties.

3. **(A) (17)** Goodwill is the intangible asset attributed to a business's reputation and the expectation of continued customer loyalty. The value of goodwill may be approximated by subtracting the value of tangible assets from the value of the business.

4. **(C) (8)** An estate for years exists for a designated period, which may be any length of time from less than a year to many years, such as a 99-year lease.

5. **(B) (10)** A township is a square six miles on each side (6 miles square). There are 640 acres in a section (not a township).

6. **(C) (5)** A fee collected from a buyer in advance of a closing is not considered to be an advanced fee because it is not collected in connection with a listing agreement. However, the fee must be placed in the broker's regular escrow (or trust) account.

7. **(A) (7)** The landlord is required to provide exterminating service, garbage receptacles and pickup, and working equipment for heat plus running water. The landlord is allowed to charge tenants for services provided, if the charges are a part of the rental agreement.

8. **(A) (11)** Section 475.25(1)(r), F.S. indicates that a listing agreement must include a definite expiration date, description of the property, price and terms, and fee or commission. However, there is no requirement that the listing be in written form.

9. **(B) (15)** The highest and best use of land as though vacant is the legal (permissible) use of the site that would produce the greatest value.

10. **(C) (7)** The Fair Housing Act only prohibits discrimination based on race, color, religion, national origin, gender, familial status, and disability. College students are not a protected class.

11. (A) (5) Brokers must deposit earnest money no later than the end of the third business day following receipt of a deposit by a sales associate or employee of the brokerage firm.

12. (D) (4) Chapter 475.78, F.S. requires real estate licensees to submit all offers up until title closing unless instructed otherwise by the seller.

13. (C) (4) It is fraudulent and dishonest dealing by trick, scheme, or device for a licensee to knowingly sell or offer for sale any property covered by a mortgage that also covers other property sold, unless the particular property offered for sale may be released from the mortgage any time before foreclosure sale on payment of an amount less than the remaining due from the purchaser after the sale.

14. (D) (5) Rule 61J2-5.015 states that "No registration shall be issued to the corporation or licenses to any officer or director, unless the corporation shall cause to register, and biennially renew the license of at least one active officer."

15. (C) (4) Licensees must provide prospective buyers a copy of the no brokerage relationship notice before the showing of property.

16. (D) (6) Conversion is the unauthorized control or use of another's personal property, including misappropriation of an employed sales associate's commission.

17. (D) (2) Salaried employees of an owner of an apartment community who work in a leasing capacity are exempt from licensure. However, they must use only approved lease forms.

18. (D) (7) The Real Estate Settlement Procedures Act (RESPA) requires that, at the time of application for a loan or within three business days thereafter, the lender provide the borrower with a good-faith estimate of probable closing costs.

19. (D) (8) A tenancy at sufferance is said to exist when the tenant, after rightfully being in possession of the rented premises, continues possession after his or her right has ended.

20. (A) (5) Rule 61J2-10.032(2)(c) requires brokers to notify the FREC within ten business days.

21. (B) (18) The Save Our Home amendment of the Florida Constitution caps how much the assessed value of homesteaded property can increase in a given year.

22. (D) (2) Section 475.01, F.S. requires that anyone who performs real estate services for another for compensation of any type must be licensed. Compensation is defined as anything of value.

23. (C) (13) The GNMA (commonly known as Ginnie Mae) was created by Congress in 1968 and is part of the Department of Housing and Urban Development (HUD).

24. (D) (4) A licensee is obligated to disclose facts regarding a property's true worth.

25. (D) (18) Mrs. Allday is entitled to a $500 surviving spouse exemption and a $5,000 veteran disability exemption in addition to the $25,000 base homestead exemption.

26. (D) (6) Rule 61J2-24.001 states that, in the case of a licensee who renews the license without having complied with Rule 61J2-3.009 and the licensee's act is discovered by the DBPR, the usual action of the Commission is a penalty of suspension or revocation.

27. (A) (5) $88,000 deposits collected – $9,000 disbursements = $79,000 trust liability. Violation of 475.25, F.S. pertaining to proper handling of escrow funds is punishable by suspension or revocation.

28. (B) (12) The defeasance clause is a provision in a mortgage that specifies the terms and conditions to be met in order to avoid default and thereby defeat the mortgage.

29. (A) (6) If probable cause is found to exist, the Probable Cause Panel will direct the Department to file a formal complaint against the subject of the complaint.

30. (D) (2) It is a violation of Chapter 475 to pay an unlicensed person for performing the services of real estate. Compensation is anything paid or expected to be paid associated with performing real estate services.

31. (D) (5, 6) Sales associates are prohibited from initiating any suit or action for compensation in connection with a real estate transaction against anyone except the person registered as their employer.

32. (D) (5) Rule 61J2-10.023(2) states that a mere temporary shelter on a subdivision being sold by the broker, for the protection of the sales staff and customers, and where transactions are not closed, is not considered to be a branch office.

33. (C) (8) A deed is a written instrument used to transfer title to real property from one party to another.

34. (B) (3) A sales associate who is employed by an owner-developer may be issued a group license according to Rule 61J2-6.006.

35. (C) (5) The broker must deposit the earnest money in his escrow account by the end of the third business day following receipt of the funds.

36. (A) (5) If a buyer of a residential condominium unit timely delivers to a licensee written notice of the buyer's intent to cancel the contract as authorized by the Condominium Act, the licensee may return the escrowed property to the purchaser without notifying the Commission or initiating any of the settlement procedures.

37. (D) (6) It is a violation of Section 475.25, F.S. for a licensee to share a commission or pay a fee to a person not properly licensed under Chapter 475, F.S. and to practice without a valid and current Florida license.

38. (B) (5) All general partners who expect to deal with the public on behalf of the limited partnership must be licensed as active brokers, with at least one of the general partners personally qualified and licensed as an active broker at all times.

39. (D) (5) If a broker receives conflicting demands on escrowed property, the broker must notify the FREC, in writing, within 15 business days and institute one of four settlement procedures (mediation, arbitration, litigation, or escrow disbursement order) within 30 business days.

40. (C) (9) In a quitclaim deed, the grantor makes no warranties about the quality or extent of the title being conveyed. The grantor does not warrant to defend the title interest conveyed.

41. (B) (7) Blockbusting is the illegal practice of inducing homeowners to sell their property by making misrepresentations regarding the entry of certain groups of people in order to cause a turnover of properties in the neighborhood.

42. (D) (20) Setbacks are restrictions established by zoning or deed on the space required between lot lines and building lines.

43. (B) (17) When the interest paid for borrowed money is higher than the overall return from an investment, the result is negative leverage.

44. (B) (2) According to Chapter 475.011, F.S., salaried employees of business entities who sell, exchange, or lease real property for their employer are exempt from licensure, provided they are not paid a commission or compensated on a transaction basis.

45. (A) (8) The Time-Share Act applies to all time-share plans consisting of more than seven time-share periods over a span of at least three years.

46. (A) (7) Section 83.62(2), F.S., states that the landlord or the landlord's agent may remove any personal property found on the premises to or near the property line.

47. (B) (12) The doctrine of caveat emptor has been held to apply in foreclosure sales. The purchaser is presumed to know that she is purchasing subject to any prior liens of record or interests for which there is constructive notice.

48. (D) (9) A purchase-money mortgage is any new mortgage taken as part of the purchase price of real property by the seller. Technically speaking, any mortgage on real property executed to secure the purchase money by a purchaser simultaneously with acquiring legal title is a purchase-money mortgage. The fact that a mortgage is made by a third party does not prevent it from being a purchase-money mortgage.

49. (D) (15) Active real estate licensees are allowed to perform a comparative market analysis (CMA) for the purpose of obtaining a listing.

50. (D) (5) Section 475.25(1)(d), F.S. requires that all parties consent before the broker can submit the escrow dispute to arbitration.

51. (B) (11) The elements of a valid real estate contract are competent parties; offer and acceptance; legal purpose; consideration; and that the contract be in writing and signed.

52. (C) (12) In a subject to the mortgage arrangement, the buyer makes regular periodic payments on the mortgage but does not assume responsibility for the mortgage.

53. (A) (8) An estate for years is a leasehold or nonfreehold estate.

54. (D) (8) Real property owned by a husband or wife prior to the marriage with the spouse having no present rights in the property is called separate property.

55. (D) (2, 6) An unlicensed individual may not perform real estate services for compensation. Compensation is defined as anything of value or a valuable consideration, directly or indirectly paid, promised, or expected to be paid or received.

56. (C) (2, 6) The promise or expectation of compensation for performing real estate services without a license is illegal. The unlicensed practice of real estate is a third-degree felony.

57. (C) (15) If correction of a defect results in greater added value than the cost to correct, the defect is curable.

58. (C) (4) A listing that is not reasonably priced will attract very few prospects in relation to the carry costs, including MLS fees, advertising, and so forth.

59. (D) (4) The term *principal* is used to mean the party with whom a real estate licensee has entered into a single agent relationship.

60. (D) (6) False advertising and culpable negligence are misdemeanors of the second degree. Unlicensed practice of real estate is a felony of the third degree. Failing to provide accurate and current rental information for a fee is a first-degree misdemeanor.

61. (D) (1) Dedication is the gift of land by a developer to a governmental body for a public use.

62. (B) (12) A note is a promise to repay that makes the borrower personally liable for the obligation. The mortgage note serves as evidence of the debt for which the mortgage on the property is the security. If the security is insufficient to cover the indebtedness, the holder of the note can obtain a deficiency judgment against the debtor.

63. (A) (4) A broker who purchases property from the listing seller and subsequently sells it at a higher price and keeps the profit may be considered to be guilty of fraud, misrepresentation, concealment, and/or dishonest dealing and could expose the broker to liability for the full amount of the secret profit and disciplinary action.

64. (D) (15) The principle of substitution is the basis for all three approaches to market value. It means that a prudent buyer or investor will pay no more for a property than the cost of acquiring, through purchase or construction, an equally desirable alternative property.

65. (D) (7) A condominium is created by recording a declaration in the public records. Buyers own an undivided fractional share of the buildings and land known as common elements. Condominium owners are responsible for mortgage payments on their units. Shares of stock are associated with cooperatives.

66. (C) (12) Novation is the substitution of a new party and/or new terms to an existing obligation.

67. (D) (14) The closing agent prepares and disburses the appropriate checks.

68. (D) (17) Financial risk, also called operating financial risk, is associated with the ability of a property to cover operating expenses from funds provided from operations, borrowing, and equity sources.

69. (D) (11) Consideration is the obligation that each party makes to the other to make the contract enforceable.

70. (C) (11) Once a counteroffer is made, the buyer's original offer is no longer available for acceptance.

71. (C) (2) The intent of the Florida Legislature is that professions and occupations should be regulated to protect the health, safety, and welfare of the public *only* when their unregulated practice can harm the public, the potential harm is recognizable, and the danger outweighs any anticompetitive impact that might result from regulation.

72. (B) (9) Recording a properly executed and acknowledged instrument of conveyance puts the world on notice regarding an owner's interests in real property.

73. (A) (9) The bargain and sale deed consists of the granting and habendum clauses and the covenant of seisin. In a quitclaim deed the grantor makes no warranties about the extent of title being conveyed.

74. (D) (18) Taxable value is the assessed value less allowable exemptions resulting in an amount to which the tax rate is applied to determine property taxes due.

75. (D) (6) It is legal to pay an out-of-state broker a referral fee, provided the out-of-state broker does not come to Florida and practice real estate services in this state.

76. (C) (6) Culpable negligence is the inadequate attention to duties and obligations by one who knows, or should know, what is required of him or her.

77. (C) (18) To calculate the dollar amount of property taxes owed, the taxable value of the property is multiplied by the appropriate tax rate.

78. (C) (6) The promise or expectation of compensation for performing real estate services without an active or current license is a violation of Chapter 475, F.S.

79. (B) (4) A provision providing for the broker to retain the deposit would need to be disclosed and agreed to by all parties.

80. (D) (18) To prevent foreign sellers from avoiding the payment of taxes due on the sale of real property, the IRS requires that buyers withhold 10 percent of the gross sale price (including cash paid and any debt assumed by the buyer). The buyer must report the purchase and pay the IRS the amount withheld.

81. (D) (6) If a broker requested an EDO and complied with it, the Commission is authorized to pay the broker's reasonable attorney's fees and court costs. The Commission is also authorized to pay the plaintiff's reasonable attorney fees and court costs.

82. (C) (11) The Florida Landlord and Tenant Act provides that, upon a change in the designated rental agent, the security deposits and advance rents being held for the benefit of the tenants must be transferred to the new agent with an accounting statement showing the amounts to be credited to each tenant's account.

83. (A) (15) The sales comparison approach is typically used for vacant lots or for valuing a site as though vacant.

84. (B) (12) The VA uses a total monthly obligations ratio of 41 percent. The VA total obligations ratio is determined by dividing total PITI and other monthly payments by the total monthly gross income.

85. (A) (10) In the government survey system, certain north-south longitudes were designated principal meridians and certain east-west latitudes were designated base lines.

86. (D) (12) A buydown is a financing technique in which points are paid to the lender by the seller or builder that lowers (buys down) the effective interest rate paid by the buyer-borrower, thus reducing the amount by the monthly payment for a set period of time.

87. (B) (18) The amount realized (or adjusted sale price) is the selling price minus selling expenses.

88. (D) (15) Situs refers to relationships and influences created by location of a property which affect value, such as accessibility and personal preference.

89. (B) (20) To plan efficiently beyond local community boundaries, a comprehensive plan (or master plan) is developed for the purpose of guiding future growth.

90. (D) (14) Amount made on sale divided by total cost equals percent profit
$125 per foot × 300 feet =
$37,500 sale price;
$37,500 sale price – $15,000 orig cost =
$22,500 ÷ 15,000 = 1.5 or 150% profit

91. (A) (14) $30,000 loan × .13 interest =
    $3,900 annual interest;
    $3,900 ÷ 12 months =
    $325 interest month 1;
    $325 × 3 months = $975

92. (A) (14) The exact number of days owed
    by the seller are January 31 + February 28 +
    March 31 + April 30 + May 31 + June 30 +
    July 31 + August 31 + September 10 =
    253 days;
    $1,700 ÷ 365 = 4.6575342 per day;
    $4.6575342 per day × 253 days =
    $1,178.3562 rounded to $1,178.36 (debit
    seller; credit buyer)

93. (B) (12) $66,000 sale price × .20 =
    $13,200 down payment;
    $13,200 – $2,200 deposit =
    $11,000 cash at closing

94. (D) (14)
    1,452 × 1,200 = 1,742,400 sq. ft.; 1,742,400 ÷
    43,560 = 40 acres;
    40 × $3,000 = $120,000 sale price;
    $120,000 ÷ 100 × .70 =
    $840 doc stamps on deed

95. (C) (13)
    $6 × \frac{1}{8} = \frac{6}{8} = \frac{3}{4}$;
    $9 + \frac{3}{4} = 9\frac{3}{4}\%$ or 9.75% yield

96. (D) (10)
    640 ÷ 4 ÷ 4 ÷ 4 ÷ 4 = 2.5 acres

97. (C) (18)
    ($24,000,000 budget – $8,000,000
    nonproperty revenue) ÷ ($1,050,000,000
    total value – $100,000,000 exemptions) =
    $16,000,000 ÷ $950,000,000 =
    .1684211 or 16.8 mills

98. (B) (15)
    $90,000 ÷ 40 total economic life × 7 years =
    $15,750 accrued depreciation;
    $90,000 – $15,750 + $20,000 land value =
    $94,250

99. (B) (14)
    $50,000 × .10 = $5,000;
    $100,000 × .05 = $5,000;
    $60,000 × .03 = $1,800;
    $5,000 + $5,000 + $1,800 =
    $11,800 total commission;
    $11,800 × .90 = $10,620 remaining after
    listing commissions paid;
    $10,620 × .65 =
    $6,903 Sarah's commission

100. (C) (15)
    $70,400 PGI × .04 = $2,816 V&C;
    $70,400 PGI – $2,816 V&C = $67,584 EGI;
    $67,584 EGI – $12,770 op. exp. =
    $54,814 NOI

Practice Exam 2 Answer Key

Note: Correct letter answer is followed (in parenthesis) by
Florida Real Estate Principles, Practices & Law chapter number(s) and
a brief explanation of the correct answer.

1. (B) (9) A completed and signed deed transfers title to the grantee when the grantor voluntarily delivers it to the grantee and the grantee willingly accepts it.

2. (B) (5) Brokers associated with a brokerage entity are not required to have an ownership interest in the company. However, Rule 61J2-5.016 requires each active broker to be registered as an officer or director of the brokerage corporation or partnership. Rule 61J2-10.024 mandates that the name of *at least* one of the brokers be included on the office entrance sign.

3. (B) (2) Joshua completed his post-licensing education in a previous renewal cycle. If Joshua completes his 14-hour continuing education requirement and renews within 12 months following the expiration of his license, he will be charged a late fee.

4. (C) (4) In nonresidential transactions where both the buyer and seller have assets of at least $1 million each, the buyer and seller may request that the broker designate one licensee in the firm to be a single agent representative of the buyer and *another* licensee to be a single agent representative of the seller. For an individual to represent both the buyer and the seller as a single agent representative is a dual agency relationship, which is a violation of Section 475.272(1).

5. (D) (4) Designated sales associates may be used only in nonresidential transactions. The buyer and seller must each have assets of $1 million or more. Designated sales associates have the duties of a single agent, including disclosure requirements.

6. (A) (5) A real estate licensee must verify that a telephone number is not listed on the national do-not-call registry before cold calling for potential listings. Violators can be fined up to $11,000 for each illegal call.

7. (A) (5) If sales associates create promotional materials such as refrigerator magnets and notepads, they must include the licensed name of the brokerage firm.

8. (B) (4) Section 475.5015, F.S. requires the broker to retain for at least five years brokerage relationship disclosure documents in all transactions that result in a written contract to purchase and sell real property. The law does *not* stipulate only "closed" transactions.

9. (C) (5) Buyer paid fees must be placed in the broker's escrow (trust) account.

10. (B) (6, 15) Section 475.25(1)(t) requires real estate licensees to abide by the USPAP. Rule 61J2-24.001(3)(t) sets forth the usual disciplinary guidelines for violating the USPAP.

11. (C) (5) Sales associates are prohibited from initiating a suit or action for compensation in connection with a real estate transaction against anyone except the person registered as their employer.

12. (A) (2) Broker Bertha could have paid a flat fee for the HUD list. However, to tie the compensation to transactions that close is a violation of Chapter 475, F.S.

13. (D) (11) Buyers of homes built prior to 1978 are required to sign a "Lead Disclosure" form before signing the sale contract. Sellers are required to disclose the presence of any known lead-based paint in the home, and buyers and renters must be given an EPA pamphlet regarding lead-based paint.

14. (B) (4) Brokerage relationships extend throughout the business entity and include any branch offices of the firm. However, they do not extend to other real estate brokerage entities.

15. (C) (5) Entrance signs must include the name of the broker, trade name (if applicable), and the words "Licensed Real Estate Broker." In the case of a corporation, the sign must include the name of the corporation.

16. (A) (11) Although it is desirable to have a closing date on the contract, it is not a required element to make a real estate contract enforceable. If necessary, the courts interpret the closing to be accomplished in "a reasonable period of time."

17. (B) (3) Rule 61J2-10.038 states that real estate licensees must notify the DRE in writing of a change in mailing address within ten days after the change.

18. (D) (8) An important characteristic of joint tenancies with right of survivorship is that the property automatically belongs to the surviving joint tenant on the death of the other joint tenant.

19. (C) (5) If a broker desires to conduct business from additional locations, the broker must register each additional location as a branch office and pay the appropriate registration fees.

20. (A) (7) A landlord is the owner or lessor of a dwelling unit. Section 83.49(1), F.S. specifies that landlords must account for rental deposits regardless of the number of rental units.

21. (D) (5) Escrow accounts may be established in a Florida-based title company having trust powers, Florida commercial banks, credit unions, savings associations, or, if designated in the sale contract, a Florida attorney.

22. (B) (5) A broker is not required to maintain an escrow account. However, without one the broker cannot hold funds belonging to others.

23. (D) (13) Discount points are an extra, up-front fee to increase the real yield, or annual percentage rate, to the lender.

24. (C) (7) Section 760.23(9)(a), F.S. prohibits landlords from refusing to allow a tenant with a disability to make reasonable modifications to a residential dwelling at the tenant's own expense.

25. (A) (10) Ranges are numbered east and west of the principal meridian. The range due east of R1E is R2E, so the township due east of T1N, R1E would be T1N, R2E.

26. (C) (2) The question on the application for licensure requires Mary to disclose the crime regarding the unemployment checks even if adjudication was withheld. See Section 475.25(1)(m), F.S. and 61J2-24.001(n), F.A.C.

27. (B) (15) The comparable property is superior to the subject regarding number of bathrooms. The value of the extra half bath is subtracted from the comparable's transaction price.

28. (C) (2) The question requires applicants to disclose if they have ever been convicted of a crime, found guilty, or entered a plea of guilty or nolo contendere, even if adjudication was withheld. The question applies to violation of laws without regard to whether an individual was placed on probation or had adjudication withheld, or was paroled or pardoned. Failure to answer truthfully could result in denial of licensure.

29. (C) (18) Loreen is entitled to the surviving spouse and blind exemptions for a total tax exemption of $26,000.

30. (B) (7) Section 83.67(2), F.S. of the Florida Landlord and Tenant Act prohibits a landlord from preventing a tenant reasonable access to the dwelling unit. The landlord must seek legal remedy through eviction procedures.

31. (D) (2) The post-licensing education requirement has the effect of placing initial licenses in a probationary status because failure to complete the post-licensing education will cause the license to become null and void.

32. (D) (7) Regulation Z of the Truth-in-Lending Act requires certain disclosures when triggering terms are included in advertisements. Other triggering terms include the period of repayment and the amount of any finance charge.

33. (A) (9) A net lease requires the tenant to pay property expenses, including property taxes, hazard insurance, and utilities.

34. (C) (7) Muffy's financial status is not a protected classification. The landlord, however, is obligated to use uniform criteria and screening practices with all prospective tenants.

35. (A) (10) A township is a square six miles on each side (6 miles square) containing 36 square miles (36 sections).

36. (C) (6) Section 475.48(2)(d), F.S. mandates that a claim cannot be made against the Real Estate Recovery Fund if the license was not a valid, current, and active one at the time of the transaction.

37. (D) (3) Quasi-legislative responsibilities of the Commission include the power to enact administrative rules and regulations and to interpret questions regarding the practice or real estate.

38. (D) (5) Florida law does not prohibit licensees from recording judgments.

39. (C) (15) The potential highest and best use of a site determines the site's value.

40. (B) (15) Choices A and C apply to the cost-depreciation approach. Choice D applies to the sales comparison approach. The income approach is based on present value of expected income. Information regarding expenses is necessary to calculate projected net operating income.

41. (B) (10) The most common type of legal description used for single-family dwellings located in developed subdivisions is the lot and block method of land description, which can be used only where plat maps have been recorded in the public records.

42. (C) (6) The licensee is entitled to an informal or formal hearing. A licensee may choose an informal hearing only if there is not disagreement regarding the material facts of the case. A stipulation is a voluntary agreement between the petitioner (DBPR, DRE) and the respondent (licensee).

43. (C) (11) Death of the buyer or seller will usually be considered a reason for impossibility of performance unless the real estate contract provides otherwise.

44. (A) (6) The Smiths may not recover punitive damages from the Real Estate Recovery Fund. The Smiths may seek reimbursement of $30,000 in actual damages. The maximum amount that may be paid by the Real Estate Recovery Fund for a single real estate brokerage transaction is $50,000.

45. (C) (5) The best advice is to request the buyer to write a check payable to the broker's escrow account.

46. (C) (4) An arm's length transaction is one in which the parties are dealing from equal bargaining positions. Choices A and D involve transactions where there is a business relationship of some sort. Choice B is a transaction between relatives.

47. (B) (8) Fixtures are objects that were personal property but have been permanently attached to or made part of real property and thus are now real property.

48. (D) (5) Tom can be compensated only by his employing broker, ABC Realty Company. XYZ must pay the selling portion of the commission to XYZ Realty.

49. (A) (9) Condemnation is the taking of private real property for a public purpose under the right of eminent domain for a fair price.

50. (D) (8) Homesteading the principal residence protects the property from personal debts such as lawsuits, credit card debt, medical expenses, and so on. It does not protect against expenses associated with the principal residence such as property taxes, mortgage payments, and improvements made to the property. (See Chapter 222.10, F.S.)

51. (B) (9) A percentage lease is a proportional sharing of the monthly or annual gross sales made on leased premises.

52. (A) (11) An express contract is an actual written agreement of the parties in which the terms have been stated clearly.

53. (D) (18) Homeowners may deduct property taxes and interest paid on a mortgage on a principal residence.

54. (C) (11) No commission is due because it has not been earned under the terms of the listing agreement. The broker is entitled to damages for out-of-pocket expenses incurred while marketing the property prior to the seller's cancellation of the contract.

55. (C) (5) A corporation is an artificial or fictitious person formed to conduct business activities. A major advantage of a corporation structure is protection of personal assets.

56. (A) (6) Section 455.224, F.S. provides that a licensee has 30 days from the day a citation is served to dispute it. After that, the citation becomes a final order and constitutes discipline.

57. (B) (2) Licensees are required to successfully complete a prescribed post-licensing education requirement *before* the first renewal of their licenses.

58. (D) (5) When the closing or consummation date of a sale has not passed, but one or more of the parties has expressed intention not to close and the broker has not received conflicting or identical instructions from all parties concerning disbursement of escrowed funds, good-faith doubt exists.

59. (B) (4) A broker may have an office(s) in another state, provided the broker agrees in writing to cooperate with any investigation initiated under Chapter 475, F.S. The broker must maintain his or her escrow account with a title company bank, credit union, or savings association located and doing business in Florida.

60. (C) (12) Section 877.10, F.S. prohibits entering into a dual contract for the purchase of real property when the purpose of the higher priced contract is to secure a loan commitment. This is an illegal transaction.

61. (C) (7) The Real Estate Settlement Procedures Act (RESPA) was enacted to ensure that buyers are informed regarding the amount and type of charges they will pay at closing.

62. (D) (4) The licensee working in a nonrepresentative capacity may provide a CMA to a buyer or seller. However, "the licensee should refrain from making recommendations or consulting with the buyer or seller when in a nonrepresentative role and may not represent the CMA as an appraisal.

63. (C) (8) An elective share consists of 30 percent of the decedent's net estate. Homesteaded property is in addition to that received by elective share because a surviving spouse is already entitled to a life estate in the homestead.

64. (D) (9) An easement in gross is a type of easement that is not related to a specific adjacent parcel. Utility easements and railroad easements are easements in gross.

65. (C) (9) An acknowledgment is a formal declaration before an authorized official, by the person who executed the instrument, that it is a free act.

66. (B) (18) The current tax law eliminates the tax deferral of gains by no longer allowing the gain to be rolled over into a new home. However, gain up to $500,000 is excluded when filing a joint return ($250,000 when filing a single tax return). Any gain in excess of the exclusion is taxable.

67. (B) (12) The due-on-sale clause and granting clause apply to deed instruments. The mortgagor (not mortgagee) signs the mortgage instrument. A legal description is included in all mortgage instruments.

68. (D) (7) See Chapter 627.776(1)(j) and 626.9541(1)(h). Federal regulations also apply.

69. (B) (20) Building codes are enacted by local governments to protect the public health and safety from inferior construction practices. They establish minimum standards for a building's design, construction, use and occupancy, and quality.

70. (A) (3) Rule 61J2-10.038 requires licensees to notify the DBPR of a change in current mailing address within ten days after the change.

71. (C) (19) Availability of skilled labor is a variable that influences supply.

72. (D) (2) Chapter 475.180(b) requires that any resident licensee who becomes a nonresident must notify the Commission within 60 days of the change of residency and comply with all other F.S. 475 requirements and FREC rules. A licensee must notify the DBPR within ten days of a change in mailing address.

73. (C) (2) The definition of real estate includes business opportunities; therefore, individuals who market business opportunities must hold real estate licenses.

74. (A) (4) The signature is recommended but not required on all of the residential disclosure forms with the exception of the consent to transition to transaction broker notice. Section 475.278, F.S. requires the buyer or seller to sign the consent in order for the broker to transition from a single agent to a transaction broker.

75. (D) (4) Loyalty is a duty associated with single agency.

76. (B) (5, 11) Brokers handling the sale of HUD-owned properties are exempted from the notice and settlement procedures in Chapter 475, F.S. However, the broker is required to follow HUD's Agreement to Abide, Broker Participation Requirements.

77. (C) (4) Both the buyer and seller must agree to transition to a transaction broker relationship in order for the buyer to be shown property listed by Little Mo Realty.

78. (A) (11) The lead-based paint disclosure law requires that the disclosure be given prior to contract.

79. (B) (7) Religious organizations may restrict dwelling units they own or operate to members of their religion if the organization does not otherwise discriminate in accepting its membership.

80. (C) (6) Chapters 475.482 and 475.483, F.S. specify who is eligible to seek reimbursement from the Real Estate Recovery Fund.

81. (B) (8) The required notice for a month-to-month tenancy at will is not less than 15 days prior to the end of the monthly period.

82. (C) (9) A property owner, such as a developer, can restrict the future use of a property by recording deed restrictions.

83. (B) (9) Each section is 1 mile long on each side. Beginning at the south boundary of section 1, cross sections 12, 13, 24, and 25 (4 miles) to reach the north boundary of section 36.

84. (D) (10) Meridians run north and south.

85. (B) (11) The contract for sale and purchase of real estate must be in writing. However, a specific form is not required.

86. (B) (11) In homes built prior to 1978, the buyer must sign a lead disclosure form prior to signing the sale contract. Sellers are required to disclose the presence of known lead-based paint hazards, and the buyer must be given a copy of an EPA pamphlet regarding lead-based paint.

87. (A) (9) An encroachment occurs when a building or other improvement such as a fence extends beyond the land of the owner and illegally intrudes on land of an adjoining owner. A survey will reveal if there is an encroachment.

88. (C) (5) A corporation sole is an artificial or fictitious person formed by an ecclesiastical body and as such may not register as a broker. Chapter 475 does not restrict a not-for-profit corporation from registering as a broker. However, to do so may create other issues with the Florida Department of Revenue and the IRS.

89. (D) (13) The discount rate is the interest rate charged member banks for borrowing money from the Fed. If the discount rate is lowered, member banks pay less for borrowing money from the system.

90. (C) (8) To have a joint tenancy, the words "with right of survivorship" are required. Without right of survivorship, a tenancy in common exists.

91. (D) (14) Jan 31 + Feb 28 + Mar 31 +
    April 30 + May 31 = 151 days;
    $1,460 ÷ 365 = $4.00 per day;
    $4.00 × 151 days =
    $604 debit to seller and credit to buyer

92. (C) (11) $120,000 × 1.05 = $126,000 year 1;
    $126,000 × 1.05 = $132,300 year 2

93. (B) (15) $87,900 × .30 = $26,370;
    $88,500 × .50 = $44,250;
    $82,750 × .20 = $16,550;
    $26,370 + $44,250 + $16,550 =
    $87,170 indicated value

94. (D) (15) $9,200 × 12 mo. = $110,400 NOI;
    $110,400 ÷ .095 = $1,162,105

95. (D) (9) 640 ÷ 4 ÷ 2 = 80 acres;
    640 ÷ 4 ÷ 4 ÷2 = 20 acres;
    80 + 20 = 100 total acres

96. (B) (15) 80 × $750 × 12 mo. =
    $720,000 × .90 = $648,000;
    50 × $950 × 12 mo. =
    $570,000 × .95 = $541,500;
    $648,000 + $541,500 = $1,189,500

97. (C) (14) $98,500 sale price × .08 =
    $7,880 total commission;
    $7,880 × .55 = $4,334 Ted's commission

98. (B) (20) $47.00 × .70 homeowner's share =
    $32.90;
    $32.90 × 110' = $3,619;
    $3,619 ÷ 2 sides of street = $1,809.50

99. (C) (12) $129,500 sale price × .75 =
    $97,125 loan amount;
    $129,500 – $97,125 =
    $32,375 down payment

100. (B) (12) $92,000 × .075 = $6,900 ÷ 12 mo. =
    $575.00 interest, mo. 1;
    $643.28 – $575.00 =
    $68.28 principal, mo. 1;
    $92,000 – $68.28 =
    $91,931.72 remaining loan balance;
    $91,931.72 × .075 = $6,894.879 ÷ 12 mo. =
    $574.57 interest, mo. 2;
    $643.28 – $574.57 =
    $68.71 principal, mo. 2.

Index

Thank you for mailing or faxing* this form.

_____
(date)

EVALUATION FORM

1. ( ) I took the review course at_____

(name of school or college)

    I completed the course in _____   _____

(month)   (year)

    ( ) I bought this book and studied on my own.

2. I found your "Exam-Taking Strategies" to be _____

3. I found your Internet Web site to be _____

4. I found your 400+ "Sample Exam Questions" to be _____

5. I found your "Sample Math Questions" to be _____

6. My scores on the "Practice Exams" were _____

7. My score on the State licensing examination for ❐ sales associate or ❐ broker was _____

8. The parts of this book that were *most helpful to me:* (Please rank 1, 2, and 3.)

    _____ Exam-Taking Strategies

    _____ Review Outlines

    _____ Sample Exam Questions

    _____ Sample Math Questions

    _____ Practice Exams

9. Overall, I found this book to be:

    ❐ excellent

    ❐ very helpful

    ❐ fairly helpful

    ❐ not very helpful

10. Other *comments/suggestions* that I would like to pass along are:

P.S. I ❐ did ❐ did not use your REAL ESTATE MATH workbook during my study/review.

Florida Real Estate Exam Manual, 30th Edition
by Linda L. Crawford
2006–2007

* Fax to: 312-577-2467

NOTE: This page, when folded over and taped, becomes a postage-free envelope that has been approved by the United States Postal Service. It has been provided for your convenience.

Important—Please Fold Over and Tape Before Mailing

Important—Please Fold Over and Tape Before Mailing

Return Address:

_____

_____

_____

NO POSTAGE
NECESSARY
IF MAILED
IN THE
UNITED STATES

BUSINESS REPLY MAIL

FIRST CLASS MAIL   PERMIT NO. 88176   CHICAGO, IL

POSTAGE WILL BE PAID BY ADDRESSEE:

Dearborn™
Real Estate Education
30 South Wacker Drive
Suite 2500
a division of Dearborn Financial Publishing, Inc.
Chicago, Illinois 60606-7481

Attn: Editorial Department